Praise for *Coaching Across Cultures*

"This unique book introduces a new and more creative form of coaching to meet the demand's of today's diverse and international workplace. Philippe Rosinski breaks new ground in the first book to bridge the gap between coaching and cultures.
Coaching Across Cultures is a rich read for anyone to wants to coach, whether professionally or inside a multinational corporation, and it is a valuable contribution to understanding what coaching is."
Business Executive, Spring 2003

"Although the concept approach of culture often suggests values and behaviours of nations, this book expands the concept to consider differences of every kind including corporate cultures and professional groups. the author wants to sensitise readers to the cultural impact in the coaching dynamic.
The author introduces important cultural dimensions via the Cultural Orientations framework that apply in the workplace worldwide. The author enriches the approaches described with plenty of illustrations, workplace examples and case examples."
Forum magazine

"This clearly written book is a serious read. It is thoroughly researched, it bursts at the seams with examples, diagrams and case studies...no intercultural stone has been left unturned."
The Weekly Telegraph

"This book is gently persuasive and challenging. The essence of the book is that difference needs to be noticed and that it can be a powerful positive force within the coaching relationship - a journey for both coach and coachee. Rosinki's passion shows through and he ends with a heartfelt and topical reminder of the potential of all of us to deal with cross-cultural differenees with an attitude of openness, curiosity and eagerness to learn."
People Management

"*Coaching Across Cultures* is a rich read for anyone who wants to coach, whether professionally or inside a multinational corporation. Philippe Rosinski has woven a tapestry of contexts to sensitize the reader to the cultural impact in the coaching dynamic. I enjoyed the practical exercises, tools, and worksheets, which I plan to use with my international clients. The idea of leveraging a sense of power and responsibility for harmony is new. This book is a synthesis of models and wisdom, very much the same as the makeup of its author, a brilliant engineer and engaging coach!"

DJ Mitsch, Master Certified Coach
President, The Pyramid Resource Group, Inc.
Past President, International Coach Federation

"*Coaching Across Cultures* brings new light to managing performance in business by integrating two important domains of leadership: coaching and diversity. Through integrating these two leadership subjects, business [leaders] will generate new energy to boost high performance. This book offers a set of new insights, tools and ideas. With most businesses moving global, this new book is a valuable resource for all business leaders and professionals in the domain of leadership and management development."

Mia Vanstraelen
Director of Learning, IBM

"...I was surprised at the high level of application these groundbreaking concepts have in my area of work—namely diversity—as well as for...coaching and human resources disciplines."

Jenifer L. Rinehart
Chief Diversity Officer, Chubb Corporation

"For those [of you] who are managing across countries and regions and who are
willing to get the best out of that rich melting pot of cultures across all operating companies, just read *Coaching Across Cultures*! You will find Philippe Rosinski's book highly stimulating."

Olivier Desforges
Senior Vice President, Unilever

Coaching Across Cultures

Coaching Across Cultures

New Tools for Leveraging National, Corporate and Professional Differences

Philippe Rosinski

nb

NICHOLAS BREALEY
PUBLISHING

LONDON
YARMOUTH, MAINE

First published by Nicholas Brealey Publishing in 2003.
Reprinted in 2003, 2004

Nicholas Brealey Publishing
3–5 Spafield Street
London, EC1R 4QB, UK
Tel: +44-207-239-0360
Fax: +44-207-239-0370

100 City Hall Plaza, Suite 501
Boston
MA 02108, USA
Tel: (888) BREALEY
Fax: (617) 523 3708

www.nbrealey-books.com

www.CoachingAcrossCultures.com

© 2003 Philippe Rosinski

ISBN: 1-85788-301-2

British Library Cataloguing in Publication Data

A catalogue record for this book is available from the British Library

Library of Congress Cataloging-in-Publication Data

Rosinski, Philippe.
    Coaching across cultures: new tools for leveraging national, corporate, and professional differences/Philippe Rosinski.
        p. cm.
    Includes bibliographical references.
    ISBN 1-85788-301-2 (alk. paper)
    1. Corporate culture. 2. Multiculturalism. 3. Organizational behavior. I. Title.
    HM791.R67   2003
    306-dc21

                                                                            2002038450

With love to my daughter, Arielle, born while I was writing *Coaching Across Cultures*. Your appetite for life, ceaseless curiosity, and radiating joy have been a wonderful source of inspiration throughout this journey.

Table of Contents

Preface xi
Acknowledgments.. xv
Introduction... xvii

Part I—Coaching and Culture 1

Chapter 1—The Recent Discipline of Coaching 3
    What Is Coaching?.. 4
    Fundamental Perspectives 6
    The Coaching Process 7
    Types of Professional Coaching... 8
    Leadership Development.. 12
    Coaching Tool: Starting a Learning Journal 15

Chapter 2—Integrating the Cultural Dimension 17
    What Is Culture?.. 20
    Layers of Culture 23
    Dealing with Cultural Differences... 29
    Ethnocentric Pitfalls.. 31
    Ethnorelative Approaches 34
    Case Studies: Leveraging Cultural Differences 41

Part II—Leveraging Cultural Differences 47

Chapter 3—The Cultural Orientations Framework.......................... 49
    Categories in the Cultural Orientations Framework 51
    Determining a Cultural Profile Using the COF............................ 52
    Methodological Considerations for Using the COF Effectively 53
    Application: Assessing Cultures 61
    Application: Bridging Cultural Gaps.. 69

Chapter 4—How to Leverage Our Sense of Power and Responsibility....... 75
    Control 76
    Harmony.. 77
    Humility 78
    Coaching Tool: Visioning Model... 85

Chapter 5—How to Leverage Time Management Approaches 91
    Scarce/Plentiful 92
    Monochronic/Polychronic 95
    Past/Present/Future 100
    Coaching Tool: Timeline 103

Chapter 6—How to Leverage Our Definitions of Identity and Purpose...105
    Being/Doing 105
    Individualistic/Collectivistic 110
    Coaching Tool: Collages to Reveal Your Common Purpose 114

Chapter 7—How to Leverage Organizational Arrangements 117
    Hierarchy/Equality 119
    Universalist/Particularist 125
    Stability/Change...129
    Competitive/Collaborative..133
    Coaching Tool: Building Alliances..138

Chapter 8—How to Leverage Our Notions of
Territory and Boundaries...141
    Protective/Sharing 141
    Exchanging Feedback 146
    Protecting Our Territory 148
    Coaching Tool: Feedback and Self-Disclosure 151

Chapter 9—How to Leverage Communication Patterns 153
    High Context/Low Context 154
    Direct/Indirect...161
    Affective/Neutral 165
    Formal/Informal 168
    Coaching Tool: Coaching Videotaped Role Plays............................172

Chapter 10—How to Leverage Modes of Thinking...............................177
    Deductive/Inductive..177
    Analytical/Systemic 183
    Coaching Tool: Creative Problem Solving 187

Part III—Facilitating the High-Performance and
High-Fulfillment Journey 193

Chapter 11—Conduct Your Assessment...197
    Coachee's Self-Assessment..199
    Others' Expectations 207

Chapter 12—Articulate Objectives with the Global Scorecard..................209
    The Global Scorecard..211
    Self: Taking Great Self-Care...214
    Family and Friends: Sharing Love and Friendship............................218
    Organization: Adding Value to the Organization's Stakeholders..........220
    Community and World: Improving the World....................................223
    The Case for Sustainable Development/Corporate Citizenship...........228
    Leveraging Economic, Social, and Ecological Cultures.....................235
    The GLOBAL Goal-Setting Principles...238

Chapter 13—Progress toward Target Objectives.....................................241
    Roles of the Coach..243
    Effective Learning...245
    Structure of Coaching Sessions...247
    Ongoing Feedback..250
    Achieving Global Success..251

Final Words—Bringing Disciplines, Cultures, and People Together........253

Appendix 1—Transactional Analysis..259
Appendix 2—Neuro-Linguistic Programming..267
Appendix 3—Soliciting Written Feedback on Your Coaching..................273
Glossary...277
Notes and References...281
Bibliography...301
About the Author...305

Preface

Coaching and interculturalism[1] have existed as separate disciplines, missing cross-fertilization opportunities. Having worked as a professional coach for the last ten years and having lived across cultures all my life, I have been eager to systematically integrate these two domains. In this endeavor I have greatly benefited from the innovative experiences and insights of my client-partners. I have also learned from participants at international conferences.[2] Their input has helped me refine the models and ideas you will find in this book. My goal is to build bridges between coaching and interculturalism to the benefit of both professions.

I have written *Coaching Across Cultures* for all of you: coaches, executives, managers, and professionals from all kinds of organizations aspiring to become coaches, and interculturalists who want to add coaching skills to your consultation or training sessions. What I imagine you have in common is a desire to help people, including yourselves, to make the most of human potential. You want people to honor their true desires and live happier and more productive lives. You seek to foster genuine commitment, which is essential for sustainable peak performance. You participate in building thriving teams and organizations. You want to achieve success in your work *while* helping to make the world a better place.

This book will show you how to integrate the cultural dimension into coaching and coaching skills into intercultural work. You will learn how coaching can then allow you to deal most productively with cultural differences. You will find out how coaching can deploy more human potential and enable greater success by making the most of alternative cultural perspectives. If you are an interculturalist, you will learn some coaching theory and practices in chapter 1 and will be able to integrate these processes into your work.

Many carmakers dream about producing cars that, year after year, have the special aesthetic and technical qualities of a BMW. Moreover, fewer perhaps have matched BMW's ability to remain profitable. In the Harvard Business Review, *Chris Bangle, BMW's global chief of design, explains how coaching designers, and mediating between these artists and the engineers and business managers, has enabled BMW to "turn art into profit."[3]*

While other companies succumb to the business pressure of shifting from design to engineering too soon, Chris Bangle repeatedly explains to nondesigners that a "BMW, like a fine wine, cannot be hurried." Everyone at BMW understands that without its classic quality, a BMW would not be a BMW and customers would not pay a premium price for the car. The artistic culture therefore has to be honored and nurtured. "For designers to do their best work, they must be guided by their strong sense of artistic quality.... They need support and empathy—they don't respond well to dictatorial management."

Chris Bangle refers to his leadership style as coaching. And as a coach, he tries to draw the best design out of each artist. "When their work isn't going well, I can't prod them the way a manager in another department might. Artists don't respond to traditional dictums or push tactics. I can't say, 'Your last design lost, so do it my way.' I have to let the art manage the artist. This means making the artist come to terms with his design. I tell the designer to listen to his creation and to talk back to it; the brilliant car hiding inside his head will somehow speak loudly enough to get itself built and sold."

It may seem paradoxical that business success is achieved when artists are allowed to be fully themselves. However, this is only part of the story. BMW is also known for superior engineering and for being profitable. The success has come from valuing those technical and business perspectives as well, by leveraging these different mindsets. Using a mechanical metaphor (after all, this is the automobile industry), Chris Bangle says,

The design group, the engineers, and the business managers are like three meshed gears. If the gears are separated and spinning solo, nothing happens. If the gears turn the same way, they freeze up. They have to be interconnected and turning in opposite directions. But as we rotate, we transfer power to one another.

I invite you to hold this metaphor of meshed gears in mind as you read *Coaching Across Cultures*. The designers, engineers, and business managers are three separate *professional cultures* within BMW and constitute a "set of meshed gears." Now consider an international dimension, say BMW's operation in Germany and in the United States, and another set of gears, *country cultures*, are added. If BMW engages in an alliance or merger with another corporation, then its respective *corporate cultures* become a third set. And that is not all. *Socio-political cultures* are an important four set of gears, bearing in mind the necessity to serve society overall, notably by reconciling business and ecological cultures (achieving profitability while, in our example, reducing cars' toxic gas emissions). In each set, all the gears should ideally interconnect, each transferring power to the other.

Coaches (including managers and interculturalists acting as coaches) help their coachees leverage cultural differences (professional, national, etc.). They seek to provide valuable tools for discovering creative solutions to problems, increasing the human potential of all involved, and achieving greater success in a journey toward high performance and high fulfillment.

Acknowledgments

I am very grateful to all those who have allowed me to make the book *Coaching Across Cultures* a reality. I have mentioned many names in the text, but I am still lacking the space to pay tribute to all the people and diverse cultures I have benefited from.

Here, I would like to thank my clients in particular. I really appreciate their continuous trust and long-term partnership. These excellent leaders, teams, and corporations have been a source of inspiration for me. They have kindly allowed me to share their real-life experiences, best practices, and insights, thus enabling me to write a much richer book than I could have otherwise. In addition, they have given me their unstinting support and encouragement along the way. For that I am also grateful.

For their benevolence and confidence over the last years, I want to express my special thanks to Peter Leyland from Baxter Healthcare, Christopher Hamilton and Jenifer Rinehart from Chubb Insurance, Bonnie McIvor and Angela Hall from Unilever, and Annie Martinez from IBM. I would also like to thank Didier Dallemagne, Bart Wille, and Olivier Desforges from Unilever, Deby Bradley and Chris Giles from Chubb Insurance, Saheed Rashid and Mireille Smets from Baxter, and Mia Vanstraelen from IBM. They have all given me their valuable help.

Several friends and colleagues have offered me their positive energy and advice. Let me acknowledge in particular the enthusiastic support and competent help of Talane Miedaner, Katrina Burrus, and DJ Mitsch throughout my journey in writing this book, a journey that has spanned several years. I wish to also thank Geetu Orme, Michael Hoppe, Françoise Bacq, Janette Howell, Mary Devine, Olivier Putzeys, Jason Winder, Sharon Hickman, and Maryvonne Lorenzen, who all offered me a significant contribution somewhere along the way, sharing relevant information or their feedback about my drafts.

My sincere thanks go, of course, to my editors at Nicholas Brealey Publishing and Intercultural Press. Nicholas Brealey expressed his interest the first time we talked, when I proposed *Coaching Across Cultures* and told him about my project of bridging coaching and interculturalism. He helped me, notably, to structure the book in a manner that speaks to managers, professional coaches, interculturalists, and in fact anyone eager to leverage human potential in its rich cultural diversity. Judy Carl-Hendrick has contributed her editorial and intercultural expertise, not to mention her constructive feedback, helpful suggestions, and encouragement. Let me also acknowledge Toby Frank for her warm support, and specifically also for her copy editing, Patty Topel for her book design, and Sally Lansdell for her final proofreading. My thanks also go to Edwin Meulensteen who made useful remarks on the original manuscript.

Last but not least, I am grateful to my family, and particularly to my wife Anne for her love and patience while I was working on this project, and to our daughter Arielle. I have dedicated this book to her. Hopefully by the time she is able to read it, humanity will have made progress in tapping more effectively into its vast potential, to the benefit of everyone on our planet.

Introduction

Coaching as a profession is a relatively new phenomenon in organizations. It started just over a decade ago in the United States and has since emerged as an important leadership practice and a distinct profession, and many leaders are recognizing the benefits of adding coaching to their repertoire.

Rather than telling people what to do, coaches[1] act as facilitators. They assume people have more potential than they are currently able to use. Coaches help clients unleash this potential, just like good sports coaches enable athletes to access the champions within.

Facing increased competition and changing conditions, corporations and other organizations have to achieve more output with fewer resources. They need creativity and flexibility to deal with unexpected challenges and to seize new opportunities. They can no longer afford to waste their human talent. Instead, they must nurture, develop, and deploy their human capabilities, while making themselves attractive to the best talent.

Until recently, coaches have relied on common sense, communication techniques, and psychological perspectives (such as behavioral psychology and emotional intelligence). Given the amazing challenges in a global and turbulent environment at home and abroad, this is no longer sufficient. Traditional coaching has assumed a worldview (i.e., American and, to some extent, Western European) that doesn't hold true universally. Culture must now become part of the equation.

Let me clarify something upfront. Although the concept of culture sometimes evokes nations (e.g., British culture, French culture), this book considers cultural groups of various kinds, the most common ones (apart from nations) being corporations (e.g., Unilever and Bestfoods) and professions (e.g., artists, teachers or professors, engineers, and business managers). In other words, *Coaching Across Cultures* is not solely written for those of you who work across cultures in an international sense but also for everyone who works with people from different organizations and backgrounds.

This said, *Coaching Across Cultures* is in fact more concerned with *cultural perspectives* (e.g., alternative ways to communicate) and what can be learned from them than, say, describing the cultural characteristics of particular nations, corporations, or professions.

By integrating the cultural dimension, coaches will unleash more human potential to achieve meaningful objectives. Likewise, enriched with coaching, intercultural professionals will be better equipped to fulfill their commitment to extend people's worldviews, bridge cultural gaps, and enable successful work across cultures.

The Intercultural Approach

Culture, which is defined in depth in chapter 2, is a group phenomenon. A group's culture represents its unique characteristics and these include observable behaviors as well as underlying norms, values and beliefs. For example, the Germans[2] tend to be direct in their communication. To avoid misunderstanding, they believe it is preferable to say what you mean and mean what you say. This can sometimes be perceived as aggressiveness. In contrast, the Japanese have devised indirect forms of communication, notably relying on hints and on mediators. Their belief is that preserving harmonious relationships and "saving face" are key. This could equally be misinterpreted as a lack of self-confidence and assertiveness.

Whether you are a manager using coaching or a professional coach, whether you are coaching other people or just yourself, you cannot ignore these cultural components in communication. Moreover and beyond communication, culture has an impact on every human activity: how we view time, think, organize ourselves, define our purpose, relate to power, and so on.

This book is written to help you become more aware of your cultural orientations as you engage in your activities. You will learn to appreciate how your cultural inclinations affect the way you coach. You will acquire a vocabulary to pinpoint specific cultural differences between you and people you interact with, or between your coachees (or clients) and their stakeholders. If you are an interculturalist, you will learn some alternative ways to interpret familiar cultural orientations. Beyond raising your awareness, this book suggests how to use those differences constructively. This ability is of utmost importance in our interconnected and increasingly global society.

Coaching across Cultures: A Creative Approach

However, *Coaching Across Cultures* is not only about techniques to deal productively with cultural differences. Coaching across cultures is in essence a more *creative* form of coaching. Whereas traditional coaching tends to operate within the confines of your own cultural norms, values, and assumptions, coaching across cultures challenges your cultural assumptions and propels you beyond your previous limitations to discover creative solutions that lie "outside the box."

Because coaching is about helping people to unleash their potential, coaching across cultures makes it possible to deploy even more potential by tapping into various possible worldviews and also by expanding your repertoire of options. Coaching across cultures should not be viewed as a new coaching specialty. It is, rather, a "paradigm shift," an enlargement of coaching as most people have practiced it to date.

I have done my best to provide you with numerous ideas, frameworks, tools, and examples to help you systematically leverage alternative cultural orientations for the crucial human activities.

Coaching Across Cultures will help you to adopt a broader view (using the "Cultural Orientations Framework"), articulate success in a global fashion (using a new model, the "Global Scorecard"), and apply the lessons from various cultural perspectives from the Framework to make it happen.

In our international and intercultural society, coaching across cultures represents a positive and inevitable evolution of coaching. Consequently, it is destined to become mainstream.

By the time you finish reading this book, you will have

- become acquainted with coaching and cross-cultural concepts,
- gained a systematic framework (the "Cultural Orientations Framework") that will allow you to integrate cultural perspectives into your coaching, and will have learned—or reviewed—some basics about coaching,
- learned numerous cultural orientations that can be considered within companies or organizations and across national cultures,
- internalized a cross-cultural development model that will help you work effectively across cultures,
- developed familiarity with a three-step process ("Global Coaching Process") to facilitate a high-performance and high-fulfillment journey with individuals and teams,
  - learned to set objectives that promote business success while encouraging you to take care of yourself, nurture relationships, and serve society at large (the "Global Scorecard"), and
  - learned to apply the last step of the cross-cultural model to leverage cultural differences to achieve the best possible coaching results.

This concept of leveraging differences, which will be explained in more detail in chapter 2, means making the most of the richness that lies in diverse cultural views. You proactively embrace cultural differences, and this is where coaching and interculturalism can unite.

As you learn how to leverage cultural differences, you will read about best practices from respected organizations such as Unilever, Chubb Insurance, Baxter Healthcare, and IBM. Because most of my experience is with international corporations, most of my examples come from organizations that cross national boundaries (country culture), but many of the cultural orientations presented in this book will be equally effective *within* organizations or companies.

Road Map for the Book

In this section, I have outlined the structure of *Coaching Across Cultures*, together with a summary of what you will find in each part.

Part I, "Coaching and Culture," lays a foundation for the book. Coaching concepts and practices are introduced in chapter 1. Culture is presented in chapter 2, with an emphasis on linking the two domains.

Part II, "Leveraging Cultural Differences," features universal challenges and the corresponding responses in the form of *cultural orientations*. Chapter 3, "The Cultural Orientations Framework," is devoted to introducing a model comprising seven categories and seventeen cultural dimensions that are of practical importance for coaches. The model will help you assess your cultural orientations profile and pinpoint specific differences between the individuals, teams, and organizations you interact with.

The next seven chapters each focus on one category:
- Sense of power and responsibility,
- Time management approaches,
- Definitions of identity and purpose,
- Organizational arrangements,
- Notions of territory and boundaries,
- Communication patterns, and
- Modes of thinking.

You will be introduced to various cultural orientations, and will find specific ways of leveraging these to effectively address your challenges (and help your coachees address theirs). Moreover, a range of coaching techniques and models will be laid out so that you can make the most of cultural differences in concrete situations.

In Part III, "Facilitating the High-Performance and High-Fulfillment Journey," I will show you how to systematically put these ideas into practice. You will learn about a three-step process, namely the "Global Coaching Process," to facilitate your journey. You can employ this methodology with your coachees—individuals and teams. However, I suggest you also use it to embark on a personal journey if you want to credibly and competently coach other people.

The three chapters in Part III provide frameworks, tools, and examples for each of three "Global Coaching Process" steps: starting with an in-depth assessment, articulating target objectives, and then progressing toward them. Part III will help your coachee gain clarity about his* desires and honor them, and it will demonstrate how to achieve business objectives while doing something useful for humanity.

The "Global Scorecard" is one of the new tools you will discover. It encompasses classic indicators of business success while going beyond the traditional corporate culture bias and scope to achieve global success.

What You Should Not Expect from This Book

In this book, I hope you will find valuable insights, perspectives, and frameworks. However, a book can never replace a coach. As an author I can write about coaching, but I cannot claim to coach you via this book. When I work as a coach, I deal with a person or a team, and I have the opportunity to help that person move on his unique journey. I can use my intuition and my experience to provide only what seems most relevant in a particular situation (see "coaching defined as an art" in chapter 1) and to do that on a just-in-time basis (see chapter 13). My ambition therefore is not so much to coach you as it is to share what I believe can help you coach yourself and others more effectively.

Second, some of the words I use, such as *global*, may give you the impression that I am aiming at unrealistic goals. That is not my intention. By global coach (i.e., a coach able to function successfully across cultures), I do not mean to suggest perfection. Who could leverage all cultural differences? Who could have worldwide capability? Global coaching, in an absolute sense, does not exist. It would be very presumptuous for me to suggest this book could

---

* Throughout the book, I want to avoid making the text unnecessarily cumbersome with formulae such as he/she, him/her, or his/her. Therefore, please bear in mind that unless explicitly stated otherwise or obviously not applicable in the context, the coach, coachee, or person I am referring to can be either a man or a woman.

help bring about a utopian world! My ambition is more modest. By suggesting a destination where cultural differences are leveraged, full human potential unleashed, and a better world fostered, I am stating that I believe in progress and am inviting you to advance on a journey to make it happen. Every step forward is significant. Your commitment is what makes you a global coach.

Third, I have yet to find a truly intercultural society or company where members have embraced cultural differences and made the most of them. To my knowledge, such an entity is yet to be built. The book does, however, relate encouraging experiences and best practices that can inspire us, and from which we can learn.

Fourth, coaching across cultures is a source of richness, but it does come with a price. It is much more comforting and reassuring to stay in your community and to live in a "ghetto." By exploring alternative worldviews and mixing with people from different cultures, you will often feel challenged and may experience higher stress. You are venturing into new territories. Who said expanding our horizons was easy? The benevolent presence of a coach and a support network can help you on that journey. The promise of a richer future and the excitement of learning should also help you accept and surmount the obstacles along the way.

Finally, some issues will inevitably not be addressed. I intend to lay a foundation for cross-fertilizing coaching and interculturalism. This implies stepping back from our current paradigms. The discipline I describe is merely emerging at this stage. Your creativity will help bring it to life. However, being a coach myself, I recognize that coaches are action oriented and cannot be satisfied with a mere intellectual exposure to concepts. You will find many ideas, models, and tools that you will be able to apply. Some of you may find there is more information than you can use. Others may wish there were more. I have had to make some choices, and there is still a lot that I have to learn! I have tried my best to find the right balance, sharing what I know and think would be most beneficial to you.

I hope *Coaching Across Cultures* will inspire you to deploy more human potential, leverage cultural differences, and promote global success.

Part I
Coaching and Culture

Chapter 1
The Recent Discipline of Coaching

Coaching is a *pragmatic humanism*. Coaching values well-being and fulfillment. It emphasizes self-care, quality of life, and human growth. I call this the "being" side. Coaching is also a method to enhance performance and a leadership style that gets results. This I call the "doing" side. In other words, well-being is important, and human development is the prime method for getting results (see chapter 6 for more on being versus doing).

The emphasis on self-care should not be confused with selfishness. By giving themselves permission to take great care of their own needs and dreams (perhaps thanks to your coaching), coachees increase their energy level, connect with their passions, and enhance their capacity to serve fellow humans.

Coaches help people find practical solutions to the concrete challenges they face: how can people make the most of their time, improve leadership and communication, achieve ambitious work goals, have a better life balance, understand and use emotions, develop their creative thinking, overcome harmful stress, establish constructive relationships, and so on?

More fundamentally, coaches help coachees step back, take in the "big picture," and craft the life they truly want, in other words, design a future they desire. In fact, both quality of life and productivity can be achieved when people embark on a journey that respects and builds on their aspirations and talents. Moreover, successful coaches help coachees find creative ways to serve their clients, colleagues, and society, while honoring their own wishes.

Coaches aim for concrete impact and tangible results. They enable peak performance. The best athletes have worked with coaches for a long time. Pete Sampras would not have conquered seven Wimbledon crowns and a record fourteen grand slam tennis titles without superb coaching. Today, in a fast-paced and competitive world, the demands on all professionals are greater, not only on athletes. Managers in particular, like sports champions, need to perform near-miracles. To that end, they increasingly use coaches to help them deploy their talents. They also become coaches themselves to unleash the potential of their staff.

Coaching has indeed become an important component of leadership. Lou Gerstner, as Chairman of IBM, declared in 1998, "In the past, it may have been sufficient for managers to deliver the numbers and close the deal. Today the definition of leadership at IBM is broader than that. You lead programs and projects, of course. But you're also in the job to *lead people, build a team, coach, and create a culture of high performance.*"[1]

It will not be a surprise therefore that many excellent companies, including those depicted in this book, have utilized coaching. They consider coaching a key leadership competency for their executives.

What Is Coaching?

I define coaching as **the art of facilitating the unleashing of people's potential to reach meaningful, important objectives**.

The key elements of this definition constitute the essence of coaching.[2] I will begin with "objectives."

1. Objectives

Coaching is oriented toward concrete impact and results; it is about helping to articulate and achieve objectives. The focus is on the current lives and future plans of the coachees.

2. Meaningful, important

Coaching seeks to engage coachees in an authentic way. To create real commitment, objectives cannot be artificially imposed or "sold." Instead, they must resonate with coachees' inner motives and values. Before helping to build an action plan, the coach helps coachees identify what is specifically important to them and what can make their lives truly meaningful and enjoyable. In addition to enabling coachees to serve themselves, the coach helps coachees serve others and pursue concrete objectives in the service of various stakeholders such as clients, employees, shareholders, and society.[3]

3. Potential

Coaches are deeply convinced that people have more potential than they are currently able to display. Great coaches often have a vision of what that potential might be, but more importantly, they are devoted to mastering the art of helping people discover, develop, and overcome obstacles to realize that potential.

4. Facilitating

Coaching is an interactive and developmental process where the coach enables coachees to find their own solutions, discover new opportunities, and implement actions.

5. People

Coaching can be applied to individuals and to teams. In the latter case, the coach works at two levels: helping the team achieve synergy (overall performance superior to the sum of individual contributions) and helping each individual team member separately reach his personal objectives. For the team overall, great coaches seek win–win solutions—opportunities that exist at the intersection between team and individual needs.[4]

6. Art

Coaching is the art of choosing an effective approach in a given situation, of creatively combining technical tools, models, and perspectives to address specific challenges, and of devising innovative processes to serve coachee needs. Technical mastery alone is not sufficient to produce excellent coaching. Because it is authentic in essence, coaching cannot be performed automatically or superficially. Intuition and synthetic intelligence[5] are key competencies of great coaching.

Coaching versus Mentoring, Therapy, Consulting, and Teaching

Mentoring. Although leaders can act as coaches, I have found that this role is often confused with mentoring. Coaches act as facilitators. Mentors give advice and expert recommendations. Coaches listen, ask questions, and enable coachees to discover for themselves what is right for them. Mentors talk about their own personal experience, assuming this is relevant for the mentees. Coaches provide frameworks to help coachees build their own support networks. Mentors often open doors and put their protégés in contact with key people. With experience, any leader can act as a mentor and proffer advice and a hand up. It takes additional empathy, and skills to be a coach. Mentors can leverage their experience more effectively to the benefit of mentees by learning how to coach, notably for building ownership and responsibility.

Therapy. Therapy usually aims at healing emotional wounds from the past (and in some cases may be complementary to coaching). Coaching may help identify blockages from past personal history but with the intent of providing new ideas, resources, and options to address present challenges. The conversation in coaching is about "what" and "how to" (future) more than "why" (past).[6]

Consulting. Coaching, with its emphasis on process, differs from traditional consulting, which prescribes solutions. The rationale for using coaching is that coachees become better equipped, increase their ownership and ultimately their confidence, satisfaction, and performance. Consulting can be a complement to coaching when additional expert knowledge is desirable.

Teaching. Coaching starts with coachees' desires and challenges; teaching, is centered on a curriculum that trainees need to try to apply in their situations.

Fundamental Perspectives

You will discover a variety of coaching methods throughout this book. Additional models have been very well described by other authors, some of whom I will evoke later. Let me recommend Richard Kilburg[7] and Frederic Hudson,[8] who have both proposed inventories of coaching foundations and methods. Frederic Hudson distinguishes psychological and social theories of adult development as the theoretical roots of coaching. Richard Kilburg mentions several coaching methods, including Cooperrider's appreciative inquiry.

Permit me a brief overview/review of a few fundamental coaching perspectives. Coaching is an advanced form of communication. Consequently, if you want to excel at it, you first need to master communication. I can recommend Transactional Analysis (TA) and Neuro-Linguistic Programming (NLP) as models, both of which are helpful. Although these models have been around for a long time, they are still important as coaching foundations. Unfortunately, they are often overlooked. What matters in coaching is not the models per se but the ability to leverage these theoretical perspectives in real situations.

In the appendices, you will find descriptions of TA and NLP that I have found particularly helpful in my coaching practice. I also indicate how I have applied some of these concepts in a real coaching situation.

At this stage, however, let me just share one insight from TA, which refers to how you view yourself, how you see others, and the resulting impact. The model describes a mindset all coaches need to develop; it is also a useful tool for replacing destructive or ineffective communication strategies with productive and enriching ones. *And it works across cultures.*

You can choose, regardless of the situation, to adopt an "OK (self)–OK (others)" mindset: you trust yourself and tend to trust other(s). OK refers to our image of someone worthy of respect, with positive intentions, and able to make a difference. OK does not mean faultless. This mental outlook will naturally lead you to engage in constructive communication and actions, and enable you to develop richer and more productive relationships.

The important point is that OK–OK is a subjective choice, independent of "objective" reality. It does not matter that you could rationally also make a case for the other mental combinations (OK–not OK, not OK–OK, not OK–not OK). For example, if you distrust people (OK–not OK), your attitude will typically alienate them or lower their self-confidence. You foster vicious circles when you interpret their lack of commitment and poor results as a validation of your initial belief. Coaches prefer the OK–OK perspective, because self-fulfilling prophecies also work positively: when you trust yourself and others, you enable virtuous circles of respect, productive behaviors, and creativity.

One perspective that has not yet been a part of coaching is *culture*. In chapter 2, I will explore the cultural dimension of communication and discuss how it can be integrated into coaching.

The Coaching Process

A typical coaching process[9] involves three steps and embeds several essential coaching features: conducting your assessment, articulating target objectives, and then progressing toward them.

Conducting Your Assessment. First, coachees are invited to systematically explore and honor their desires. Desires are essential because they house energy and passion. Consider the difference between *wanting* to do something and *having* to do something. As André Comte-Sponville noted, *"When love is present, one does not have to worry about duty."* This being said, the assessment is also an opportunity for coachees to examine opportunities to serve others; thus the assessment includes the expectations of various stakeholders and their feedback.

The assessment phase typically includes making your coachees aware of the "mental filters" that exist, often unconsciously, between the external reality and their mental representation of it.[10] In the same way that optical lenses can alter shapes and colors in photography, mental filters can create a unique subjective perspective that is different from objective reality.

In traditional coaching, the focus is on determining *psychological* filters. For example, the Myers-Briggs Type Indicator (see chapter 11) provides a concrete example of these kinds of filters and suggests our biases in the form of psychological preferences.

Coaching Across Cultures, however, invites you to consider both psychological and *cultural* filters, which are unfortunately often ignored in traditional coaching. The "Cultural Orientations Framework" presented in Part II will help you determine your personal cultural orientations (influenced by your nationality, profession, etc.) and establish a cultural profile. Recognizing and understanding these filters and how they influence our perception of people and events is the coachees' first step; they then can consciously try to alter these filters and possibly overcome obstacles to their own effectiveness and success.

Articulating Target Objectives. Coaching is results oriented; therefore, coachees next project themselves into the future and define the objectives they will later strive to reach. In traditional coaching, the focus is on personal or corporate objectives. *Coaching Across Cultures* invites you to consider success globally, helping coachees to set target objectives beneficial to them, while serving their organizations and helping to make the world a better place. The "Global Scorecard" presented in chapter 12 will help you visualize a wide range of possible objectives, which are interconnected. Coachees will typically be more inspired and committed when they see how their work positively impacts society at large.

Progressing toward These Target Objectives. The third step is the journey toward those targets, and coaching is centered on coachees' challenges during this journey. Coaches offer tools and help coachees apply them to deal with real issues as they arise. In other words, the coachees' challenges drive the agenda; learning occurs "just-in-time." Coaches also help coachees tap into their desires, leverage their strengths, overcome their weaknesses, and build on their successes along the way.

Types of Professional Coaching

In this section, I will concentrate on three coaching professions (personal, executive, and team coaching). However, let me first bring up a difficulty with coaching. Because it is a fairly new profession, many people are tempted to jump on the bandwagon and start offering "coaching services." Such fly-by-night operations raise serious issues of quality and ethics, which could potentially harm coachees and damage the profession altogether. To my knowledge, these questions have been best addressed in an international context by the International Coach Federation (ICF).[11]

Personal Coaching

When a professional coach works with an individual who pays for the intervention, the process is called "personal coaching." Thomas Leonard,[12] who has trained many personal coaches,[13] urges coachees to honor themselves and remake the world on their own terms. Leonard proposes "practical guidelines" to help coachees meet these objectives. Personal coaches have traditionally emphasized the notion of self-care, which has been mentioned earlier and has had an impact on the entire coaching profession.

Moreover, they have insisted on congruence and I have found that the best coaches do indeed strive to practice what they preach (for example, Talane Miedaner, Laura Berman Fortgang, and Cheryl Richardson). They try to live in coherence with their ideals, believing that, to paraphrase Gandhi, "You must be the change you want to see in the world."

Executive and Corporate Coaching

Executive coaching is a form of coaching in which
- the coachee is an executive,
- the organization employing the coachee pays for the coaching intervention,
- the sessions are strictly confidential to ensure candidness and openness in interactions, which are essential to effectiveness, and
- the intervention is in service of multiple stakeholders: the coachee and his organization.

Incidentally, the same criteria apply to corporate coaching, but the coachee is not necessarily an executive in this case. Some say that a balance needs to be struck between the needs of the executive and those of the organization.[14] My view is that good executive coaches go beyond finding a compromise. They help identify creative solutions and synergies where all parties can discover new ways to make the most of their relationship. Although all executive coaches recognize that they serve multiple stakeholders, not all agree on how to handle conflict between stakeholders' interests.

I typically indicate upfront that my goal is to help everybody win. To that end, I learn about the organization and its context. I get a feel for the challenges and opportunities ahead. I seek to understand the expectations for leadership development and how these connect with the overall vision, strategy, and culture of the organization.[15] At the same time, I make clear that I shall be serving the coachee's best interests during our sessions. I want the conversation to be authentic. The worst approach would be to manipulate the executive, in other words, try to influence him to do something he does not truly want to do.

The vast majority of coachees will be more committed, passionate, and effective at leading their organizations as a result of the coaching process. Some, however, having gained clarity about their motives, may realize the poor match between their own desires and objectives and those of the organization. If they cannot identify a way to bridge the differences, they will probably decide to leave the organization. In this case, the best I can do is to help ensure the departure is graceful and respectful.

The flow of information in this triangular partnership is represented in the figure below.

All parties are responsible for communicating on an on-going basis. Since the coach cannot comment on the coachee's progress (because of the confidentiality agreement), he encourages feedback exchanges between the executive and his organization. This ensures that progress gets noticed and that issues don't turn into blind spots.

Contracting concerns the general conditions and the intervention process. However, sometimes it also includes a discussion about specific target objectives, which are agreed on among the coach, the coachee, and an orga-

Partners in the Executive Coaching Process

nizational representative (typically the coachee's supervisor and/or a human resources executive). I have found this practice to be less common at the senior executive level. In any event, the coachee's progress and results should speak for themselves, and the coachee always has the option of keeping certain objectives confidential with his coach.

In October 1999, Laura Whitworth initiated the first Executive Coaching Summit for the purpose of identifying the primary distinguishers of executive coaching, which was emerging as an important profession within the coaching field. We met for two days in Orlando with a group of thirty-six senior executive coaches she had invited and who were viewed as leaders in the field.

The published conclusions[16] included a list of advanced proficiencies, which highlighted how executive coaching is distinguished from the basics of coaching. The following points are from that list:

- Ability to have conversations beyond the obvious. May include global issues, philosophical items, sociological issues, or business issues of the day and of the future. Executive coaches are comfortable coaching around complex issues and international agendas.
- Ability to be a risk taker by challenging individuals at high levels. Executive coaches speak the truth when no one else will.
- Ability to be a confidant with whom executives can share all sides of themselves: their hopes as well as their fears, their egotistical desires as well as their social needs, their dreams for themselves as well as for their organizations.

Team Coaching

Coaching teams is about helping a team achieve superior performance while also helping team members create more fulfilling lives for themselves and for others.

Football fans know that putting together a group of talented players does not by itself make a winning team. Nobody would dream of such a thing. Coaching is indispensable. Yet, when it comes to executive groups, I have often noticed managers who entertain the fantasy that somehow they can achieve high performance by concentrating solely on the business agenda and without any coaching.

Team coaching differs from "masculine" (business imperatives, task objectives) consulting and "feminine" (human values, relationship objectives) team building in that it leverages both parts for greater business results and improved relationships. Coaching that does not include the relational part is merely facilitation. Coaching without the business discussion would not be coaching. It could take the form of outdoors team games, which are fun and useful but insufficient for tackling the business issues. Coaches will, for instance, help team members realize how they behave as they do the real job. They will help ensure all learnings are transferred to enhance the way team members perform the work.

I have described elsewhere the aims and practices of team coaching, considering executive team coaching in particular.[17] Team coaching involves an elaborate intervention process; it includes interviews with each team member, team assessment, customized design, and a feedback session with the team leader before any team retreat takes place.

As a team coach, I believe I can best serve the team overall to the extent that I am able to serve each member individually. Genuine commitment is found where team and individual objectives intersect. This creates congruence, a resonance, which is the basis of true synergy. Coaches help unleash individual and collective potential in pursuit of the team's mission.

Here is how Peter Leyland of Baxter Healthcare describes his experience of team coaching:

> This process has supported and met the needs it was intended to address beyond the expectations of the whole team. Not only have the issues previously identified been positively dealt with, but the group has been able to move on, capable of dealing with increased levels of complexity as we combine two new businesses onto the core. The core business has also experienced a fifty percent increase in growth since the start of the intervention process.... Looking back over the past 18 months...the team has moved a long way and passed many milestones. The old self-confidence has returned. People are enjoying their jobs. We continue to invest in training, new people and competitive tools. Last but not least we have established a new and exciting future together.[18]

Leadership Development

Rebecca Ganzel, in her article "Hard Training for Soft Skills," describes the "golden days of American management," when "life was easy for workers who preferred dealing with facts, figures, and numbers rather than with messy human relationships." She goes on to explain, "Workplace rules were simple: Show up on time. Keep your head down. Get the job done." Then, she writes, "came the bad stuff. Stuff like empowerment, team building transparency, accountability. The analytical skills you'd been hired for were glanced over like so much garage-sale rubbish; the data you'd counted on turning to throughout your career was no longer a safe haven."[19]

Coaching is part of this new "bad stuff." Coaching is in fact a new management leadership philosophy that invites creativity, authenticity, and ownership in the workplace. Whereas in the old days, management would secure compliance and suboptimal performance, *coaching strives to unleash people's potential and to obtain full-hearted commitment.*

Leadership and coaching have only slowly found their way into business school training programs. Likewise, the main strategic consultancies ignored for a long time the soft side of organizational leadership, proposing brilliant strategic plans but leaving the executive or manager with the challenge of bringing employees on board to implement recommended changes, which often resulted in enormous frustration if not open social conflict. Today, even hard-nosed corporations understand that authoritarian or paternalistic management styles will not win the war for talent, nor will they elicit the best performance needed to stay competitive.

Daniel Goleman researched "Leadership That Gets Results"[20] and found that it came in the form of six leadership styles, one of which is, precisely, coaching. His research indicates that coaching has a positive impact on the organization's working environment, which in turn affects business performance.[21]

In my view, executive coaching involves developing personal leadership. Executive coaches help leaders to grow, notably by demonstrating their own leadership skills. Part of the growth is leaders' ability to act, themselves, as coaches. Unilever, for example, expects coachees to be able to act as coaches after they have completed their one-year individualized executive coaching process. If a leader is still unable to be an effective coach, Unilever makes it clear that the executive coaching process should continue. While coaching is key, leadership encompasses many other *activities*. Executive coaches should be equipped to help leaders perform a variety of *tasks*.[22]

Coaches know that even the best leaders cannot reach perfection in all areas. Welcome to humanity! A more realistic objective is then to help executives become aware of their strengths and weaknesses, to make the most of the former and minimize the effects of the latter.

Frequently, organizations define their own set of competencies, which employees need to exhibit to promote overall success. A few examples — Unilever, IBM, Chubb, Baxter — follow.

Unilever's "Path to Growth"

Unilever's "Path to Growth" includes the development of world-class leadership competencies. For example, Unilever expects its executives to demonstrate the following qualities:

- developing others (particularly by acting as coaches)
- exhibiting a passion for growth
- thinking creatively
- demonstrating political acumen
- seizing the future
- being a catalyst for change
- holding people accountable
- empowering others
- influencing strategically
- demonstrating team commitment
- exhibiting team leadership.[23]

Leadership development training and coaching are designed to develop these competencies. The reward system and promotions are also aligned to ensure that desirable leadership behaviors are reinforced.

I have been personally involved in some parts of the comprehensive curriculum Unilever has put together to develop executives at all levels. I designed the "Foundations of Leadership" and "Leadership Development" programs in collaboration with Unilever,[24] and I am now working as an external coach with senior executives. As part of their leadership training, they take part in a seminar in which Chairmen Niall FitzGerald and Antony Burgmans personally speak with participants and offer them the option of working for one year, one-on-one with an executive coach.

IBM — "A Strong Coaching Style"

Coaching is one of IBM's core leadership competencies. An IBM leader behaves as a coach when he

- expresses pride in others' accomplishments,
- enjoys seeing subordinates grow and move on, even at a cost to himself or the team,
- provides coaching and inspires the long-term development of others, and

- has substantial positive impact on others' professional growth and development.[25]

Furthermore, IBM found that its leaders with a strong coaching style created high-performance climates 100 percent of the time. This is of utmost importance considering IBM also established that organizational climate accounts for 28 to 36 percent of the company's results![26]

Effective Leaders as Good Coaches

At Chubb Insurance the same commitment to coaching is evident and starts again at the top of the organization. Dean O'Hare, chairman, insists that "effective leaders are good coaches and mentors; they provide feedback and motivate others to exceed expectations."[27] Building coaching skills has become a key part in Chubb's Leadership Development Seminar.[28]

Peter Leyland from Baxter has engaged his Baxter Renal U.K. team in a long-term developmental journey. I acted as the external coach while Peter and his team were learning and demonstrating proficiency as leader coaches. Peter was subsequently promoted to a vice president with global responsibility.

In fact, and to summarize, it has become apparent that many of the most successful organizations today have embraced coaching as both a key means and a core goal of their leadership development efforts.

Coaching Tool: Starting a Learning Journal

If you don't currently use a learning journal, I suggest that you visit your local stationer. You may opt for a refined, leather-covered version or a simple book-let with empty pages. You may prefer a flexible format, where you can remove pages you consider obsolete and gradually replace the old pages with new ones as you gain clarity or as your projects progress. What matters is that your journal is inviting and *right for you*.

A coaching journal is a valuable tool to help you reflect on your own personal journey, to aid your thinking about what is truly important to you. It is a place where you can capture insights and learn from experience. It can act as a catalyst to helping you step back to enhance your self-awareness, expand your worldview, and formulate your goals. You may jot down personal beliefs, ideas, questions, thoughts about your values, strengths, weaknesses, the ways you interact with fellow team members, and so on. However they come, and whether they seem to be logical or illogical, complete or incomplete, your thoughts and feelings in real time can be captured in your journal for later reflection and allow you to gradually move toward clarity.

You will want to go back to these notes, identify key themes, and articulate actions you will commit to take. Even if in your culture, people tend to openly share personal information, I recommend that you treat your learning journal as a secret garden. You always have the option of verbally disclosing select parts with trusted confidants.

The "Global Coaching Process" (more specifically, the assessment or the "Global Scorecard"), which will be detailed in Part III, can provide a structure for your journal if you choose to read chapters 11 and 12 at this time. But there is not a unique way to use the tool.

A book can never replicate the rich human interaction that typically takes place during coaching sessions. The learning journal, however, will enable the active learning mode I encourage you to adopt. You can then learn to coach yourself and engage in fruitful internal dialogue.

Chapter 2
Integrating the Cultural Dimension

As mentioned in the Introduction, the concept of culture applies not only to "those out there," the "others," people from foreign nations. Countries have cultures, but so do corporations, organizations in general, professions, and so on.

Within groups there are individual differences, class and educational differences, ethnic and racial differences, personality type differences, and gender differences. Furthermore, groups develop their own cultures. All of us know this to be true if we have changed jobs and found the feel of things—how people act and communicate, the "climate" of the place—to be different from our previous experience.

The various aspects or kinds of culture share many similarities. What applies to country cultures also has applications to corporate, organizational, or academic cultures. And once differences can be seen as cultural, there is the possibility of understanding and developing skills to manage, or better yet leverage, those differences.

In this chapter I begin our exploration of culture, and in Part II I delve deeper into cultural orientations. Here, I offer two case studies. The first involves a clash between the values of two professional cultures within a company; the second is about the misunderstandings that can lead to stereotyping and agitation across country-culture lines.

Case Study 1: Professional Cultures

When Peter Leyland was appointed business unit director of Baxter Renal in the United Kingdom, he asked me to act as the external coach to his management team. The coaching role was described to the team as facilitating a long-term, high-performance journey. The journey that started in 1997 has indeed come a long way since then; we had a fifth retreat in 2001. Saheed Rashid, previously marketing director, replaced Peter Leyland in 2000. In the meantime, Baxter Renal had further reinforced its dominant market position in the U.K. by devising innovative ways to prolong and enhance hundreds of patients' lives.

Baxter Renal U.K. became a model for the entire Baxter organization, and the story of this success has been featured in the *Sloan Management Review*.[1] Back in early 1997, however, the team could not have, by any stretch of the imagination, qualified as high performance.

One challenge was the clash between *profit-driven* and *people-driven* values. The team was really composed of two subcultures, with a divide along educational backgrounds: business professionals, typically holding MBA degrees, and nurses who had left the National Health Service to join Baxter. The nurses strongly valued helping to improve patients' lives. Despite having made the transition to Baxter (usually for better pay and better management), the nurses harbored a sense of uneasiness and almost betrayal, because they were a part of the corporate universe and its relentless pursuit of profit.

Through team coaching, the nurses learned that the rest of the team was also genuine and serious about enhancing patients' lives. The nurses learned to appreciate that sound business management would enable Baxter to better serve these patients. The nurses on the team became convinced that they could have a great impact as *nurses* within Baxter. Business professionals, on the other hand, learned to better hold patients' needs to heart. Used to impersonal marketing plans, they developed the values of caring and empathy. They found pride and inspiration knowing that their work would make a real difference for patients.

The team set out to make renal patients' lives as easy as possible. Baxter offered to take care of various tasks that patients would normally have to worry about, such as the disposal of dialysis bags, water purification, or the update of prescriptions.

To stimulate their thinking before engaging them in goal setting and action planning, I invited team members to put themselves in the shoes of their various stakeholders, drawing graffiti on flip charts representing each group's hopes and concerns. Cultural differences became a source of richness rather than frustration. Mutual trust and passion for a common mission united members. The team was now ready to begin its journey to high performance.

Case Study 2: National Cultures

Mark Philips,[2] a British director of the U.K. operation of an international corporation, was asked to manage the European Nordic Region. The regional head office was based in Stockholm, and most employees were Swedish.

These Swedes had acquired a negative reputation among other European staff members, resulting from a series of misunderstandings due to poor intercultural awareness on all sides. During our one-on-one coaching sessions, I encouraged Mark to learn more about the Swedish culture. Rather than assuming a lack of commitment from the Swedes, I challenged Mark to view the puzzling behaviors he had observed through the lens of the Swedish culture itself[3] and to proactively look for the merits of their cultural orientations rather than the pitfalls.

Mark realized, for example, that the Swedes' absence of agitation and frenzy (which he was accustomed to) had some advantages. For Swedes, being referred to as *kolugn* (calm as a cow) is a compliment. It suggests virtues of patience and of maintaining one's cool no matter what happens. Mark had initially been infuriated seeing Swedish employees calmly sipping their cups of coffee and taking a lot of time off, apparently unaffected by the business pressures to deliver results quickly.

As it turns out, this is not laziness; Swedes simply value their leisure time highly. Furthermore, Mark found that independence is also important to Swedes, who want to be their own masters. They do not show off or try to appear different. Yet, they simply back out when coerced. However, Swedes are comfortable with very direct communication and in fact expect straightforwardness. Consequently, Mark stated his expectations precisely and quietly, while offering his support if they needed help. He gave the Swedes time to reflect on how they would go about meeting specific business challenges. They eventually agreed on a plan. The Swedes proved very reliable at carrying out the project as stated. Their European colleagues started to appreciate them.

Mark was able to earn the respect of Swedish employees. Even more important, Mark went beyond adapting his behaviors to fit into the Swedish culture. I asked him regularly how he was inspired by the Swedes and what he was learning from them. Life balance is something Mark decided, having seen the Swedish example, to make a top priority for himself. Moreover, he learned from the Swedes the virtues of being patient and of calmly putting issues on the table without beating about the bush. He blended these traits with his own British cultural traits and thus enhanced his leadership repertoire.

Following the examples of Peter Leyland and Mark Philips, culturally trained coaches aim not only to unleash human potential (this is what traditional coaches already do), they also aspire to make the most of alternative worldviews. In reality, coaches and leaders may not always be able to emulate individuals who manage to find richness in cultural differences. But *Coach-*

ing Across Cultures will help you, at a minimum, become aware of your own cultural characteristics, decipher underlying worldviews of others, and use cultural differences constructively.

Coaching with a national and corporate cross-cultural focus does not yet prevail. It should become apparent in the next pages that traditional coaching has implicitly reflected particular norms, values, and basic assumptions that reflect the originating culture of the field of coaching, the United States, and do not necessarily hold true universally. From notions of time and hierarchy to patterns of thinking and communicating, all human endeavors are influenced by culture. An acknowledgment of this cultural reality has been missing in coaching. This chapter provides the theoretical "glue" for integrating the cultural dimension and enlarging the coaching discipline. "Coaching across cultures" allows coaching to become fully effective in all business and organizational environments—across the hallway and across the world.

What Is Culture?

I do not claim any pioneering role in interculturalism. For years, cultural anthropologists, cross-cultural scholars and consultants, and other experts have studied and worked with the concept of culture. My aim is not to compete with these specialists.

However, I do want to offer a working definition geared toward practitioner coaches (managers using a coaching style or professional coaches). I will first share this definition and then explain how it compares with the interculturalists' view.

> A group's culture is the set of unique characteristics
> that distinguishes its members from another group.

This definition encompasses both *visible* (behaviors, language, artifacts) and *invisible* manifestations (norms, values, and basic assumptions or beliefs). This definition goes to the essence of culture: it is a *group* phenomenon as opposed to an *individual* reality. In the Baxter Renal case, the business professionals and the nurses constitute two groups, each with its set of unique characteristics, or culture.

Furthermore, we belong to multiple groups. Therefore, we each operate within multiple cultures. Sometimes the nation is the only group taken into consideration to identify us culturally (we Brits, Germans, Brazilians). But our nation is only one of the groups to which we belong. These groups originate from various categories:

- Geography and nationality, region, religion, ethnicity
- Discipline: profession, education
- Organizations: industry, corporation, union, function
- Social life: family, friends, social class, clubs
- Gender and sexual orientation

You can simultaneously be French, work in the corporate world, be Catholic, be a Grande Ecole alumnus, and so on. Some researchers, such as Gilles Verbunt, insist on the diminishing importance of nations among our cultures. Verbunt argues that "individuals characterize themselves culturally less and less in relation to a nationality and more and more with respect to a values system, social and political aspirations, modes of production and of consumption."[4] Our *identity* could be viewed as this personal and dynamic synthesis of multiple cultures. Our behavior will typically vary depending on the group we happen to be associated with. Just like you, I am always the same person; I have a certain personality. Yet, my behaviors change depending on the group I am interacting with at the moment. For example, some of my friends and I tend to kid with each other in a way that would be totally inappropriate when I meet a new potential business partner. People adapt to groups by choosing to express or repress emotions like joy, anger, humor, and sarcasm. Someone could yell epithets in one context and remain totally silent in another.

The fact that our behaviors depend in part on the particular cultural context further justifies the need for coaches to integrate the cultural perspective into their practice. In some cases the obstacle to someone's progress may be cultural rather than psychological, thus calling for a different coaching dialogue.

For example, a Japanese manager may start a presentation by proffering apologies to his audience: "I would like to apologize for the fact that I am utterly unprepared to speak in front of this distinguished group." He may be bowing and speaking with a low voice and a soft tone. From a Western behavioral perspective, this manager could be perceived as lacking assertiveness resulting from low self-esteem and a lack of confidence. The Japanese manager may not, therefore, be viewed as credible and knowledgeable to a Western audience. Yet, in a Japanese context, the same behavior would be not only totally appropriate but also expected and rewarded.

Without being able to view the Japanese manager's cultural value of modesty through a cultural lens, a coach would not be able to put the observed behavior into perspective. The Western coach would be tempted to help the Japanese manager solve an imagined sense of low self-esteem—with disastrous results!

When I analyzed various definitions of culture, I noticed that most cross-cultural authorities tended to refer to two basic levels of culture: external (all visible manifestations) and internal (such as the largely invisible values and basic underlying assumptions); hence, my similar division on page 23. Not everyone, however, includes the visible aspects in their definitions of culture.

Edgar Schein[5] proposes a definition that excludes overt behaviors. He studies only the "deeply embedded, unconscious basic assumptions" and defines them as the "essence of culture." He argues that overt behaviors, on the other hand, are not solely determined by cultural predispositions. He warns the reader therefore about the potential risk of misinterpreting these behaviors. Likewise, Hofstede defines culture as "mental programming" that evokes an inner reality (norms, values, and basic assumptions) rather than its observable manifestations. Fons Trompenaars uses an "onion ring" model of culture similar to the one Schein proposed, with different cultural layers. However, he refers to both explicit and implicit cultures.[6]

This duality—the external/internal representation of reality—is actually an essential part of how a number of us approach coaching. Imagine culture as an iceberg, which numerous interculturalists have been doing for years (see the figure on page 23). To make an impact on the visible tip of the iceberg, you often need to work below the water's surface, with the immersed part of the iceberg. Adding a cultural dimension to coaching enables us to access and address parts of the iceberg that are otherwise inaccessible. In other words, understanding invisible (deep) culture offers new levers that allow us to access and affect the visible part, by fostering concrete and observable actions.

As a coach, you need to make certain hypotheses in real time. Noticing certain behavior, for example a direct way of communicating, you may *choose* to interpret the behavior as a cultural manifestation rather than as a psychological phenomenon.

Viewing such behavior through a cultural lens may lead to new insights and may pave the way to new possibilities, even though you may not know for certain that the behavior was a cultural manifestation. Likewise, a mathematician, faced with the prospect of resolving a complex equation, will intuitively attribute a value to a certain variable and move forward with the problem solving *as if* his hypothesis were true. If he reaches a satisfactory solution, the mathematician will *a posteriori* be comforted with his initial choice. If he does not solve the problem, he will select a new working hypothesis. The coach does not pretend to decide between the primacy of psychology or culture for explaining behaviors. Coaching from multiple perspectives attempts instead to shift views, in a kaleidoscopic manner, to look at issues from various angles, each with potential merits, to facilitate progress.

Layers of Culture

What do we specifically mean by a set of unique characteristics?

I like the onion ring explanation best, because it is a simple and useful way to answer the question. It emphasizes the different layers of culture,[7] proceeding from visible and conscious to buried and typically unconscious.

Culture as an onion ring   **Culture as an iceberg**

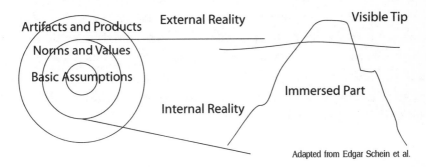

Adapted from Edgar Schein et al.

Artifacts and Products

Artifacts and *products* are the visible manifestations of a culture. Examples are language, food, etiquette, architecture, fashion, and art, to name but a few. They are the visible tip of the iceberg. All the *observable behaviors* belong to this layer as well.

Imagine you were an anthropologist studying a population of professional coaches.[8] You would listen to what they said and how they spoke. You would pay attention to nonverbal behaviors such as their tone of voice, gestures, and postures. You would examine the overall coaching process unfolding over a period of time. You would look for common patterns among all coaches but would probably also notice variations, especially among subgroups.

For example, you would detect that many coaches use the phone to conduct their sessions. They ask direct questions such as "What is holding you back?" or "What will you do specifically as a result of our conversation?" Their tone of voice conveys warmth and firmness. You may also observe variations in the total coaching process. Contracting could result in an elaborate written document between the parties, with comprehensive legal clauses, or in a simple and short agreement form. Coaching itself could focus on specific and measurable targets or be more open-ended, and so on.

Noticing diversity in artifacts and products is interesting. For example, McDonald's launched an advertising campaign in Belgium. Cruising in their vehicle, two visiting reps shared their astonishment: "These Belgians eat french fries with mayonnaise!" (a Belgian habit indeed). One of the men continued, "Aren't you supposed to eat french fries with ketchup like in the USA?" The point seemed to be: "This is a strange habit, but McDonald's pledges nevertheless to adapt to consumer desires." Focusing all the attention on this visible layer of culture may have worked in this instance, but often it does not. For example, while emphasis is often placed on following local etiquette, our experience indicates that a mistake in this area is often of far less consequence than a failure to appreciate the deeper levels of a culture. Gardening serves as a helpful metaphor. If you want your plants to blossom, you need to pay attention to the soil. Each plant requires a specific soil to thrive.

Coaching across cultures moves beyond looking at the observable manifestations of culture to consider the inner layers.

Norms and Values

The next layer toward the center of the onion is composed of norms and values. *Norms* refer to what is considered right, appropriate, and acceptable by the cultural group. *Values* are the ideals shared by that group. Norms and values vary cross-nationally, but they also vary by other cultural groups: corporate, professional, ethnic, age, class, and so on.

For example, an important coaching norm is the *rule of confidentiality*, which typically applies to personal and executive coaching. All conversations between the coach and the coachee should be kept strictly confidential. Confidentiality ensures candid exchanges. Such a norm would exclude the possibility of confusing coaching with auditing. Coaching is a developmental process, not an evaluation or a selection.

The notion of confidentiality is a part of the International Coach Federation's[9] Ethical Guidelines. The norm is ethics rather than law. In fact, unlike conversations with attorneys, confidentiality is not protected by law. Legislation, of course, varies from country to country.

Consider a second example. Sessions over the *phone* may be a norm for personal coaching in the United States, but in Europe *face-to-face* dialogues are preferred, especially to discuss important and sensitive topics. On the other hand, in the U.S. just as in Europe, face-to-face sessions seem to be more common for executive coaching. Country is not the only cultural variable. Here, professional (executive coaching) culture also plays a role.

Note that sometimes *abstract* norms have to be distinguished from *real* ones. For example, *nondiscrimination* could be the abstract norm (i.e., the right thing to do *in principle*). However, *discrimination* may be the real norm (i.e., the rule usually applied *in practice*).

When abstract norms differ from real ones, the dissonance engenders confusion or alienation. Coaches should help raise awareness about these norms and possible gaps. On the positive side, abstract norms can represent aspirations. The goal is to change the real norms so that they match the abstract ones (e.g., nondiscrimination made real) or to change abstract norms so that they have the potential of becoming real (e.g., "Do the best you can" versus "Never fail," which is often unrealistic).

Values refer to what is important for members of a particular group.[10] Hard work and perseverance are examples of common coaching values, as is the ideal of human *growth*. These values are not absolutes. Many people simply enjoy living.[11] They have settled for a routine job, and they take life as it comes. In their view life unfolds with moments of happiness and times of suffering. If presented with a coaching opportunity, such people may refuse it. Should we blame them? Most people I know achieve fulfillment through self-questioning and being proactive, and coaches facilitate this process. But I also know individuals who have a special talent for life. With humor and grace, they accept whatever the universe offers them, and they find contentment. Still others have not found this to be a recipe for the good life but still refuse to trade off their present condition, as difficult as it may be, for a hypothetical better future, achieved through personal growth. In the movie *Alexandre le Bienheureux* (literally, "well happy"), actor Philippe Noiret spends his days tranquilly. Through ingenuous devices he minimizes his efforts and enjoys delicious meals while lying on his bed. The film celebrates the alternative value of doing as little work as possible.

To effectively coach across national and even organizational cultures, coaches need to accept the relativity of their own norms and values, even the core ones like growth. After all, everyone can benefit from shifting our perspective from time to time. For sure, growth is inherent to life itself. Yet coaches' emphasis on growth can sometimes turn into an obsession. By always wanting more fulfillment and more performance in our lives, we may indeed fail to appreciate what we have, and, paradoxically, eventually become desperate. There is also wisdom in accepting life as it comes.

We are not here to *judge* values, but we do want to *challenge* their universality.

The insatiable *quest for money* is another ideal, shared by some or most individuals within a country. In 2001, the TV series *Who Wants to Be a Millionaire?* was shown on TV networks throughout the Western world. An old man with Raybans appeared on an advertisement during the *Millionaire* frenzy. He looked like a New Orleans jazz player, serene and happy. The ad read, "I don't want to be a millionaire." Translation: Money is not a universal value. I am happy living a simple life…and wearing Rayban glasses!

Deciphering norms and values will enlarge our understanding of culture. It will open up new horizons and options. The study of culture, though, cannot be complete without examining basic assumptions, the central and most buried layer of culture.

Basic Assumptions

Through time and space, we have all faced and will continue to be confronted with *universal challenges*. Among these is the implacable passage of *time*. Whether you live in London, Nairobi, or Moscow, whether you practice engineering, performing arts, or carpentry, time is passing. It is our common challenge to deal with time. Time is universal; conversely, our experience of it is not. Fundamentally, you can view time as a scarce resource (a Western and particularly U.S. assumption): there is never enough time to do all the things you want to do. Therefore, you should not "waste" time but pay attention to how you "spend" it. You should manage time carefully and learn to be efficient.

This notion that "time is money" is not a fact. It is an assumption, or belief,[12] which has implications for coaching. For example, you could conclude that, because you don't have much time, coaching sessions will last thirty minutes. Imagine your coachee telling you his story. He has not prepared a neat summary. He speaks spontaneously and openly about his experiences. You can feel his hopes and fears. You start to discover the coachee's different challenges and opportunities. But you only have thirty minutes. There is never enough time. You may think, "I would like to hear your entire story, but I cannot afford to let you go on and on because we only have a half hour. I want us to stay focused and reach our objective in the short amount of time we have."

After all, when this session is over, the coach or the coachee may still need to finish a report today, respond to fifty e-mail messages, pick up the children, and then save a couple of hours to exercise or enjoy a dinner with friends.

The assumption that time is scarce is a useful outlook, inviting you to savor every moment, or stimulating you to increase productivity. It can also be a pernicious belief, pushing you to struggle to keep up with a hectic pace.

In other cultures people believe that time is plentiful. There is a lot of time, so you take your time. You can enjoy a more relaxed relationship with time. When I coach people, I usually set aside two to three hours. Other colleagues in Europe share a similar norm. I say to my clients, "Let's plan for two or three hours, and I want you to know that I will not make an appointment right after our session. In case we are in the middle of a good conversation, I would hate to rush the dialogue and finish it abruptly. If we need the time, we will take it." Incidentally, taking time does not cancel out efficiency, which I also happen to value. It may even yield increased impact. Holding the belief that time is plentiful, even for a moment, can help you to get off the treadmill, slow down, and take a welcome break. It is an alternative and refreshing way to look at time.

Another example of an assumption or belief is our *relationship to nature*. Are you in control of nature or are you controlled by it? Some believe that life is what you make it. "Just do it!" If you work hard and persevere, your dreams will come true. It is very much up to you to make it happen. On the other hand, you could assume that external forces are controlling you. Life may be a matter of luck or fate. As coaches, your goal is not to judge either of these assumptions. Rather, you can try to understand the different perspectives. You can examine the potential advantages and disadvantages each entails.

The positive virtue of assuming you are in control is that it will lead to proactivity and self-fulfilling prophecies. You make dreams happen. On the negative side, this belief can be viewed as naïve or even arrogant. It can also trigger guilt when things don't happen as planned. After all, if you think you are in control, you are also to be blamed when success is elusive.

Conversely, the benefit of assuming that nature is in control of humans is that it removes the burden of worry about always feeling responsible for what happens. However, the negative effect of believing that external forces are in charge is that it can lead to passive acceptance of what happens, "fatalism."

The nature of the coaching profession implies the assumption that you can steer your lives, deploy your talents, and reach success. However, it is useful to keep a sense of humility. You can do your very best, but it is also all you can do. You still need luck. After all, you could have died in a plane crash or a car accident.

In Part II, I will explore these examples and many others in more detail within a framework for categorizing cultural differences. I will also examine the implications for coaching in a systematic fashion. But for now, let us note that each cultural group has organized itself to deal most effectively with its environment by choosing to address universal challenges in a certain way. The basic assumptions, values, and norms are the group's collective answers to these challenges. Having suffered through floods and hurricanes, again and again, Venezuelans have come to believe that nature is very much in control. Businesspeople in the fast information age think that time is scarce. Over time these assumptions typically become internalized, unconscious, unchallenged; they are confused with reality and become our undisputed truth. Our global world and changing environment is an invitation to reevaluate our fundamental assumptions.

The question becomes, How can we deal with those differences in our collective mental programming? What is the development path? What are the steps we must take before we can leverage cultural differences? How can we help coachees develop their ability to deal with people who do not recognize their cultural biases? How can we help them discover new solutions to their challenges? The following section, "Dealing with Cultural Differences," proposes a roadmap.

Norms

What do you consider right/wrong, proper/inappropriate?

What rules do you live by in practice?

Values

What is important to you?

How do you manifest those values?

Basic Assumptions/Beliefs

What is your truth?

What do you regard as true/false?

Dealing with Cultural Differences

The model in the table on page 30 is adapted from the work of Milton Bennett.[13] He has devised an interesting six-stage model for the development of intercultural sensitivity. Albeit not a coaching model per se, I have found it useful as a *development path* both for coaches and their coachees. In this section, building on Bennett's model, I suggest the ultimate goal of *leveraging cultural differences as a seventh developmental stage*. This stage is consistent with the coaching notion of unleashing people's potential.

The model provides a step-by-step method for advancing your ability to recognize and deal with cross-cultural differences. You can assess which stage you have reached, identify what the next developmental level looks like, and then move forward. While you probably have a "default" current stage, you may be operating from different stages in various situations.

Using this model, you will be able to help your coachees determine how they work with cultural differences and what they could do differently. It will, however, be hard to coach them effectively beyond stages you have not first mastered yourself.

As you read the following pages, I invite you to think of a challenging situation where you have been confronted with some kind of cultural differences. You may be in the middle of a merger, where clashes occur between alternative values and assumptions. You may be part of a remote team involving members from different countries, with cultural habits that are unusual to you. You may be coaching a group of engineers who are frustrated with their company's designers.

1. Try to reconnect emotionally with this situation. What was different about the other culture(s) and what was your experience of the differences? Were you puzzled, did you feel frustrated, offended, amused, or excited?

2. Reflect on how you managed those cultural differences. What was your mindset in this situation? And what was the impact of your attitude and behaviors?

Dealing with Cultural Differences

Culture as a Process →

Ethnocentric* Pitfalls

1. Ignore differences
   - be physically or mentally isolated/separated
   - deny

2. Recognize differences but evaluate them negatively
   - denigrate others
   - feel superior
   - place others on a pedestal

3. Recognize differences but minimize their importance
   - trivialize
   - fail to notice uniqueness—"we are all the same"

Ethnorelative** Approaches

4. Recognize and accept differences
   - acknowledge, appreciate, understand
   - acceptance ≠ agreement, surrender
   - acceptance needs to be instinctual and emotional as much as intellectual

5. Adapt to differences
   - move outside one's comfort zone
   - empathy (temporary shift in perspective)
   - adaptation ≠ adoption, assimilation

6. Integrate differences
   - hold different frames of reference in mind
   - analyze and evaluate situations from various cultural perspectives
   - remain grounded in reality; essential to avoid becoming dazzled by too many possibilities

7. Leverage differences
   - make the most of differences, strive for synergy
   - proactively look for gems in different cultures
   - achieve unity through diversity

*Ethnocentric coaching

**Ethnorelative coaching
= Global coaching
= Coaching across cultures

← **Culture as a Given**

Sources: Milton Bennett, "Toward Ethnorelativism: A Developmental Model of Intercultural Sensitivity," 1993, and Philippe Rosinski, "Beyond Intercultural Sensitivity: Leveraging Cultural Differences," 1999.

The model on page 30 should help you determine your attitude vis-à-vis cultural differences. Before examining specific ways to leverage cultural differences, you first need to be honest about your level of development and make a conscious decision to raise it if necessary.

Ethnocentric Pitfalls

Traditional coaching and leadership often fall into the trap of adopting an ethnocentric view. What is *ethnocentrism?* According to Bennett, it is "the assumption that one's own culture is central to all reality." There is no evil intent, simply a naïveté or a lack of awareness of culture.

Ethnocentrism occurs in three forms: ignoring differences, evaluating them negatively, and downplaying their importance. In my experience, the first form of ethnocentrism is rare among coaches and leaders, the second is not uncommon, and the third is frequent.

Ignore Differences

At this stage there is no recognition of cultural differences. Ignorance or denial[14] occurs from a position of isolation or separation. This can happen if you live in a remote community or if you intentionally erect physical or social barriers to create distance from cultural difference. In any event, you don't pay attention to cultural differences.

In the eighteenth century, French Queen Marie-Antoinette, wife of Louis XVI, lived a life of pleasure and luxury. She didn't want to see the harsh lives people were enduring or recognize the deterioration of their condition. When she was told that people did not have bread to eat, she suggested they eat brioche instead. Needless to mention, the fancy brioche was not an option for the lower class. Marie-Antoinette's separation from her people led her to ignore the differences between her and them. She created resentment and ended up paying a high price for ignoring cultural differences. She had to kneel at the guillotine.

Ghettos (e.g., rich/poor, black/white, Christian/Jew) have played the role of creating separation in urban areas, enabling an attitude of denial toward cultural differences. But barriers can also be mental; you can travel abroad without noticing fundamental differences. A Westerner may say, "Tokyo is just like home; there are lots of cars, tall buildings, and Coca-Cola."

I have not met coaches who effectively practice coaching while also operating at a denial stage. But I have seen "soft" forms of denial, which exist whenever one avoids mixing with different cultural groups and adopts a paro-chial attitude. For example, a group of professionals from the same country might not pay attention to a colleague from another country. They may not express any curiosity in how his culture is different, behaving as if that differ-ence did not exist.[15] If the foreigner were to offer an alternative viewpoint, the dominant group of professionals would fail to acknowledge it, as if they were simply deaf to anything outside their worldview.

If your coachee denies cultural differences, your goal as a coach is to help him recognize them. It would probably be overly ambitious to expect anything more initially. You certainly can't expect your coachee to leverage differences he can't even see! Organizing visits, creating opportunities to come into contact with cultural artifacts, is a place to start. Your coachee can discover artistic creations (architecture, music, painting, film, literature, etc.), taste food, learn about political and social systems, and more.

Recognize Differences but Evaluate Them Negatively

As Bennett pointed out, this happens in three situations: denigration, superi-ority, and reversal.

Denigration means you see other cultures as inferior, and it can take the form of negative stereotyping and racism. Hostile behaviors are frequent in this case. Mild yet dangerous forms of denigration are unfortunately com-mon: intellectuals looking down on manual workers, executives showing little respect for clerks, the older generation viewing the younger one as irrespon-sible, the young people considering the old as reactionary, farmers seeing foreign migrant workers as inferior.

At the superiority stage, you see your cultural group (nation, religion, profession, gender, etc.) as superior, really the flip side of denigration. Superi-ority goes beyond a healthy pride. The negative side to patriotism is extreme nationalism. Similarly, the shadow side of religion is called fundamentalism. These negative attitudes have survived into the twenty-first century, continu-ing to cause horrors and suffering in the world.

In coaching situations, believing in the superiority of your culture could lead you to impose your approach (time is money, achievement is vital) without regard for the coachee's culture. You would then likely frustrate the coachee and miss an opportunity to learn from him.

Reversal is a more subtle form of negative evaluation. I have known West-erners who have become fascinated with Asia. They contrast Eastern spiritual wisdom with Western materialistic decadence. In a simplistic manner, they place the other culture on a pedestal while denigrating their own. As Bennett indicates, "This may appear to be a more culturally enlightened position…but it is actually only changing the center of ethnocentrism."

For Bennett, to develop out of what he calls the defense half of the model implies a passage through a third stage, minimization. This means emphasizing commonality rather than differences.

Recognize Differences but Minimize Their Importance

At this stage, people recognize cultural differences and moreover do not evaluate them negatively. This represents progress from previous stages. Focusing on what we all have in common can favor communication. We all have biological needs; we all face similar universal challenges. After all, the word *communication* itself suggests finding intersections and bringing together.

Still, minimization is characterized as ethnocentrism because people "bury differences under the weight of similarities"; in other words, cultural differences are trivialized.

The golden rule "Do unto others as you would have them do unto you" may sound like a wise and humanistic statement, but it also reveals an assumption of underlying similarity.

For example, imagine one female manager among a group of male managers. If the men say "She's just like the guys" or "We are all the same," they may be conveying their inability to appreciate her differences. They perceive her as a valuable team member—as long as her uniqueness is ironed out. Corporate women who first broke the glass ceiling had to embrace a "masculine" culture, which stresses return on investment and competition. Only slowly have corporations started to appreciate collaborative and relational feminine-type values and their importance to organizational success.

Minimization is a preferable form of ethnocentrism to the two previous stages, but it is ethnocentrism nonetheless—and it is, as I mentioned earlier, quite common among coaches. As an executive coach, I am often confronted with managers who tend to project their own values, norms, and beliefs onto others. They simply assume that what is relevant to them is necessarily pertinent to others. They fail to appreciate the variety of people's drivers and sources of motivation. As a result, they are not nearly as effective as they could be in bringing diverse people on board with their projects, in fostering genuine commitment, and in liberating efforts.

For example, managers driven by a desire to achieve task objectives may overlook the importance of human relationships as a key motivator for other collaborators. They may offer you a bigger car when in fact you long for more social interactions and a better quality of life. Managers who have not gone beyond minimization have likely alienated many employees, probably without even being aware of it, and are thereby achieving far less than possible.

I have found that I can help coachees move from negative evaluation directly to acceptance, skipping minimization altogether. In essence, the goal is to evaluate differences positively instead of negatively. As a coach, you can help coachees to value differences by showing them the merits of the other perspective, as the Baxter nurses and business professionals came to see.

Such a jump is easier with coaching than it is with teaching. Coaching is action oriented, driven by coachees' actual projects, rather than by an education curriculum. Another reason is that coaching is a process, not an isolated event. It takes place over a period of time during which tendencies to fall back into old patterns (regression) can be readily dealt with and target objectives achieved. Coaching will in fact speed up the developmental journey.

Ethnorelative Approaches

The next four stages avoid ethnocentric pitfalls and take on ethnorelative or cross-cultural approaches. I have already referred to this type of coaching using the terms *coaching across cultures* or *global coaching*.

In the ethnorelative stages, you perceive cultural differences as inevitable, and you acknowledge that your worldview is not central to everyone's reality. Yet you don't feel threatened but instead become curious and eager to learn about differences you had recognized but evaluated negatively earlier (stage 2). As a cross-cultural coach, you start to accept, appreciate, and then adapt to differences. Importantly, you do it without giving up your own integrity. You become more flexible without changing who you are. In fact, you can now be more fully yourself. You grow by expanding your consciousness and by enriching your repertoire.

Let us use an analogy. Bjorn Borg was one of the all-time great tennis champions. He won a record six consecutive Wimbledon championships. The Wimbledon lawn surface favors natural volley players. Björn Borg was not one of them. He preferred to play from the baseline, hammering forehands and backhands. At ease on clay, he won five Roland Garros (French Open) titles, a competition the great Pete Sampras, who enjoyed seven victories at

Wimbledon, did not win even once. Björn Borg enhanced his game by venturing to the net and volleying. He avoided sticking with what was comfortable and natural. He chose not to place a narrow limit on his tennis identity. By adapting, he unleashed more potential and achieved greater success.

Recognize and Accept Differences

Acceptance is characterized by a respect for and appreciation of cultural differences relating to all cultural layers: artifacts and products, values and norms, and basic assumptions. Accepting the inner layers is usually harder to achieve. Tasting a different food may be easy; respecting a different belief is another story.

In the area of communication, for example, you may prefer to be explicit. As a coach, you may like to put everything on the table, so there is no misunderstanding. In some cultures, though, communication is more implicit. What really matters is not just what you say, but how you say it, what you do not say, your tone of voice, posture, and gestures.

You can develop an appreciation for implicit communication, and it has interesting implications for coaching. You will realize that you can only go so far with e-mail or even with the phone. If you are dealing with a coachee whose orientation is implicit communication, you need to understand the importance of face-to-face communication and become attuned to subtle messages.

An executive based in the United Kingdom and I, based in Belgium, were having difficulties scheduling our next face-to-face appointment. I suggested an exceptional phone conversation instead. I wanted to make sure we could keep in contact and not wait for another three weeks for our next coaching session. My client said he preferred to meet face-to-face. He came to Brussels by plane, spent three hours with me, and then flew back.

He felt much more comfortable having a coaching session face-to-face than by phone and our coaching was more effective. He knew I could notice his smiles, frowns, and other facial expressions. He was confident I could observe him leaning forward or backward, see him suddenly sit up straight or sink into the chair. He wanted me to capture all the nonverbal, implicit signals, which were clues for how he really felt. I could then act as if I were holding a mirror and invite him to acknowledge his feelings, which would guide his decisions.

A valid concern about acceptance is that it may lead to surrender, but appreciating another culture does not imply renouncing your own. Acceptance does not mean agreement. You can respect a different cultural trait without making the same choice in your life. You can see that it may be right for another person, even if it is not right for you. For example, while you may value informality and wear blue jeans and running shoes, you can also respect that some cultures are more at ease with formality.

Another concern is that all cultural differences are relative and therefore we should accept any culture on the grounds that we should be tolerant of cultural differences. No. Accepting alternate cultural views should not go as far as accepting a cultural view that would promote intolerance: racism, xenophobia, or antisemitism. Acceptance does not mean naïveté.

In the vast majority of cases, however, accepting cultural differences is desirable. And apart from intolerance itself, we should tolerate and encourage alternate worldviews.

Finally, acceptance needs to be instinctual and emotional as well as intellectual. A mere intellectual acknowledgment of difference is not sufficient. You need to become convinced in your heart and in your guts that a different truth or ideal is legitimate.

Adaptation to Differences

Adaptation is the stage where you are willing to venture outside your comfort zone. You adapt your behaviors when appropriate. You are willing to take a different perspective and to hold different values and assumptions. You put yourself in a person's shoes, looking at reality from his viewpoint. *Empathy* is an essential human quality, and adaptation requires a lot of it.

I have found the notion of comfort zone an extremely useful metaphor in the context of human development in general.

Comfort Zone

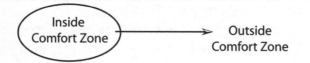

The cross-cultural environment provides a valuable opportunity to step outside your comfort zone. Coaches should motivate coachees to embrace this opportunity to grow while urging them to regularly come back inside to recharge their batteries. Recognizing and accepting differences keeps you within the comforting boundaries of the familiar. Adapting to difference requires you to bravely step outside and experiment with changing some of your behaviors: letting go of control, trying silence on like a new coat, taking the nurses' perspective in the Baxter Renal example.

Each person needs to find the right dynamic balance between being inside or outside his comfort zone. Stretching your or your coachees' comfort zone is constructive, but obviously you can only progress so far and so fast. Beyond a certain limit, going "against the grain" becomes counterproductive, possibly causing burnout or simply reducing the coachees' ability to experience any joy during the coaching journey.

Some people suggest that empathy is sufficient to coach across cultures. If you are open, curious, respectful of differences, and ready to learn, they argue, this is all you need to be an effective coach. There is some truth in this assertion. After all, your role as a coach is to enable the coachee to devise his own solutions. The coachee is the expert. But is coaching that simple? Can you *really* be empathetic across cultures without learning about cultures? I don't think so. The danger is in overlooking the necessity to engage in your own cross-cultural development.

I remember talking to several individuals in the U.S. during the Bill Clinton–Monica Lewinsky scandal. These people were regarded as highly empathetic in their own culture. But in the following instance their empathy did not extend across cultures, and was therefore not sufficient to adapt to cultural differences. When I mentioned the fact that French President Mitterand had once had his mistress and illegitimate daughter living in the Elysée palace (equivalent to the U.S. White House) and that this fact remained quiet and never became a scandal, I noticed a shock. When I told them that furthermore the French press thought that President Clinton did not have any choice but to lie by omission about the affair, because of the puritanical U.S. culture, the natural empathy gave way to severe judgment: "These French obviously do not share our same level of moral standards!" This reveals an ethnocentric attitude: those expressing the judgment do so from the perspective of their own cultural context. Morality manifests itself indeed in different cultural ways. As a generalization, inevitably inaccurate, some say that sex may be shocking in the U.S. just like money and wealth may shock the French! In this example, I portrayed Americans. I could have chosen other cases. No culture is immune from ethnocentric temptation.

What is particularly useful is to immerse yourself in different cultures in various organizations and corporations as well as in foreign countries. Working as an expatriate in a foreign country provides a great opportunity but by no means guarantees that intercultural adaptation will automatically develop very far. For example, I was in close professional contact with two couples from the United States living in Belgium. The first couple made an effort to learn the local languages and socialize with Belgians and Europeans living in Brussels. The second couple rented a secluded house and spent most of their time alone or with American friends. Even the couple that remained secluded discovered differences they could not have known had they stayed in the U.S., but overall they were still judgmental about Belgians by the end of their stay. In contrast, the couple who had made the effort to experience the local culture learned to appreciate and even try out new behaviors: the Belgian sense of derision, resourcefulness, and straightforwardness. In other words, they adapted to the Belgian way of life.

To help you adapt to different cultures, you could also consider two very helpful resources. One, the Society for Intercultural Education, Training, and Research (SIETAR),[16] is a premier international network of interculturalists. The second, Intercultural Press,[17] publishes guides to specific cultures and countries and culture-general books on adapting to an overseas posting.

Importantly, adapting does not mean assimilating. Referring to the Trans-actional Analysis vocabulary from chapter 1, the distinction is that adaptation implies an OK–OK mindset, while assimilation suggests a not OK–OK frame of mind. Assimilation occurs when you give up your own identity, when you let it be absorbed by the new culture. While adaptation supports coaching, which attempts to leverage potentials and achieve synergy, assimilation, on the contrary, eliminates differences and fails to notice uniqueness.

Integrate Differences

Adaptation means a temporary shift in perspective, adaptation of behavior when needed. Integration, Bennett's final developmental stage, occurs when you are able to hold different frames of reference in your mind at any time. You can look at a situation from various angles. You have acquired knowledge and developed mental agility, which are both very useful when working with your coachees.

You can "analyze and evaluate situations from one or more chosen cultural perspectives." You can therefore switch cultural perspectives and suggest alternative ways.

You have become, as Peter Adler describes, a person whose "essential identity is inclusive of life patterns different from his own and who has psychologically and socially come to grips with a multiplicity of realities."[18]

For example, a coachee may fail to see patterns and interconnections. He may tend to break a problem into smaller pieces that are more easily manageable but that also create artificial silos. The coach, at the integration stage, is able to see the process itself unfolding while also focusing on the coachee's issue and will realize, for example, that his coachee may be experiencing the limitations of Western analytical thinking.

This consciousness is possible because the coach also knows the existence and applications of an alternative mode of thinking, Eastern systemic thinking (see Part II, pages 183–87). Equipped with this knowledge, the coach can invite his coachee to become aware of how he is thinking. Through questions, suggestions, and other coaching techniques, the coach helps the coachee adopt a more systemic approach.

Integration is an advanced form of cultural development, and it comes with a price. Self-questioning is more difficult than living with certainties. When you understand that culture is a process and that there is more than one "right" way, you are no longer a passive spectator who can blame others without being accountable. You are an actor who can contribute to dynamically shaping culture. You have choices and, therefore, you have a responsibility to build the right cultural environment.

You can also, however, become dazzled by too many possibilities. Bennett writes: "[At the integration level,] you are outside all cultural frames of reference by virtue of your ability to consciously raise any assumption to a metalevel (level of self-reference)." You experience "your self as a constant creator of your own reality." This is constructive, yet "vulnerability, diffuse identity, inauthenticity and anomie are dangers that loom beyond an unprepared departure from cultural boundaries…. People may experience a kind of void where they cannot feel a part of any culture, nor can they clearly feel themselves as constructive actors outside of culture."

Remaining grounded in reality is critical. Don't just embrace a "meta" position. Also immerse yourself in cultures and enjoy the experience. When you do step back, you will have the benefit of familiarity with real life.

A mere intellectual understanding of the concepts described here is not sufficient. You cannot simply skim through stages 4 to 6. It takes significant life experience and self-questioning to really accept other worldviews as viable alternatives. Your understanding needs to be instinctual, emotional as much as intellectual.

When you have developed a willingness and ability to accept cultural differences without feeling that your integrity is threatened, then you can move to stage 5, adaptation. Your cross-cultural sensitivity as a coach is probably already greater than most. The transition to stage 6, integration, is almost natural, just like new tennis strokes may seem odd at first but then become second nature with practice. At stage 6, the tennis player has not only mastered multiple strokes, but has developed an uncanny ability to choose the optimal stroke in a split second during a match. Likewise, the coach's repertoire has expanded together with his capacity to call upon multiple cultural perspectives as needed.

Being able to juggle—being comfortable with different cultural perspectives—and shedding light on the coachees' issues with cross-cultural rays is certainly remarkable. Yet I suggest you can move even further, toward a new stage (stage 7), where you can leverage the differences to great advantage.

Leverage Differences

Leveraging cultural differences is a proactive attitude. You look for gems in your own culture(s) and mine for treasures in other culture(s). You encourage your coachees to do the same. The riches appear in the form of useful insights, alternative perspectives on issues, and can be collected from human wisdom accumulated through space and time.

Although I have mentioned *leveraging* in earlier chapters, I have not defined it specifically. In mechanics, a lever is "a rigid bar resting on a pivot, used to help move a heavy or firmly fixed load with one end when pressure is applied to the other."[19] The *lever effect* is the multiplication of force that occurs by using a lever. In other words, leveraging your force means obtaining a stronger force than the one you are exerting, thanks to the lever.[20]

I believe the concept of leveraging is essential in coaching. Leveraging means *achieving more output with a given input.* The input is *human potential*—individual or collective. Moreover, for coaching across cultures, the input is also different cultural orientations. The richness that lies in cultural diversity is part of our potential. Simply stated, leveraging cultural differences means making the most of these differences. The coaching process is the lever that helps to achieve greater success and to overcome complex challenges.

Leveraging is associated with a dynamic view of culture. It implies proactively studying cultures, and looking for creative ways to find the best of different cultural views. Leveraging is about building *synergies*, creating a *synthesis* bigger than the sum of cultural components taken separately.[21]

Paradoxically, in this process you will at last discover *unity*. This is not a bland version. It is not a stage 3, "We are all the same" type of situation where uniformity is confused with unity and where a dominant view or a lowest common denominator prevails. Unity refers to a form of completion, wholeness, or globality. Unity is the synthesis of differences. In this context, becoming whole means developing a mindset that honors cultural differences.[22] Moreover you can never become complacent because unity in a changing world is fragile, unstable, and thus requires being constantly reinvented and reestablished.

This brings us full circle to where we started in chapter 2. Baxter Renal UK leverages profit-driven and human-driven values to achieve both superior profit and human performance. Mark Philips became more effective by blending Swedish traits with his own British culture. In the next part, you will learn many different cultural orientations, with definitions of these orientations, examples of cross-cultural stumbling blocks, instances of leveraging differences, and applications to and advice for coaches.

Finally, let me recognize that leveraging differences is not always possible, for practical or moral reasons. Sometimes choices need to be made between alternatives. Compromises or tradeoffs may be the best you can hope for. In certain instances, you have to take a strong stand: this cultural view is right and the other one is not. For example, holding life as sacred is right, and murdering innocent victims is unacceptable.

Case Studies: Leveraging Cultural Differences

Coaching across cultures means looking for opportunities to unleash more human potential by leveraging cultural differences. The outcome is increased performance and fulfillment. The following case studies illustrate how this can be done in a variety of situations.

Leveraging Unilever and Bestfoods Cultures

Research has shown that "over one merger out of two fails. Two out of three do not produce the value creation promised during the operation. The question of people and company culture is by far the number one failure factor."[23]

In 2000, Unilever acquired Bestfoods for just over US$25 billion. The operation was among the twenty largest mergers and acquisitions worldwide that year.[24]

Rather than de facto imposing its culture, Unilever understood that to make the merger work, cultural differences between the two companies had to be well understood.

A task force, with the help of the Hay Group, identified the following differences, realizing that there were many exceptions to those generalizations:

	Unilever	Bestfoods
Mindset/Behaviors	Conceptual/intellectual focus Egalitarian/risk averse Diffuse/collective accountability Stretch the mold Reflective observation Rational	Operational focus Work to high risk/reward equation Sense of personal accountability Break the mold Active experimentation Intuitive
Decision-Making Style	Consensus decision making Slower decision making Decentralized, but with strong corporate influence	Individual/small group decisions Instant decisions Decentralized, high level of regional autonomy
Influencing/Politics	Question decisions and analyze Adept at managing corporate politics	Just do it (compliance/coercion) Naïve in managing organizational politics

The integration team recognized that all the orientations had potential merits. They considered amalgamating the best of both cultures but soon realized that a context was necessary to make that evaluation. The overall vision and strategy provided that context. What was called for was *a new corporate culture* that would draw characteristics from Unilever and Bestfoods.

To that end, an enriched cultural repertoire has started to develop, leveraging Unilever and Bestfoods cultures. For example, Unilever executives are learning to make quicker decisions whenever extra analysis would only impede action. Bestfoods executives are developing a habit of constructively challenging decisions to avoid engaging in a hasty, inadequate course of action.

I noticed the intellectual versus operational focus with several senior executives I coached from both companies. I urged them to learn from the other culture to enrich their original company culture. For example, I challenged one Unilever executive to describe his vision in more specific terms and to spell out his operational priorities. Meanwhile, I invited a Bestfoods executive to articulate a general philosophy and a compelling business case, building on his intuitive ideas and concrete initiatives in order to bring his colleagues on board with his novel approach.

Time will tell how successful the Bestfoods acquisition will prove to be. But it is clear that this eagerness to learn from the other merging company has already strengthened Unilever–Bestfoods. Talent from the acquired Bestfoods has been retained and developed, rather than alienated, as is too often the case.

Synthesizing Western and Asian Cultures at Chubb Insurance

Chubb's operation in Asia has been very successful. In 2001, the Asia Pacific operations of Chubb achieved an overall growth rate of over 37 percent (representing a total of just over US$158 million), way above the 3–7 percent general market growth estimate of March 2002. While many factors made this possible, top leadership's commitment to synthesize Western and Asian cultures has, I believe, played an important part.

Chris Giles, president of Chubb Asia/Pacific, and Chris Hamilton, senior vice president of human resources, have always been convinced that to build a thriving business operation, Chubb executives would have to be excellent leaders. They knew that this meant in particular a capacity to act as coaches and to do so across cultures.

Chris Hamilton asked me to help his team design and deliver a leadership development program in Singapore for Chubb's senior Asian and Australian executives. We all wanted to avoid coming across as arrogant Westerners who impose our way and show Asians how to lead. Chris Hamilton expressed the more humble view that we can all learn from each other and that difference is a source of richness.[25]

During my experience of the first Leadership Development Seminar with Chubb Asia Pacific (October 2001), I noticed, for example, that within the Asian group, many forces converged to create unity at the top, which constitutes an important asset to drive the company and build Chubb's presence in Asia. The forces included a cultural inclination for harmony, a preference for internal cooperation, and the sense of belonging to a community. Preserving harmony entailed relying on indirect forms of communication, ensuring that everyone could save face and being careful not to hurt anyone's feelings. It also implied more comfort with discipline (e.g., following instructions consistently and rigorously) as a way of providing impeccable service to the organization and its clients.

During the seminar, I saw the Australian executives (who are closer to the West culturally and who also constitute an important part of Chubb Asia Pacific) being more outspoken on average, spontaneously sharing their thoughts and feelings with the group. They later learned from the Asians the virtues of listening and of keeping silent. Conversely, they showed the Asians how to speak up, risking challenging the group's harmony when they felt the group was heading in the wrong direction.

Mutual respect and eagerness to learn from one another enabled the group to cross-fertilize Western and Eastern cultures in a highly effective and synergistic way. This resulted in the development of a new culture of high performance and high fulfillment, synthesizing Asian and Western characteristics.

Chubb Asia Pacific's executives have learned to blend Western individual leadership with Asian collective harmony; for instance, to give direct feedback (which may feel more natural to Westerners) while relying on the Asian culture to avoid potentially damaging effects. They would, for example, always build sufficient trust, mutual respect, and appreciation before giving negative feedback. To avoid loss of face, they would focus on describing behaviors and their impact, insisting that this feedback was not a judgment of the person per se. Furthermore, they would always conduct delicate conversations "between four eyes" (one-on-one).[26]

Chubb Asia Pacific's executives have learned to ask more questions of their subordinates as a way of empowering them. Chris Giles had insisted that this was critical to achieve business results. They have acquired a habit of fostering autonomous decision making, yet still counting on their subordinates' sense of discipline and collective harmony to preserve overall alignment with Chubb's goals.

One Chinese executive told me that despite their collectivist reputation, Chinese heroes had always been individuals (i.e., Confucius, Mother Meng, Zhu Bolu, Sun Tzu…).[27] So, he said he did not have any difficulty embracing both individualistic and collectivistic orientations!

Of course, leveraging cultural differences is not straightforward and may not always be possible (e.g., sometimes you have to make tradeoffs). Moreover, one can never become complacent. It will be up to all of Chubb Asia Pacific's people to continue to look for ways to leverage their human potential and their cultural differences to achieve success beyond expectations.

We now move into Part II of this book, where we will explore important cultural dimensions via the "Cultural Orientations Framework." Those of you who are interculturalists learning how to coach will be very familiar with these dimensions, although you may find some different definitions for familiar variables.

Part II
Leveraging Cultural Differences

Chapter 3
The Cultural Orientations Framework

To integrate culture into coaching, what is needed first is *a language to talk about culture*. Without language, it is as if cultural reality does not exist. Eskimos possess a myriad of words to describe varieties of snow, for example. Most of us don't master that language and are therefore unable to decipher subtleties. The same is true for every discipline and human activity. For the unaware, a tennis serve is just a serve. But for a connoisseur, you have the topspin, slice, and flat versions. You can serve into the body, wide on the backhand or forehand sides, and so on.

Language is essential, but the problem is that culture is a vast subject. There are an almost infinite number of possible values, norms, and behaviors. When we learn a foreign language, we cannot expect to readily master thousands of words and expressions. Likewise, it would be unrealistic for coaches to try to suddenly become interculturalists. Even during an entire lifetime, one could only hope to begin exploring various civilizations across space and time!

The good news is that eminent interculturalists have identified key cultural features, which allow us to distinguish fundamental characteristics. Exploring all aspects of a culture is beyond our reach. However, we can focus on a set of *cultural orientations* and *cultural dimensions*, relying on the findings of anthropologists, communication experts, and cross-cultural consultants, including Florence Kluckhohn and Frederick Strodtbeck, Edward T. Hall, Geert Hofstede, and Fons Trompenaars, among others.

A *cultural orientation* is an inclination to think, feel, or act in a way that is culturally determined. For example, in the United States people tend to communicate in a direct fashion, saying what they mean, and meaning what they say. The message is clear, but it can also be perceived as offensive. Their cultural orientation, then, is "direct communication," in contrast with Asians' typical indirectness. Asians don't necessarily spell out what they mean, at the risk of being misunderstood, because they wish to avoid hurting someone's feelings.

Cultural orientations are not black and white. In other words, no one is totally direct or indirect, but individuals and cultures lie somewhere on a continuum bounded by the extreme on both ends. For example, you may be inclined to be direct 70 percent of the time and indirect the remaining 30 percent. In other words, your cultural orientation, on the "direct–indirect communication" *cultural dimension*, is primarily "direct communication."

Example: Direct–Indirect communication cultural dimension

```
X————————————X——————————0————————————————————X
100% direct            70%           50%                      0% direct
<Direct communication orientation>       <Indirect communication orientation>
```

In order to *assess and compare cultures*, coaches need an *integrative framework* that includes a range of cultural dimensions/orientations that are of practical importance to their work with coachees. Here again, several authors have proposed models building on cultural dimensions that had been previously identified, largely by the authors mentioned earlier. The "Cultural Orientations Model" by the Training Management Corporation (TMC) is a useful source.[1] TMC has also devised a psychometric instrument called the "Cultural Orientations Indicator." The "Learning Framework" by the Center for Creative Leadership is another valuable reference.[2]

In this chapter and throughout Part II, you will discover and become familiar with an integrative framework, the "Cultural Orientations Framework" (COF), which maps out regions of cultural territory important for coaches, in particular, and for coachees working in organizations. The framework has a number of uses:

- *Assess cultures.* The COF provides language to describe the salient traits of a culture and focuses your attention on key cultural variables and tendencies.
- *Discover new cultural choices.* You may recognize an orientation for, say, hierarchical organization and compare it with a preference for a flat structure. Patterns that seemed so natural and universal suddenly appear relative and even biased when contrasted with their opposites. Orientations that had been overlooked or undiscovered offer new choices for dealing with challenging situations.
- *Assess cultural differences.* As Stewart and Bennett's research indicated, "The core difficulty in cross-cultural interaction is—simply stated—a failure to recognize relevant cultural differences."[3] When several cultures are involved, the COF gives you a systematic approach for clarifying the nature of cultural differences as well as similarities among them.

- *Bridge different cultures.* Having pinpointed specific cultural differences allows you to focus your energy next on bridging the gaps.
- *Envision a desired culture.* The COF provides a vocabulary to describe an ideal culture. It then becomes a matter of bridging the current culture with the desired one. The challenge is still great, but it becomes manageable at least.
- *Leverage cultural diversity.* With cultural alternatives clearly identified, you can strive to internalize the best of the two or three viewpoints for each dimension. Whenever possible, you will make the most of cultural differences and achieve synergy.

The COF allows coaches to work with cultural differences without judgment or even a fixed prescription. All cultural orientations have potential merits and downsides. Coaches should encourage an ethnorelative attitude (see chapter 2) and lead by example.

Categories in the Cultural Orientations Framework

Having in mind the universal challenges coaches and their coachees face and the important cultural dimensions from the intercultural literature, I have grouped the dimensions into seven categories that correspond to critical challenges people undoubtedly face, regardless of their culture or work, but that are especially important for the coaching arena. As I mentioned earlier, every culture contains each one of the orientations; the key difference among cultures is the point of emphasis. For every dimension, the orientation *on average* will tend to lie somewhere along the continuum.

The first category, *sense of power and responsibility,* invites you to examine the question "Do you control nature or does nature control your life?" Your coachee's answer influences how you should go about engaging in the coaching process. Coaching can only begin if the coachee assumes he has at least some control over his life. If not, what would be the point of articulating personal objectives?

The second category, *time management approaches,* explores alternative ways to view time, perhaps our most precious yet limited resource (we all have to face death at some point).

The third category deals with *identity and purpose,* which directly relate to the coach's mission of helping coachees to reach important, meaningful objectives. What is meaningful to someone is largely determined indeed by his purpose, which is in turn influenced by culture.

The fourth category explores various *organizational arrangements* that are essential, since most coachees work in some form of organization.

The fifth category refers to *territory*, another precious resource. As you will discover, the way you delineate your physical and psychological territory affects the coaching dialogue.

Communication patterns, which make up the sixth category, are of obvious importance since communication is what enables us to build relationships and to exchange information.

Finally, *modes of thinking*, the seventh category, are critical for understanding how your coachees think about their problems. Their mode of thinking may indeed be part of the problem, while an alternative mode may be part of the solution.

The table on pages 54–55 summarizes the categories and dimensions of the COF.

Note that I sometimes use terms in a way that is different from that of the authors who initially introduced these cultural orientations. I may also use different terms altogether. For example, in the first category, I have chosen the term *humility* instead of *subjugation to nature*, which originated with Kluckhohn and Strodtbeck. The word *humility* indicates a value that in my experience as a coach is more likely to be easily recognized as positive. I connect the concept of humility with the philosophical notion of transcendence (there is humility in accepting that power resides outside of us) as opposed to control-immanence (see chapter 4).

Determining a Cultural Profile Using the COF

You can use the COF to determine your *cultural profile* or to help your coachees establish theirs. This is part of the coaching assessment process.

Because culture is a group phenomenon, it is possible, at least in principle, to use the COF to describe the characteristics of a particular team, division, or company.

Geert Hofstede[4] did something equivalent back in 1980 when he wrote a book based on his previous research with IBM employees in over twenty nations. Hofstede mapped out the various countries along a continuum for each of his four cultural dimensions.

However, since an individual's cultural orientation can vary significantly from national characteristics (e.g., the French may prefer hierarchical organizational arrangements in general, but I know some who favor equality), I suggest that each person, team, or organization establishes his or its unique profile.

To create a cultural profile, your coachees will need to reflect on the meaning of each dimension and think of their typical inclination in situations they have experienced. Of course, to provide useful guidance you need to have a good understanding of the dimensions, which are explained in detail in the following seven chapters. Moreover, your coaching will help bring these cultural orientations to the surface; they are often unconscious. For example, if your coachee does not realize that he views time as a scarce resource as opposed to one that is plentiful, he will probably fail to recognize opportunities to break out of the mold and live his life in a more relaxed manner. Awareness will allow for productive action.

The same method can be used to determine a group's collective profile, for example, or to depict a company culture.

It's interesting to know that establishing profiles is hardly a new phenomenon, although cultural profiling is. Psychological typologies have been a human tradition since ancient times. Allow me to give just a few examples. Hippocrates' (c.460–377 BC)[5] "humors" yielded personality types (e.g., the lymph and the associated phlegmatic, lymphatic person), while the Ancients' "four elements" can be tied to various personality attributes, represented below.[6]

Element	Personality Attributes
Earth	Stability, pragmatism
Air	Flexibility, creativity
Water	Openness, affability
Fire	Determination, passion

More recently, Carl Jung's psychological types[7] have been captured in the Myers-Briggs Type Indicator (MBTI),[8] which is probably the most widely used psychometric instrument worldwide to describe personality differences. In chapter 11, you will find a brief description of the MBTI dimensions.

Methodological Considerations for Using the COF Effectively

Cultural versus Personality Profile

While a parallel can be drawn between cultural and personality profiles, the

Cultural Orientations Framework

Categories	Dimensions	Description
Sense of Power and Responsibility	Control/Harmony/ Humility	Control: People have a determinant power and responsibility to forge the life they want. Harmony: Strive for balance and harmony with nature. Humility: Accept inevitable natural limitations.
	Scarce/Plentiful	Scarce: Time is a scarce resource. Manage it carefully! Plentiful: Time is abundant. Relax!
Time Management Approaches	Monochronic/ Polychronic	Monochronic: Concentrate on one activity and/or relationship at a time. Polychronic: Concentrate simultaneously on multiple tasks and/or relationships.
	Past/Present/Future	Past: Learn from the past. The present is essentially a continuation or a repetition of past occurrences. Present: Focus on the "here and now" and short-term benefits. Future: Have a bias toward long-term benefits. Promote a far-reaching vision.
Definitions of Identity and Purpose	Being/Doing	Being: Stress living itself and the development of talents and relationships. Doing: Focus on accomplishments and visible achievements.
	Individualistic/ Collectivistic	Individualistic: Emphasize individual attributes and projects. Collectivistic: Emphasize affiliation with a group.
	Hierarchy/Equality	Hierarchy: Society and organizations must be socially stratified to function properly. Equality: People are equals who often happen to play different roles.
	Universalist/Particularist	Universalist: All cases should be treated in the same universal manner. Adopt common processes for consistency and economies of scale. Particularist: Emphasize particular circumstances. Favor decentralization and tailored solutions.
Organizational Arrangements	Stability/Change	Stability: Value a static and orderly environment. Encourage efficiency through systematic and disciplined work. Minimize change and ambiguity, perceived as disruptive. Change: Value a dynamic and flexible environment. Promote effectiveness through adaptability and innovation. Avoid routine, perceived as boring.
	Competitive/ Collaborative	Competitive: Promote success and progress through competitive stimulation. Collaborative: Promote success and progress through mutual support, sharing of best practices and solidarity.

Categories	Dimensions	Description
Notions of Territory and Boundaries	Protective/Sharing	Protective: Protect yourself by keeping personal life and feelings private (mental boundaries), and by minimizing intrusions in your physical space (physical boundaries). Sharing: Build closer relationships by sharing your psychological and physical domains.
Communication Patterns	High Context/ Low Context	High Context: Rely on implicit communication. Appreciate the meaning of gestures, posture, voice and context. Low Context: Rely on explicit communication. Favor clear and detailed instructions.
	Direct/Indirect	Direct: In a conflict or with a tough message to deliver, get your point across clearly at the risk of offending or hurting. Indirect: In a conflict or with a tough message to deliver, favor maintaining a cordial relationship at the risk of misunderstanding.
	Affective/Neutral	Affective: Display emotions and warmth when communicating. Establishing and maintaining personal and social connections is key. Neutral: Stress conciseness, precision and detachment when communicating.
	Formal/Informal	Formal: Observe strict protocols and rituals. Informal: Favor familiarity and spontaneity.
Modes of Thinking	Deductive/Inductive	Deductive: Emphasize concepts, theories and general principles. Then, through logical reasoning, derive practical applications and solutions. Inductive: Start with experiences, concrete situations and cases. Then, using intuition, formulate general models and theories.
	Analytical/Systemic	Analytical: Separate a whole into its constituent elements. Dissect a problem into smaller chunks. Systemic: Assemble the parts into a cohesive whole. Explore connections between elements and focus on the whole system.

reader should keep in mind that these constructs refer to different realities: cultural (e.g., COF) versus psychological (e.g., MBTI).

Jung believed that we are born with a set of psychological preferences (i.e., our personality profile), which do not change[9] and are independent from culture. Thus, it is possible to determine a stable personality profile for each of us (at least in principle).

Behaviors do vary of course. Behaviors are influenced by our personality as well as by our culture. For example, Extraversion (an MBTI preference derived from Jung's work) could manifest itself in various cultural ways: more affective in Italy and more neutral in Sweden. Hence the idea of a cultural profile.

Coaches should realize, however, that the cultural profile concept is somewhat of a stretch. Our cultural orientations depend indeed to a large extent on the cultural context (unlike psychological preferences). This means that our orientations frequently change (at least to some degree) depending on the situation (e.g., low context at work, high context with family and with close, long-time friends). So how could we establish a reliable cultural profile? One solution is to devise a cultural profile for each situation. The cultural profile would be valid, but only in that situation. Another solution is to accept that an individual cultural profile is only meant to represent our default, our overall tendency. Some people in Asia, for example, may prefer to think analytically, especially if they have studied in the West, whereas most Asians think systemically. Systemic thinking is their orientation by default.

Coaches should also keep in mind that our cultural profile does not always determine our actions. For example, we might have an orientation toward competition yet choose collaboration in a particular situation. Personality profiles like the MBTI have more predictive power than the COF but still not to the extent of being fully deterministic; an Extravert will occasionally behave in an Introverted fashion. Consequently, coaches need to remind coachees that their cultural profile does not limit their potential. The opposite is in fact true. Coachees who are aware of their profile will discover new options outside their profile and tap into this unexpected potential.

Inner and External Realities

Coaching works in two complementary realms: the *inner* and *external* realities. Our inner world comprises elements such as memories, feelings, beliefs, imagination, and thinking. It also includes our representation (map) of the outer world (territory). As Alfred Korzybski[10] pointed out, however, "The map is not the territory." The outer world is where we interact, take action, and make things happen. Effective coaches facilitate the interaction of these two worlds, fostering a perpetual dance between the external reality (the territory) and our inner and filtered representation of it (the map).

For example, realizing the negative consequence of a belief such as "There is no solution to this problem" can lead to a conscious decision to adopt a more productive (inner world) belief instead, such as "There is a solution for me in this situation." This can facilitate taking new (outer world) actions, thereby actually solving the problem.

A coach can help coachees become aware of their "map of the world" (i.e., inner reality) and how it controls their actions in the world. As the poet David Whyte nicely phrases it, "Difficulties can fall away when we make our inner territory larger, while simplifying our outer work."[11]

Culture also possesses two basic aspects. Stewart and Bennett contrast *subjective culture*, the inner "features of culture, including assumptions, values, and patterns of thinking," with *objective culture*, the outer manifestations, "the institutions and artifacts of a culture, such as its economic system, social customs, political structures and processes, arts, crafts, and literature."[12] Coaches can help coachees make the connections between internal and external reality.

The COF can be viewed as a map to help you get your bearings in an intercultural and global environment. It will help you to appreciate your own current worldview and, by presenting alternatives, indicate how you can move from an ethnocentric to an ethnorelative perspective (see chapter 2).

Dialectical versus Binary Thinking

Each orientation on the COF can potentially be useful or harmful. For each dimension the key is to develop the ability to see reality from both sides (i.e., there are generally two orientations per dimension), to integrate and leverage the diversity. Richness comes from this synthesis.

The danger is using *binary thinking*, which people in the Western world have become accustomed to since Aristotle. Binary thinking leads us to choose one cultural orientation or the other, preventing us from finding new ways to consider and then reconcile alternatives.

To use the COF with positive impact, coaches need instead another form of thinking, called *dialectics*. Dialectic thinking looks for contrasts, for opposite poles and viewpoints. New ideas, solutions, and options emerge from the confrontation. Dialectic thinking itself can be opposed to binary thinking, which assumes one best way (rightly so sometimes).

Throughout history dialectics, characterized by contradiction, has been distinct from binary logic, characterized by third-excluded. The third-excluded principle stipulates that "Out of two contradictory propositions, if one is true, the other must be false." Referring to the thinkers of Ancient Greece, we could say that Aristotle could be viewed as a binary logic champion. Plato, on the other hand, applied dialectics when he claimed, "It happens that all things take part in contrary ideas and that, through this double participation, they are similar and dissimilar at once."[13]

Several contrasts can stimulate a dialectics conversation: day and night; whole and part; yin and yang; wave and particle; freedom and slavery; immanent and transcendent; sacred and profane; and so on. Stanford professor Philip Zimbardo noticed that most, if not all, human phenomena operate like a coin: heads and tails are inseparable; good can also be bad and vice versa. Jung talked about the shadow side, which we all possess.

James Collins and Jerry Porras[14] propose to shift our thinking from *or* (exclusive) to *and* (inclusive) and argue that this mode of thinking is one factor which separates the best organizations, "built to last," from the second best. Their philosophy is equivalent to choosing Plato over Aristotle. I believe the ability to think dialectically will also distinguish the most effective leaders and coaches from the others.

Distinguishing between Orientations, Abilities, and Behaviors

The COF provides a framework to systematically assess cultural orientations that matter to coaches and their coachees.

When describing a culture, however, it is easy to confuse *orientations* (What do you prefer?), *abilities* (What are you capable of?) and *behaviors* (What do you do in reality?).

Let me use a tennis example again, to illustrate the difference. I prefer to play on clay while the tennis champion Pete Sampras prefers to play on grass. If I had the chance to play a match against Pete Sampras, I, the tennis amateur, would surely lose badly, even on clay! My preference/orientation is for clay, but my ability on clay is still low. The opposite is true for Pete Sampras. Furthermore, you may see me playing on a hard court. This behavior would have no connection with my orientation. Maybe I just tried something different or maybe only hard courts happened to be available.

Differentiating between these three concepts is important for coaches. If your coachee recognizes that he was not straightforward enough when confronting an employee with poor performance (behavior), you need to determine what the issue was before you can effectively address it. Was it a belief that speaking directly is not appropriate (orientation) or a lack of skill (ability)? Re-evaluating the belief in light of the new situation may be called for in the first scenario, while increasing skill level through practice could be the right thing to do for the coachee in the second scenario.

This preference–ability distinction also applies to psychological profiles. Psychometric instruments like the MBTI (personality) or the COI (culture) are helpful to measure preferences/orientations but not abilities and behaviors. On the other hand, the following matrix, used for each COF dimension, allows one to visually represent both the orientations and the abilities. The assessment is enhanced and the resulting actions will be more appropriate and make more of an impact.

Taking the deductive/inductive dimension as an example, the assessment process would work as follows.

1. *Orientation* (What do you prefer?)

   Questions:
   - Does this individual (or group) *prefer* to think deductively or inductively?
   - What is he (are they) most comfortable with?

   An orientation is neither good nor bad. Furthermore, the individual's (or group's) orientation can be plotted on the continuum from the deductive extreme pole to the inductive extreme pole. It could be represented by a discrete number from –2 to +2 (see figure on the following page).[15]

2. *Abilities* (What are you capable of?)

   Questions:
   - What is the behavioral flexibility?
   - In other words, if the individual (or group) prefers inductive thinking, how able is he (are they) to think deductively? (Someone may be culturally drawn to deduction but equally able to use induction.)

   The behavioral flexibility could be represented by scores for each possible orientation. The scale could be from –2 to +2.

In the example in the matrix on the following page, the person's orientation is deductive thinking and this preference is mild. Moreover, the graph indicates that the person has a good ability for deductive thinking as well as a fair ability for the alternative mode of thinking, which is induction.

Orientation and Ability

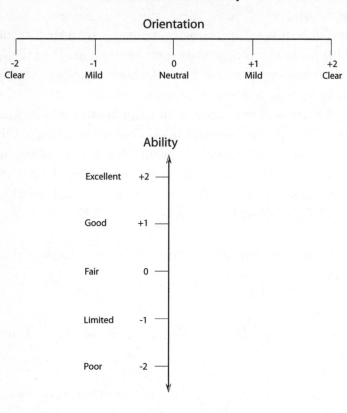

Orientation

-2	-1	0	+1	+2
Clear	Mild	Neutral	Mild	Clear

Ability

Excellent	+2
Good	+1
Fair	0
Limited	-1
Poor	-2

Orientation and Ability

Example: deductive–inductive thinking dimension

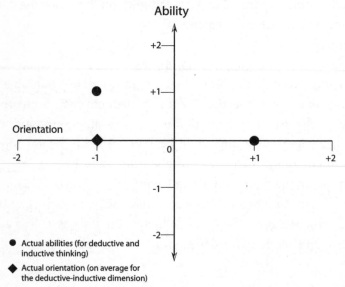

● Actual abilities (for deductive and
  inductive thinking)

◆ Actual orientation (on average for
  the deductive-inductive dimension)

3. *Behaviors* (What do you do in reality?)

   Questions:
   - What is the actual behavior?
   - What appears to be the orientation(s)?
   - How does an individual's orientation translate into his approach to solving a problem?

   We could build a 360-degree feedback mechanism to try to obtain an accurate response to these questions. Instead, I suggest adding qualitative comments and evidence to describe the styles most often used and their impact.

Application: Assessing Cultures

The following worksheet can be used to record estimates of an individual's/ group's cultural orientations. I suggest that you also complete your own cultural profile. As you read the rest of Part II, the meaning of the various cultural dimensions will become clearer and you will be able to gradually complete this assessment. This will serve as input into the "Global Coaching Process" described in Part III, where you will be invited to engage on a journey toward high performance and high fulfillment. Working through Parts II and III yourself first will greatly enhance your effectiveness with your coachees.

In practice, I have found that assessing cultures can best be done by combining inductive and deductive methods. Let me explain and illustrate how it works.

Inductive Approach—The Postcard Exercise

Intuiting, by definition, is a form of immediate knowing that does not involve logical reasoning. It can enlarge one's thinking repertoire. The postcard exercise is designed to tap into coachees' intuition. Whereas deduction—through logic—can be viewed as a sequential mental processing, induction—through intuition—provides direct access to knowledge.

The postcard exercise exemplifies an inductive approach to reflecting on culture.

It is essentially a creativity technique, which utilizes a visual stimulus—the postcard—to stimulate the imagination. The pictures evoke analogies and associations, which will typically enrich coachees' understanding of various facets of an existing culture and will facilitate envisioning their ideal culture.

Cultural Orientations Framework Worksheet

Sense of Power and Responsibility

Control/Harmony/Humility

Time Management Approaches

Scarce/Plentiful

Monochronic/Polychronic

Past/Present/Future

Definitions of Identity and Purpose

Being/Doing

Individualistic/Collectivistic

Organizational Arrangements

Hierarchy/Equality

Universalist/Particularist

Stability/Change

Competitive/Collaborative

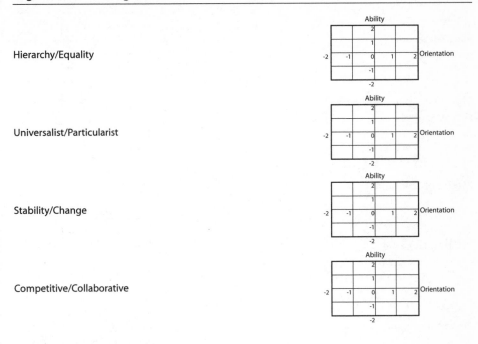

Notions of Territory and Boundaries

Protective/Sharing

Communication Patterns

High Context/Low Context

Direct/Indirect

Communication Patterns (continued)

Affective/Neutral

Formal/Informal

Modes of Thinking

Deductive/Inductive

Analytical/Systemic

The postcards enable them to circumvent their rational thinking, which sometimes prevents their intuition from expressing its farsighted and original ideas.
It is a good idea to do the exercise yourself before presenting it to a coachee.

Instructions for Facilitator's Preparation

Display a variety of postcards on the floor or on a table, some face up and
others face down (this will guarantee a purely random selection by participants later on, which quite often leads to more surprising and interesting
connections).

Instructions for Participant(s)

Before approaching the postcards, reflect on the following initial questions:
- What characterizes your culture?
- What is one aspect of your culture that enables you to be successful?
- What is one aspect of your culture that prevents you from being as suc-
  cessful as you could be?
  ### Notes
  - You need to specify which individual, group, or organizational cul-
    ture you are referring to.
  - You will need to clarify for yourself what is meant by success: for
    example, success can be defined as a combination of high perfor-
    mance and high fulfillment (for the team considered collectively
    and for team members considered individually).
  - You need to decide whether you are referring to your current culture
    or a desired culture.

Once you have clearly understood these questions, forget about them and
go to the postcards. You will not have to choose postcards. Let the postcards
choose you! When a postcard "calls you," pick it up. (We don't want you to
rationally control the process, by choosing postcards that simply illustrate the
preconceived ideas you might have already and that would not generate new
insights. Therefore, the facilitator should determine and tell you in advance
how many postcards you should pick up. He will also decide on a predetermined sequence; for example: the first postcard, face up, will be meant to
inform you about the first question; the second postcard, face down, should
tell you about question two, and so on. The facilitator will typically ask you to
pick up one or two cards per question.)

Once you have collected your cards, go back to the original questions as
well as to the initial discussion of culture and ask, "What does card 1 tell me

in response to question 1, card 2 in response to question 2, and so forth?" (following the predetermined sequence).

I have been impressed by the powerful insights participants typically generate.

There may be some reluctance at first to engage in an activity that seems irrational and like child's play, meaning "bad," at least for some people. The key is to encourage the coachees to give it a try and to have some fun in the process. Tell them that the worst that can happen is that they do not find novel and useful ideas. Invite them to accept that possibility up front and to take the risk of trying something different. Most often, even the skeptical and all-rational types will surprise themselves. Moreover the process does not typically end with the session itself. Your coachee may very well come up with new associations and analogies later, without devoting any conscious effort, for example, while falling asleep, traveling back home, or enjoying a shower.

Example

I was coaching Bart Wille, who was senior vice president of human resources, Latin America, at Unilever in 2001. He has kindly given his permission to let me share this example. One of his primary roles is to promote cultural change in the company.

I asked him to pick four postcards, having proposed the following questions:
1. What is positive in your company's culture today, enabling the company's growth?
2. What is negative in your company's culture today, preventing the growth?
3. What would the future (ideal) company's culture look like?

Bart was immediately attracted to a strange-looking postcard featuring smiling characters (elegantly dressed, apparently out of the 1950s) who looked intrigued about something. They were watching a woman trying to break a contemporary pack of Aïki Noodles with a heavy hammer. The package's yellow and red colors stood out from the black-and-white background, reinforcing the anachronic contrast.

Bart made the following connection: "I like the diversity of characters. Unilever values diversity, which brings new ideas and viewpoints." He later added, "It so happens that Unilever has sold Aïki Noodles. Unilever has decided to focus on fewer brands. In the past, we have fallen into the trap of spreading ourselves too thin. Focus is an important aspect of the culture we are putting in place. The big hits count. Eliminate small brands!" Bart also pointed out team spirit. The characters in the postcard were all in sync.

The card that was face down turned out to be a picture of a greenish character with a huge mouth, black and purple horns, and a yellow trumpet-like nose. It read "Monster!" Bart was quickly inspired to make the following remarks: "The postcard evokes fun and spontaneity, being a little crazy and wild. Let's have fun and don't take ourselves too seriously. We need to celebrate, step out of the box, let ourselves go more, let our gut feelings and our hearts speak. We too often rely on analytical methods. We need more creativity and intuition."

For the ideal culture, Bart had come across a postcard I had bought in Provence, featuring sundials. The first insights were about creating a sense of urgency: "The ideal culture should favor gut feeling because we cannot afford to overanalyze. Time is scarce in a competitive environment." When we met again, Bart showed me inscriptions in the sundials neither of us had even noticed before: "Mortal, do you know what I am here for? To mark the hours you waste!" "I pass and come back. You pass and don't come back!" "Time passes by. Words stay (*demeure la parole*)." These dramatic and provoking sentences were reinforcing the sense of urgency and responsibility Bart felt. They acted as powerful wake-up calls for making the most of the time available. Both Bart and I were touched. These words had definitely captured an aspect of the culture Unilever was setting out to build. Bart wrote, "We have only one career, one life. Let's make the best of it. We do what we say—we keep our promises—*demeure la parole*." He also mentioned building a business for the future, one that would stand the test of time, like sundials but unlike mortals.

The last postcard, face down, was showing a man handing out a present. It read: "Are you looking for alluring lingerie, silver rings, a video camera, a techno CD? Scoot and it is all found." ("Scoot" is a brand name.) Bart noticed the man was smiling. Joy certainly has to be a part of the culture Unilever wants. Moreover Bart mentioned a "can do" and service mentality as well as stretching targets.

As is often the case, even randomly chosen postcards will elicit important features of a culture. This intuitive method invites the heart to speak, not just the head. A classic pitfall of presenting this exercise is to be satisfied with the first insight and move on. Creativity requires time to look again, explore further. Advise your coachee to just calmly observe the postcard and let ideas and associations freely emerge, not censuring them. You may invite your coachee to first capture ideas and observations as they come, then look later for connections with the original question. You may let him keep the cards to refer back to until your next meeting, when you reflect on the cards again.

Bart took the initiative of building a set of visuals to represent key aspects of the new Unilever Latin America culture. Having a clear vision and sharing it often is certainly a good way to promote a culture, but it is not sufficient. He also needed to align different levers of progress, such as the reward system and work processes (a systematic approach will be presented in chapter 4). And he needed to become an example of the culture he envisioned.

Bart articulated the following seven key values. He ranked himself, Unilever South America, and Unilever overall, evaluating to what extent each value was currently being acted upon. He devised a scale with a maximum of +5 (this value is currently acted upon to a great extent) and a minimum of −5 (the opposite of this value is currently acted upon) and then rated himself, Unilever South America, and corporate Unilever.

- Do what we say: reaching objectives, living the values
- Winning together
- Stretching ambitions
- Focus
- Service mentality: mindset, effective results—client satisfaction
- Diversity[16]
- Fun/celebration

Looking at his scores, he concluded, for example, that he was well positioned to champion the value of "winning together" within Unilever. He also realized that "focusing" would allow him to do a better job at converting positive intentions into tangible results. We discussed specific ways to measure progress: bridge the gap between the current and the targeted cultures (measured notably through climate surveys and attraction/retention figures for key managers), and become one of the most admired companies in each country (with precise targets per country).

Deductive Approach—Applying the Cultural Orientations Framework

As I said earlier in this chapter, assessing cultures works best by employing both inductive and deductive methods. The postcard exercise exemplified an inductive method. The Cultural Orientations Framework comes with a deductive approach. You can systematically review the COF dimensions' descriptions and determine which ones are most relevant and provide accurate descriptors of the culture you are studying.

In the example of Unilever Latin America, certain dimensions stand out. These are salient areas where some change needs to take place:

Control/Harmony/Humility

Scarce/Plentiful

Competitive/Collaborative

Affective/Neutral

Deductive/Inductive

Using the COF can allow you to systematically explore aspects that can easily be overlooked otherwise. Bart Wille, in the spirit of harmony, initiated socially meaningful actions. For example, one hundred Unilever managers spent a day revamping a facility for underprivileged children in Brazil. Many managers said this was the best team-building experience they had ever had. Through the direct contact with the children, they gained a better sense of the social context and increased their motivation to bring a positive contribution to society through their work. The control orientation reminded Bart about other qualities such as courage, ambition, and confidence, which are so important for success.

In the next seven chapters, you will find more examples and details of how the COF can be used to describe cultures.

For now, being equipped to assess cultures, you are ready to start bridging cultural gaps.

Application: Bridging Cultural Gaps

Cross-cultural challenges arise from cultural gaps. Differences among one or many orientations can cause misunderstanding and frustration. The COF provides a vocabulary to talk about cultural differences in a nonjudgmental manner. It offers a language for discussing various viewpoints and reconciling differences. With cultural alternatives clearly identified, you can then invite your coachee to use creativity to discover ways to leverage differences and achieve synergy. I am not suggesting that you will always be able to reconcile differences and achieve synergy, but I am arguing for the dialectical approach described earlier, which favors *and* over *or*.

The worksheet on pages 71 to 73 can be used to systematically assess two cultures, say A and B, to identify the gaps (differences) to be bridged. The list of actions to bridge the gaps should be written on a separate sheet or in a learning journal. Sometimes, one action well chosen can bridge several gaps.

At the individual level, culture A may be your own, and culture B may correspond to your coachee, or culture A can characterize your client and culture B, his stakeholder.

At the team level, cultures A and B may be associated with two subcultures. Remember the nurses and business professionals in the Baxter Renal example in chapter 2?

At the organizational level, cultures A and B can represent different entities or companies to be merged.

Culture A can also be the current culture, and culture B the desired or ideal culture. Bridging the gaps in this case means moving toward the ideal culture.

In principle, the process is simple: you assess cultures A and B, identify the gaps, and determine actions to bridge the gaps.

It is not necessarily a matter of choosing one pole over the other, of replacing one orientation with its opposite. The way to bridge or leverage cultural differences was described in chapter 2. Raising awareness about differences and tolerating them is in itself a significant step. Moving outside one's comfort zone and adapting is another option. Integrating and possibly leveraging differences is ideal.

Bart Wille, for example, indicated that Unilever Latin America, starting with himself, was currently not making the most of time passing. The ideal he described combined viewing time as both scarce and plentiful. He wanted to focus, which implied managing time carefully and setting priorities. Yet he also aspired to have fun and loosen up, rather than live under constant time pressure. In fact, he wanted to have it all and live in a culture that would leverage both the scarce and plentiful perspectives! Incidentally, in chapter 5, I will discuss how this can be done.

How do dimensions within the COF manifest themselves? What is the possible merit of each orientation? And what about downsides? What does it look like to leverage cultural orientations for each dimension? How can this knowledge affect and enhance the way you coach and the way you lead people? In chapters 4 through 10, I suggest some answers to those questions. I invite you to add your own ideas and solutions. Thinking dialectically, searching for *and* instead of *or* is a challenging endeavor. It is also the best way I know to achieve high performance and high fulfillment.

Bridging Cultural Gaps

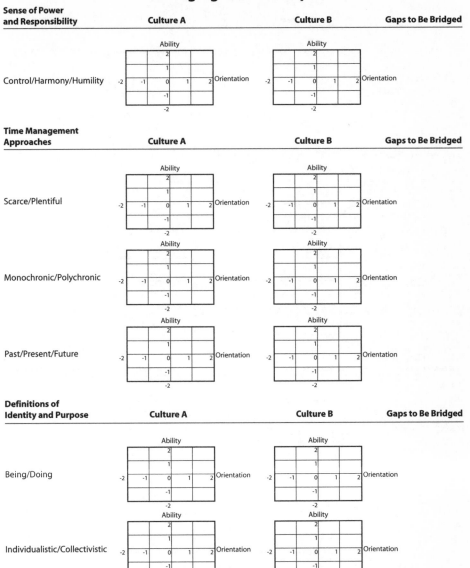

Sense of Power and Responsibility — Culture A — Culture B — Gaps to Be Bridged

Control/Harmony/Humility

Time Management Approaches — Culture A — Culture B — Gaps to Be Bridged

Scarce/Plentiful

Monochronic/Polychronic

Past/Present/Future

Definitions of Identity and Purpose — Culture A — Culture B — Gaps to Be Bridged

Being/Doing

Individualistic/Collectivistic

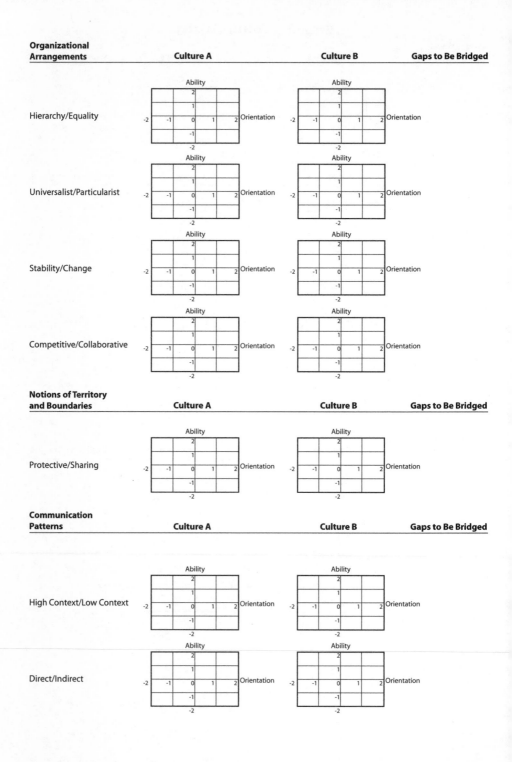

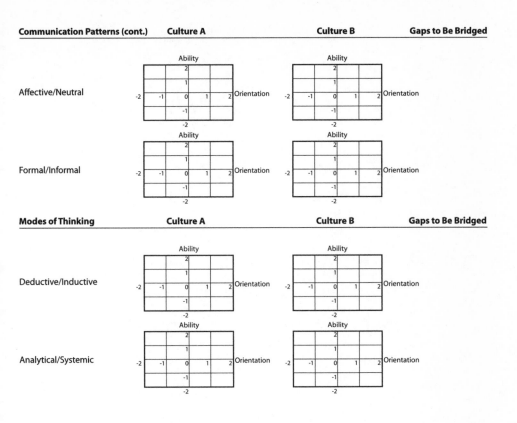

Chapter 4
How to Leverage Our Sense of Power and Responsibility

How do you view your sense of power and responsibility?

Control/Harmony/Humility

Control: People have a determinant power and responsibility to forge the life they want.
Harmony: People should strive for balance and harmony with nature.
Humility: People should accept inevitable natural limitations.

> *Sometimes, you think you have a limit and when you believe you have reached it, something happens: you feel you can go a little bit further. With your mental strength, you can fly even higher.*
>
> —Ayrton Senna

Florence Kluckhohn and Frederick Strodtbeck, in their book *Variations in Value Orientations*,[1] wrote about "a three-point range of variation in the man-nature orientation: Subjugation-to-Nature, Harmony-with-Nature, and Mastery-over-Nature, all well known from the works of philosophers and cultural historians."

Terence Brake, Danielle Walker and Tim Walker[2] used the same concepts but chose the words *control, harmony*, and *constraint* to refer to humanity's relationship with the environment. I have opted for the word *humility*, which hopefully suggests the possible virtues of that orientation. It may be otherwise tempting, from a Western perspective, to dismiss the notion of subjugation or constraint as unpalatable and pure bunk. Moreover, the word *subjugation* may come across as unnecessarily complicated.

What is important here is that to be an effective coach, you need to gain a sense of the possible merits and downsides of all three orientations. The art of coaching is helping a coachee discover new options, shifting perspectives, and possibly leveraging different orientations.

Control

The individual in a control-oriented culture is in charge of his own destiny, a primary American orientation. "There are very few givens in life, few things or circumstances that have to be accepted as they are and cannot be changed. There are no limits on what you can do or become, so long as you set your mind to it and make the necessary effort."[3] Someone who does not "take the world by the tail" is not respected like one who "makes it all happen." This orientation applies to controlling nature, one's relationships, one's happiness, and one's business or academic success (or lack of such).

> Natural forces of all kinds are to be overcome and put to
> the use of human beings. Rivers everywhere are spanned
> with bridges; mountains have roads put through and around
> them; new lakes are built, sometimes in the hearts of deserts;
> old lakes get partially filled in when additional land is
> needed for building sites, roads, or airports. The belief in
> man-made medical care for the control of illness and the
> lengthening of life is strong to an extreme; and all are told
> early in life that "the Lord helps those who help themselves."
> The view in general is that it is a part of man's duty to
> overcome obstacles; hence there is the great emphasis upon
> technology.[4]

The control orientation underpins a belief in immanence: "We have the power." This will result in statements like "Go for it!" and "Life is what you make of it!" Tony Robbins gave the title *Unlimited Power* to one of his books; not only do we have power but our power is supposedly without limit! In the Protestant Calvinist ethos, hard work and perseverance pay off. It is worth making the effort because we can turn things around.

The positive virtue of the belief in control is that it will lead to pro-activity and self-fulfilling prophecies. You can actually make dreams happen. The negative effect is that the orientation may be viewed as naïveté or arrogance. Another downside is the guilt that is often triggered when things don't happen as planned. After all, if you believe you are in control, you are also at fault when success eludes you. The control orientation, at its best, exudes a sense of optimism and ability to achieve extraordinary goals. You believe so much that you can do it that you win against all odds.

Western management concepts like autonomy, ownership, accountability, self-management, employability and empowerment reflect a control cultural orientation. Coaching itself is culturally biased. It starts with the assumption that you have at least a certain power to forge the life you want. It is no surprise that coaching originated in the United States. Coaches claim they will help you achieve your potential. You can do it!

At the end of the day, though, Tony Robbins is wrong; we do not have unlimited power. The truth is that life is fragile. We can be very careful but still we could have been in a plane crash or an automobile accident. We can try hard and take some credit for our success. But we also need luck, or the absence of bad luck. Conversely, when we fail, we might take some of the blame, but transcendence (i.e., the belief that power is outside of us) teaches us to avoid beating ourselves up over it. If we have done the best we can, we can learn to feel at peace, regardless of the outcome, which we know is not solely in our hands.

Harmony

Harmony may be viewed as the midway point along the continuum. Wisdom, from this perspective, is about balance: knowing when one must act and when it is best to let go. This balance is about mediating between the opposite poles of control and humility and is one of the basic orientations of East Asian countries, of yin and yang, opposites in balance. "Yin and yang are not necessarily opposites but are often complementary.... All things in the universe consist of varying proportions of yin and yang."[5]

Harmony is an alternative cultural angle. John Heider's *The Tao of Leadership* illustrates this perspective. His book extracts the following lessons from Lao Tzu's *Tao Te Ching*.

Heider writes about "The Paradox of Letting Go":

When I let go of what I am, I become what I might be.
When I let go of what I have, I receive what I need.
These are feminine or Yin paradoxes:

- By yielding, I endure.
- The empty space is filled.
- When I give of myself, I become more.
- When I feel most destroyed, I am about to grow.
- When I desire nothing, a great deal comes to me.
   When I give up trying to impress the group, I become very impressive.
   When I yield to the wishes of the person working, I encounter no resistance.

> This is the wisdom of the feminine: let go in order to
> achieve. The wise leader demonstrates this.

In another lesson, John Heider indicates that a "leader can act as a warrior or as a healer."

> As a warrior, the leader acts with power and decision. That is
> the Yang or masculine aspect of leadership.
> Most of the time, however, the leader acts as a healer and
> is in an open, receptive, and nourishing state. That is the
> feminine or Yin aspect of leadership.
> The leader who knows when to listen, when to act, and
> when to withdraw can work with nearly anyone....[6]

With harmony, as Kluckhohn and Strodtbeck explain,

> there is no real separation of man, nature, and supernature.
> One is simply the extension of the other, and a conception
> of wholeness derives from their unity. This orientation seems
> to have been the dominant one in many periods of Chinese
> history, and is strongly evident in Japanese culture at the
> present time as well as historically.[7]

Confucianism, Taoism, and Buddhism encourage people to maintain deepest harmony, internally and externally. This orientation is probably not conducive to the "American dream," which inspires people to pursue their dreams against all odds. On the other hand, it is likely to remind people to constantly listen to their feelings and sensations and be attuned to others' as well. We can learn to honor the signals our body sends us. We can take a rest, for example, when we are tired instead of pushing ourselves too hard and ultimately falling sick or breaking down.

Harmony can be viewed as becoming one with nature (our own nature and the external environment). This unity is achieved by relying on the yin (feminine) as much as possible and on the yang (masculine) as much as necessary.

Humility

The humility orientation recognizes that there are many things out of human control. "There are limits beyond which one cannot, indeed should not, go. These givens must be respected. Success is a combination of effort and good fortune. It is never entirely of one's doing."[8] Humility spares one of the loads of guilt for not having everything under control, for not having scaled the heights of perfection and achievement.

While harmony already represented a shift, humility is control's cultural antithesis. Idries Shah illustrates this view in the Sufi story, "The King and the Wolf":

> A certain king decided to tame a wolf and make it a pet.
> This desire of his was based on ignorance and the need to be approved or admired by others—a common cause for much trouble in the world.
>
> He caused a cub to be taken from its mother as soon as it was born and to be brought up among tame dogs.
>
> When the wolf was fully grown it was brought to the king and for many days it behaved exactly like a dog. People who saw this astonishing sight marvelled and thought the king to be a wonder.
>
> They acted in accordance with this belief, making the king their adviser in all things, and attributing great powers to him.
>
> The king himself believed that a near-miracle had occurred.
>
> One day, when he was out hunting, the king heard a wolf pack coming near. As they approached, the tame wolf jumped up, bared his fangs, and ran to welcome them. Within a minute he was away, restored to his natural companions.
> This is the origin of the proverb: "A wolf-cub will always become a wolf, even it is reared among the sons of man."[9]

Similarly, in Greek mythology, Icarus vainly hoped to escape his human condition. He wanted to fly like a bird. Yet as he rose to the sun, the wax holding his artificial wings started to melt, precipitating his fall. His legend is there to remind us about natural limitations. Those stories warn us against our own arrogance or naïveté when we believe that the "sky is the limit." If control pushes us to stretch ourselves and set higher and higher targets, humility teaches us to gracefully accept our limits.

Humility lies on the other end of the continuum, and reflects transcendence as the guiding philosophy. Nature and external forces are in charge. *Insh'Allah* (Allah willing!) "It's a matter of luck." "It's fate." "You take what life gives you."

An orientation to humility can be ineffective when it leads to passive acceptance of fate, when it prevents you from taking proactive steps to promote positive change. Such clichés as "It's not going to make a difference anyway," "Things have always been that way," and "It's not going to change" are self-fulfilling prophecies that perpetuate the status quo and cause one to miss opportunities to improve conditions.

However, a humility orientation can teach wise lessons as well. We can learn to take what life presents us with, gratefully or with a grain of salt, relieving ourselves of the burden and worries of always feeling responsible for what happens.

Examples of Control, Harmony, and Humility

I have seen humility exemplified on several occasions. In organizations, the number of positions becomes scarcer near the top. Coachees do not always get the promotion they feel they deserve. If a promotion is what they truly want and would allow them to use their unique gifts, I challenge them to keep going for it, by engaging in constructive politics (see chapter 7), for example. In this instance, the "control" belief that they can do it is stimulating. Sometimes however, an executive who was passed over for a promotion will admit that he did not really want it anyway and that, in fact, he is longing for something different. Humility can inspire an executive to acknowledge that maybe he does not have the drive or perhaps the talent to take on the next job, and that this reality is beyond his control. The failure then opens the door to new possibilities: the executive can ask himself, "What am I really good at?" and "What do I truly want?" while putting aside social pressures toward high-status and high-money jobs. As a result of this humble introspection, some former executives have gone as far as changing their lives dramatically: becoming a high school teacher, opening up a restaurant in some exotic place, and finding new ways to enjoy life and to serve society.

Harmony has been illustrated in chapter 2. Chubb Asia Pacific's success can be attributed to a significant extent to the harmony orientation, present among Asian executives especially. By striving to maintain harmony, Chubb's executives have created an atmosphere full of consideration and mutual respect. This has fostered unity, reinforcing the top team and its capacity to lead the company to success.

Finally, let me elaborate on the control orientation, exemplified by IBM's journey.

For many years IBM enjoyed an unrivaled dominant position in the computer industry. IBM executives, mostly men dressed in their famous conservative blue suits, made the classic mistake of feeling invincible. Back then uniformity, "the IBM mold," was a substitute for diversity. Working in the computer industry in the 1980s, I remember IBM rivals fighting for open systems such as UNIX, while IBM was literally locking its clients into proprietary system software. Potential buyers were encouraged not to take any chance, and to go with the safe IBM choice. Dwarfs like Microsoft then became the giants while IBM went "through a near-death experience."[10]

In May 2001, I had lunch with four IBM executives in their superb training facility at La Hulpe, Belgium. I enjoyed the company of four enthusiastic and friendly executives, all women. For sure, this was now a very different IBM. You could feel a sense of entrepreneurship and a desire to participate in continuously building a company they could be proud of. The old smug attitude had now given way to a healthy desire to learn and grow. These executives fully realized that leadership had to be earned every day. Mia Vanstraelen, director of learning with global responsibility, invited her direct reports to give her regular feedback. The old proprietary philosophy was clearly also over: IBM applications have now "to be written to open, industry standards."[11]

Fortune magazine was then citing IBM as a model, inviting the company Lucent to learn from the IBM turnaround success story:

> Starting in 1993, Louis Gerstner, Chairman of the Board
> and CEO, leveraged strength in network integration and
> consulting to transform IBM from a moribund maker of
> mainframe computers to a sexy services company that
> can basically design, build, and manage a corporation's
> entire data system. Today IBM's "solutions" business is at
> the heart of its growth strategy: About 37 percent of IBM's
> revenues come from services, which in turn help drive sales
> of IBM software, hardware, and other products to corporate
> customers.[12]

Lou Gerstner and IBM exemplify the belief that you can realize incredible ambitions. In IBM's *One Voice*, you are reminded of where the journey started:

> We said the Net was where competitive advantage is gained,
> where wealth is created. We said the coming transformation
> would affect every industry, every institution, and virtually
> every aspect of society. But we said something else that to
> many seemed even more outlandish. We said we would be
> at the centre of that revolution. We said IBM would lead.
> Again.

Today, "customers credit us with defining e-business — not just the clever term, but the whole idea that the Internet is a place for serious transactions."[13]

It has to be noted that IBM knows it needs to be realistic about the challenges still ahead: "When it comes to whom they ask to bid, IBM is still not the company customers put first." IBM is determined to do what it takes to be first, investing hugely in research, strategic acquisitions, and employees' development.

Lou Gerster writes, "Our customers and shareholders have come to expect great things from the New Blue. But I believe that in the next few years we will surprise the world with our ingenuity, our passion — and our performance. I believe we will surprise ourselves, as well."[14]

While IBM's turnaround illustrates control at its best, the danger of control is visible in many competitive sports, like cycling. These are seemingly plagued with doping.[15] The pressure for glory, media attention, and money is enormous. Average performance is not sufficient to attract sponsors' financing. To win, athletes train extremely hard, but they also sometimes turn to doping to win. In a culture lacking humility, athletes may get away with cheating. But such athletes, modern Icaruses, risk paying a steep price later: cancer, sterility, heart failure, and depression.[16] You can only go so far against nature. This phenomenon exemplifies the shadow side of "control." To break the vicious circle, the current culture could learn the humility lessons from the Sufis and Greek mythology.

The Enron scandal in 2002, fraud resulting in the biggest bankruptcy ever until then, is there to remind us that cheating is always a threat in the corporate world as well, whenever the "control" pressure to succeed at all cost is high.

Leveraging Control, Harmony, and Humility

Leveraging control, harmony, and humility means that you keep in mind the richness in each orientation, while watching for their downsides. I have alluded to this notion already. For example, you act as if you were in control, even though you know you are not really in control (in an absolute sense).

On one hand, you take responsibility for your own life. You don't blame others for your situation, using the excuse that you are not in control: "Top management, my immediate boss, politicians…are responsible, not me!" Instead, you ask yourself, "What could I do, at my level, to improve the situation?" and "What positive contribution can I bring?"

On the other hand, you accept natural limitations, starting with your own. Paradoxically, humility can lead you to achieve more, by keeping your energy focused toward goals within your reach. You also become more tolerant of other people's shortcomings, more gentle and helping with them. And you acknowledge that our planet's resources have limits as well, which need to be preserved.

Whether you take proactive steps to bring success about (control) or wait for happy circumstances to come your way (humility), harmony is essential to sustain well-being. Harmony teaches you to keep listening to your needs and to the needs of others. These needs evolve and you have to remain attuned to them. Your career may have been your priority in the past, but your family may be more important to you now.

Harmony also teaches respect for the external environment, respect for the planet's "needs," so that it too can sustain its beauty and maintain its ability to host future generations.

Costa Rica exemplifies what can happen when you leverage the three orientations. Costa Rica is a beautiful country with a dizzying array of ecosystems, from the dense rainforest to jeweled strands of coral reefs. Covering an area about the size of West Virginia, Costa Rica contains an astonishing quantity of plant and animal life—about five percent of all known species on Earth. Costa Ricans realized they could not continue to clear forests to make way for cattle but that instead, they had to actively preserve their natural patrimony. As a result, an increasing number of tourists are now attracted by Costa Rica's beauty and bring an important source of revenue (while being taught to respect nature during their visit). Diversity of species has become an object of scientific research, notably with pharmaceutical applications.[17]

In sum, Costa Ricans make their country more prosperous (control) as long as nature is preserved (harmony), keeping sight of the limited ability to regenerate ecosystems (humility). In others words, leveraging the three orientations creates an ideal scenario for Costa Ricans (and for our planet), as long as they resist giving in to pressures (e.g., urbanization, unplanned growth, large-scale commercial ventures) that could quickly turn the virtuous circle of progress into a vicious circle of destruction.

Likewise in the corporate world, organizations achieve greater financial performance on average when they are sustainability driven (see chapter 12).

Applications and Advice

Good coaches are known for eliciting peak performance. Yet we should not be so obsessed and enamored with getting to the top that it causes us to break down.

A wise coach recognizes the relativity of the all-powerful control orientation.

First, your coachee may have a different orientation. If he prefers humility, encouraging proactivity will be ineffective if you have not first brought to his consciousness underlying cultural beliefs like "You should take what life gives you," which prevent such actions. Worse would be to judge your coachee, blaming his resistance to change.

Second, you need to gain a sense of the possible merits and downsides of each orientation. The art of coaching is to help a coachee discover new options, shift perspectives and possibly leverage different orientations. On that note, let me add to what I have said already.

Sometimes in the corporate world, executives resort to living out of balance, ignoring their biological and spiritual needs in order to beat the competition, to serve clients, and to please shareholders. They assume they are in control until an accident, illness, or loss reminds them that they are not. If their sole perspective is control, coaches run the risk of merely perpetuating the system, by helping "corporate athletes"[18] cope with whatever pressure is on them. Sometimes you need to question if the game itself has turned into a rat race. Global coaches appreciate this necessity to take a different perspective, by considering harmony and humility. For overachievers and people used to taking on responsibilities, it is comforting to accept that you can only do the best you can. The final outcome is not solely your responsibility.

Harmony teaches the following lesson: Your drive to reach financial targets or achieve your ambitions cannot be so great that, to make it happen, you would crush people (including yourself), compromise safety, or destroy the planet. This is not to say that harmony implies giving up performance. It suggests adopting the kind of coaching and leadership John Heider is talking about. Performance will follow naturally. Think of times where it all seemed so easy, when you were "in the flow," playing amazing tennis shots or doing brilliant work almost effortlessly. This is when you have reached this fragile harmony, both internally and externally.

In chapter 12, the "Global Scorecard" is in essence a tool that enlarges the traditional "control"-biased corporate scorecards. The "Global Scorecard" leverages control and harmony, allowing you to set business targets, while aiming to honor the needs of people and of the planet.

Let's return for a moment to the Sufi story, which taught the king a lesson in humility. "To be a Sufi is to become what you can become, and not try to pursue what is, at the wrong stage, illusion."[19] Coaching, too, should embrace humility. The purpose of coaching is not to change anybody. Coaches should not try to turn wolves into lambs. Instead, coaches should help people to be fully themselves, by unleashing their potential and by expanding their behavioral repertoire. Stretching people and fostering ambitions may seem contradictory with humility. Yet, maintaining a humble attitude will prevent you from wasting your energy and putting lives in jeopardy by going for "pie in the sky." For sure, knowing your limits is not always obvious. But humbly accepting them is paradoxically within your control.

Coaching Tool: Visioning Model

A vision is an ideal situation a company strives to reach. For example, Baxter Renal UK's vision (as expressed in 1997) encompassed "being the leading company in the development of patient care and the support of purchasers, clinicians and organizations involved in the treatment of renal insufficiency."

Successful corporations have a habit of developing a vision for the future and a strategy for making it happen. Executive coaches are called upon to help articulate the vision and strategy, but more often, their contribution resides in enabling leaders and teams to harness their potential to make it all happen.

In this section, I will share a model to help you with the visioning process. I will explain how you can put it to use with your team and how the model relies on the three orientations: control, harmony, and humility.

The model's premise is that the best visions and strategies alone are insufficient to create excitement and whole-hearted commitment. Only strategy together with the following levers of progress can turn a vision into reality. The six levers represented in the figure on page 86 are interdependent and should be aligned, as much as possible, to unleash maximum energy toward the goal. This is how a vision can become truly compelling (i.e., resonating with people's motivators, addressing needs and opportunities in the external environment) and effective for guiding actions (i.e., supported by a specific strategy, culture, and organization).

- External forces
    Awareness of external forces at work ensures that the vision
    and strategy are grounded in reality. Michael Porter's classic
    model involves a systematic analysis of the following factors
    in a given industry: rivalry among existing competitors,

Visioning Model

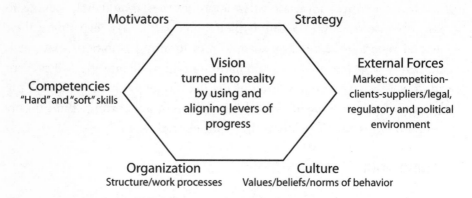

bargaining power of suppliers, bargaining power of buyers (channels and end-users), threat of substitute products or services, and barriers to entry. Michael Porter makes the case that these fundamentals are still key in the Internet age.[20]

Other forces are associated with the legal, regulatory, and political environments. Sociological and demographic trends also shape customer behavior and need to be reckoned with.

- Strategy

    The vision is the ideal endpoint a company strives to reach. The strategy captures the sources of competitive advantage to be leveraged to make the vision come true. The strategy can also be viewed as the company's chosen way to survive and prosper.

- Organization

    This lever, presented in chapter 6, has to do with modifying the structure. The basic structure can be transformed; for example, flatter or more hierarchical, decentralized or centralized, mergers and acquisitions, and downsizing. On a global basis, different international structures are possible. So are organizational practices: promotions from outside or within, demotions or terminations, and so forth. Improving and reengineering work processes also fall into this category.

- Culture

    This is an often neglected or poorly mastered lever; thus its

emphasis in this book. Executives regularly fall into the trap
of engaging in painful and disruptive restructuring, when in
fact changing people's mindset could prove more effective.
The visioning model assumes that cultures are not static
but can be dynamically shaped (to some extent at least) and
become instruments of progress.

- Competencies
  To enable success, talent must be nurtured, skills developed,
  and knowledge acquired. In the information age, human
  competencies are the main asset.
- Motivators
  Motivators are what turn people on, the internal forces
  that drive them to put in their best efforts. Our discussion
  on desires (chapters 1 and 11) suggests the primacy of this
  lever as well as the risk involved in mistakenly projecting
  your needs and dreams onto others. In chapter 6, the
  "being-doing" dimension highlights typical differences in
  motivators.

You can use the Visioning Model to facilitate a discussion with individuals
and groups. There are many possible variations, and you will need to design
one that best addresses the challenge.

Team Exercise

You should first ask participants to spell out their vision as best they can: "How
would you describe the ideal situation your company strives to reach?" Incidentally, you could use the creativity tools presented in chapter 10 to stimulate
participants' thinking around the vision itself. Your purpose here, however,
is to ensure participants can turn the vision into reality, by following these
steps:

1. Ask team members to individually identify and write down for each
   lever (motivators, competencies, culture, etc.)
   - 3 enablers of success (meaning 3 factors currently helping achieve the
     vision) and
   - 3 obstacles (3 barriers to success).
     This means you will end up with a list with a total of 18 enablers and
     18 obstacles.
     For example, for the "Culture" lever, a shared sense of caring
     could be on the list of enablers, and universalism (a tendency to treat

all cases in the same universal manner) could be a key obstacle (if tailored solutions would be more consistent with the vision). Other entries could be, for "Motivators," technical challenge (an enabler if solving technical problems is important to achieve the vision) and autonomy versus collective (an obstacle if team work is required to make the vision come true); for "Organization," international presence (enabler) and lack of decentralized decision making (obstacle); for "Competencies," strong technical skills (enabler) and poor interpersonal skills (obstacle). The list has to be as specific as possible in relation to the participants' particular vision. An enabler in one situation could be an obstacle in another.

2. Collect the answers and write them on flip charts. Group some of the items, while making sure to check whether the contributors feel their original points have been kept. The group may have a tendency to debate during this process. Assuming you want to use time efficiently, you can explain that only clarification questions are welcome at this stage.

3. Ask the team to vote on those enablers and obstacles that are most critical for success. Each participant has three votes for each lever.

4. Tally the votes and circle or otherwise highlight the chosen enablers and obstacles. The team discussion now revolves around two questions: (1) What actions can you initiate to take full advantage of the major enablers? and (2) What solutions do you propose to overcome the main obstacles?

With the visioning model, you can leverage control, harmony, and humility. The *control* orientation is apparent in the proactive nature of the approach itself (i.e., establish a vision and make it happen). The assumption is that we have the capacity to build the future by aligning the best levers in the desired direction. The *harmony* orientation is present as well. The model encompasses external as well as internal forces (motivators). Harmony suggests that both types of forces are essential and need to operate in concord. Finally, the method also invites *humility*. Obstacles are identified, and you can encourage team members to accept those obstacles they cannot remove. Humility assumes that indeed there are inevitable natural limitations. Leveraging control and humility implies that team members save their energy, focusing on areas where they can have an impact and finding ways that are within their reach to overcome obstacles.

Of course, the way you use the method will affect its applicability across cultures. For example, referring to the next chapter, you will want to be sensitive to cultural variations in the way participants expect you to manage time.

Chapter 5
How to Leverage Time Management Approaches

How do you view and manage time?

Scarce/Plentiful—Monochronic/Polychronic—Past/Present/Future

Scarce: Time is a scarce resource. Manage it carefully!

Plentiful: Time is abundant. Relax!

Monochronic: Concentrate on one activity and/or one relationship at a time.

Polychronic: Concentrate simultaneously on multiple tasks and/or relationships.

Past: Learn from the past. The present is essentially a continuation or a repetition of past occurrences.

Present: Focus on "here and now" and short-term benefits.

Future: Have a bias toward long-term benefits. Promote a far-reaching vision.

The first grand discovery was time, the landscape of experience. Only by marking off months, weeks, and years, days and hours, minutes and seconds, would mankind be liberated from the cyclical monotony of nature. The flow of shadows, sand, and water, and time itself, translated into the clock's staccato, became a useful measure of man's movements across the planet.... Communities of time would bring the first communities of knowledge, ways to share discovery, a common frontier on the unknown.[1]

—Daniel Boorstin

Hundreds of books have been written on the subject of time; we all face the reality of its passing. It is natural to ask, How do you make the most of time? How do you manage it practically (whether you do this consciously or not)? Where do you focus on a timeline going back to an ancient past and forward into a distant future?

There is a range of cultural responses that we will explore in this chapter. As always, each orientation offers pearls of wisdom worth considering. The orientations you have overlooked may be precisely the ones that could make you feel more fulfilled and more productive.

Scarce/Plentiful[2]

Scarce: In cultures where time is considered scarce, time itself is rather like a limited commodity—to be carefully spent and saved. People are often busy; there is so much to do and so little time. People learn to manage time efficiently and often rely on daily planners and engagement calendars to keep track of their busy schedules.

Plentiful: When time is viewed as plentiful, people usually slow down. They take their time, following natural rhythms rather than letting themselves feel constrained by tight schedules.

The hard-working capitalistic world, with global competition and technological progress, seems to have fostered what the *Nouvel Observateur* has called a "speed generation" (*génération vitesse*).[3]

Coping with multiple demands on time could have become easier: at home, household appliances have removed the burden of manual work; at work, technical equipment has become more sophisticated, simplifying tasks that used to be tedious or impossible to perform. But somehow, we have not always taken advantage of progress. We don't necessarily work less; we simply achieve more to stay competitive. E-mail and mobile phones are good examples of wonderful communication tools that are often misused, with the perverse consequence of enslaving some of us.

Coaches, and trainers before them, have responded to those time pressures by proffering guidance on how to cope. You have probably all heard the advice: distinguish what is important from what is urgent. You have probably also read about the "laws of time": Pareto's law says that if we don't pay attention, we spend 20 percent of time on what is essential and 80 percent on what is incidental. Illich's law suggests that beyond a certain threshold, the time we devote to a task is no longer effective; we might as well stop and relax. The Ecclesiast's message itself, "There is a time for everything," has become a top time management tip! And what about the infamous "time eaters" that we need to combat?

Once you let down your guard and stop being organized, time becomes the master again. The entropy law suggests that time will literally eat up all the space you give it. Before you know it, three hours have gone by and the meeting is still going on, with little progress made.

From a scarce time standpoint, you need to plan, delegate, learn to say no, and set priorities. Get yourself a well-designed time planner. You could conduct a systematic audit, jotting down every time you start an activity, decide to stop, or are interrupted. Then you can take some remedial actions, like closing your door to focus for time periods.

In chapter 2 I mentioned how, in the Western corporate world, particularly in the United States, people often assume that time is scarce. I also indicated how, alternatively, I prefer to consider that time is plentiful when I coach executives. We give ourselves the time we need and therefore don't have to break a productive discussion. We may have planned a two-hour session but do not let ourselves be constrained by that schedule.

Examples of the Dimension

Coaches, because of their own cultural mindset, have learned to adopt the "scarce" perspective and help coachees manage time more efficiently. I coached a client who succeeded in cutting down his workday by two hours on average, while doubling his sales volume that same year. Besides more systematic and rigorous organization, the key for him was to identify what he would really want to do if he had more time. He became an amateur theater actor, something he had dreamed of for many years. When I met him seven years later, he had kept his hobby and was still a very successful entrepreneur.

Global coaches know how to manage time efficiently and help their coachees do so too. But they can also shift their perspective. After all, why should we give in and live in a constant rush if it does not work for us? For sure, it is possible to thrive on speed. Certainly, there are so many exciting things you can do—and only so much time. Yes, time is precious. But there is an *art de vivre* in taking one's time.

Do you know what Churchill did when he was informed about the Mers-El-Kebir drama and was asked what he was planning to do about it? "First, a nap" was his answer.[4] Facing crisis, great leaders slow down! In sports like tennis, you will miss shots by rushing at the ball. You have to stay alert, taking your time as you move swiftly.

Nancy Adler tells the story of an American engineer working in Bahrain.[5] The engineer was profusely apologetic when explaining that the opening of the plant under construction would be delayed by six months. To the

American's surprise, the Bahrainian's response was, "We have lived for thousands of years without this plant; we can easily wait another six months or a year. This is no problem."

While vacationing, my wife and I were traveling through the French Provence. The highway quickly brought us closer to our destination. We then left the main road to appreciate the beauty of the region by adopting a slower pace along the little roads. We finally decided to enjoy the countryside even more by cycling or simply walking to admire the beautiful ocher and olive colors—and breathe in the incomparable lavender scents.

Jacques Brosse explains that for someone meditating, time does not count in the same way.[6] In zazen, the practice of zen, watches are no longer in charge. The time that matters is the natural rhythm of your body, heartbeat, and breathing. These become fractal symbols of the rhythm of your whole life. You become conscious of your exchange with the world, taking in and giving out.

The paradox is that when you take your time, you can appreciate the eternity in moments. Without being Buddhist, you can feel "awakened," intensely struck by beauty and grace.

Joy may not be the only experience, however. Pain is sometimes inevitable to growth. When you allow time to be plentiful, in the silence and immobility, you can also face the important questions about your existence. Perhaps your hectic pace and busy life have permitted you to mute your inner voice. But even buried, it is still alive and perhaps sapping you.

In *The Straight Story*, David Lynch opposes slowness and contemplation with the usual frenzy in American movies. Alvin Straight (played by Richard Farnsworth with emotion and sobriety) travels on a lawnmower. You could hardly go slower, but the pace enables real human encounters and keeping sight of the essential.

The Italians have a saying: *"Chi va piano, va sano; chi va sano, va lontano"* (Who goes slowly goes safely; who goes safely, goes far).

Leveraging Scarce and Plentiful

Leveraging scarce and plentiful time orientations was effectively demonstrated by several British and Italian executives I worked with. The British managers saw that living in a rush sometimes prevented them from investing the necessary time to know their Latin colleagues. They learned to shift their cultural view of time, "giving time time" when necessary (*"dare tempo al tempo"* and *"donner du temps au temps"* are Italian and French expressions, suggesting treating time as a plentiful resource). They became more patient and thus better able to connect with Latin European colleagues.

In chapter 2, we saw how Mark Philips, who already knew how to manage meetings rigorously, never wasting time, learned to become patient and calm. He leveraged British and Swedish cultural traits.

The obvious response to the lack of time (when time is considered scarce) is to help coachees manage their time more efficiently. But leveraging scarce and plentiful time means thriving on paradoxes. The best way to honor the scarcity of time may well be to savor it rather than hurry, treating time as if it were plentiful.

You can increase performance and fulfillment when you learn to view time as a plentiful resource. This should not prevent you from managing time efficiently. However, you do have to set priorities and avoid cramming too much into your life.

Applications and Advice

Joël de Rosnay advocates for "a subordination of speed to our objectives, to the meaning we wish to give to our individual and collective enterprises."[7] That summarizes my advice to coaches.

If you, as a coach, are to help people achieve "meaningful, important objectives," you need to appreciate both views of time, scarce and plentiful, making the most of each, and ask "What for?"

Monochronic/Polychronic

Monochronic: In monochronic cultures, people prefer to devote their full attention to one "thing" at a time (that "thing" could refer to an activity, a relationship, or both). Processing of tasks is sequential rather than parallel. "Time is segmented like a road or ribbon."[8] That road is divided into distinct sections that are devoted to one client, one meeting, or one project at a time.

Polychronic: In polychronic cultures, people tend to interrupt a task or a meeting in order to attend to another important task or relationship at the same time. "Immersed in a polychronic environment in the markets, stores, and souks of Mediterranean and Arab countries, one is surrounded by other customers all vying for the attention of a single clerk who is trying to wait on everyone at once."[9]

Edward T. Hall has coined the terms *monochronic* and *polychronic*. Fons Trompenaars[10] uses different words, *sequential* and *synchronic*, to refer to the same dimension, suggesting either a sequence of activities or synchronicity.

From a monochronic perspective, being professional or polite typically means devoting your full attention to one person or group at a time. From a polychronic perspective, being professional or polite means juggling different projects and people at the same time.

Let me warn interculturalists who have internalized Edward T. Hall's notions that my concept of monochronic and polychronic is not strictly equivalent to his. For example, Hall considers scheduling as an important part of monochronic time, whereas, in my experience, scheduling can be a consequence of a monochronic orientation but doesn't have to be. You can do one thing at a time without following a strict schedule. Like Hall, I regret that "there are times when things are just beginning to develop in the desired way; yet they must be stopped to conform to a preset schedule." However, in my mind, monochronicity per se is not the issue. The schedule may be too tight or too rigid, and that is what causes the problem. The crammed time slots may reveal a "scarce" time bias, and the rigidity may be the negative manifestation of a culture valuing order over flexibility.

Elsewhere, Hall suggests that "M-type people (those oriented toward monochronic time), by virtue of compartmentalization, are less likely to see their activities in context as part of the larger whole,"[11] whereas I do not see why working on one project at a time prevents you from applying systemic thinking to that project (see chapter 10).

I prefer to cling closely to the essence of the dimension, which lies in its etymology and which I have tried to capture in my definition: doing one or multiple things at a time. However, let me make clear that by *time*, I mean a "period of time," which could be anywhere from seconds to years.

Let us accept the ambiguity inherent in notions like "period of time" or "activity." Of course, it all depends on where you set the boundary. You may be working on one activity at a time during a five-minute period, but on ten different activities simultaneously over a five-hour period. The notion of activity itself is not black and white either: watching television and switching between channels could be regarded as one activity (watching television) or as multiple activities (watching several television programs at once). In other words the same culture could be viewed as monochronic or polychronic. Edward Hall had already recognized this particularity, indicating that "American time is monochronic, but in a deeper sense it is both polychronic and monochronic."[12]

We should not be disturbed by the ambiguity. It does not really matter because the point here is not to separate nations (or other cultural groups) between two categories, polychronic and monochronic. The value I see in this cultural dimension is that it allows us to contrast juggling multiple activities or relationships (polychronic) with concentrating on one activity or relationship (monochronic). This distinction is of importance for coaches because in my experience coachees often struggle with too many things to do at the same time.

Examples of the Dimension

Although Hall describes the American and Northern European cultures as monochronic, he also gives the counter-example of the frequent interruptions people experience at work.

We should recognize that certain activities are mono- or polychronic by nature. In a hospital emergency unit, for example, a doctor typically attends to several patients at once, constantly reevaluating whose situation requires the most urgent treatment. Polychronicity may not be the doctor's preferred orientation, but it is clearly the better choice here. Tennis professionals however will want to concentrate solely on their match, especially if they play a final at Wimbledon!

I remember feeling upset when an Israeli painter kept interrupting our conversations by answering his portable phone. But then I appreciated being always able to reach him, which meant that he was probably interrupting other meetings to talk to me.

In Mediterranean polychronic cultures, a corporate executive or public minister can deal with several people at once, who all feel acknowledged as having access to the top person—quite an advantage. Several meetings take place in parallel in different rooms. Since the senior person is sharing his time, specialists and lower-ranked assistants may continue the conversations until he returns.

It takes gifted people to manage an operation in this polychronic fashion, as Hall pointed out. Gary Kasparov, the chess champion, may be able to play several chess games in parallel and win, even though his opponents have to focus only on their sole match with him. Most people need some monochronic time to be successful.

The monochronic perspective allows one to concentrate one's energy on a single ambitious project. The English mathematician, Andrew Wiles, had dreamed as a child of solving mathematics' most challenging problem, a riddle that had confounded the world's greatest minds for 358 years. After a long journey, he finally and officially succeeded in 1997. He said, "I was so obsessed by this problem that for eight years I was thinking about it all the time—when I woke up in the morning to when I went to sleep at night. That's a long time to think about one thing. That particular odyssey is now over. My mind is at rest."[13] Likewise, the great architect Antonio Gaudi passionately devoted all his time during his last years to building the astonishing Sagrada Familia.[14] He even slept in his small workshop on the construction site. Still he could not complete the church, but the masterpiece he left, albeit unfinished, is breathtaking.

Leveraging Monochronic and Polychronic

In my experience, the norm of professional coaches is to focus solely on their clients. This makes the meetings more effective, providing clients with a real opportunity to step outside their normal patterns and take a fresh look without any external distraction. It seems more difficult, however, for leaders to allocate uninterrupted time. In the current, increasingly electronic information culture we live in, the span of attention is short. But when a leader does make the commitment to give his undivided attention to coaching sessions, his management style has a better chance to actually help develop people under his supervision.

Of course, working across cultures, coachees will have different expectations and habits. Once, I was coaching an Egyptian manager. We were interrupted twice for three minutes in two hours. As it turns out, one phone call enabled him to secure his biggest commercial deal of the year. Clients appreciated his availability. More importantly, he seemed at ease with the interruptions because they were an integral and accepted part of his way of life. In this case, it seemed to me that I had no mandate to push this manager to change his behavior as long as it did not interfere with his success and fulfillment, and as long as it did not prevent me from effectively doing my work as a coach.[15] We have to be willing to make some adaptations ourselves to be credible when inviting our coachees to consider possible changes in their habits.

To summarize, leveraging monochronic and polychronic time could come in the following forms:

- being able to rely on both orientations depending on what is required in the situation
- making room regularly for quality monochronic time to focus on something or someone significant for a few hours, weeks, or more
- making room for exciting polychronic time, attending to multiple tasks and relationships without losing sight of what is important to you

Applications and Advice

Beyond what has already been said, and without contesting the virtues of polychronicity, I would like to insist on the need for more monochronicity. The United States and Northern Europe have often been regarded as monochronic by interculturalists. Yet in my view, the danger is not too much monochronicity but rather too little of it.

We are faced with a constant and abundant flow of information, through the Internet and television in particular. "Zapping" (i.e., originally meaning "moving suddenly and rapidly, especially between television channels"[16]) has become a favorite tactic for dealing with the sheer quantity of information — e-mail, journals, newspapers, and so on. By doing so, we risk spreading ourselves too thin. We might want instead to go into more depth, devoting our full attention to select tasks and people. Unless zapping is used as a screening device, superficiality may be the unfortunate consequence.

A recent cultural trend exemplifies making the most of monochronic time. Sabbaticals are now made available in the corporate world and are no longer the sole privilege of university professors or those enjoying retirement at forty. In some Western countries, maternity leave has become longer and, equality obliging, fathers are getting time off as well. These options are made available as a result of pressures to attract and retain good professionals in a tight labor market ("the war for talent"), and by political action to promote better quality of life through social regulation.

Business Week reported, "More Silicon Valley hotshots are taking extended periods of time off—and getting away with it." For example, with hundreds of job offers pending, Mark Breier set off with wife and kids for eighteen months in a Winnebago, and Stacey Stillman took three months off from her law firm to be a contestant on CBS Television Network's smash hit *Survivor*.[17] Incidentally, the comment "getting away with it" demonstrates how taking time off to stop juggling multiple obligations and focus on one project instead is far from being engrained in Western cultures.

As you coach, your priority indeed is to encourage coachees to do what is important and meaningful to them, rather than to keep putting these projects off to a hypothetical future.

Past/Present/Future

Past: In many countries with long histories, the past is, understandably, very important. Lessons learned from mistakes with costly consequences are remembered and applied to current situations. In East Asia, for example, past events, great scholars, artists, and one's ancestors are valued and honored in ways foreign to younger countries. Historical contexting is vital to many European countries, where nearly every speech, book, or article begins with background material giving a historical perspective. This irritates Americans, who wonder, "What does this have to do with our planning session?"

Present (and near future): Many so-called "traditional" cultures live in a sort of eternal present. Many such peoples, for example African and Native American groups in former times, reflect this orientation to the present with languages that have no verb tenses to indicate past occurrences or future events. Of those nations where the near future is valued, the United States is probably the best example. Instant gratification and short-term benefits propel Americans ever forward—but not too far. Business planning intervals range from the quarter to the year. Five- or ten-year planning is virtually unheard of.

Future (long term): A long-term orientation often coincides with relationship- and obligation-based cultures. The reasoning behind Chinese and Japanese careful building of mutual obligations in relationships, for example, is the knowledge that five or ten years from now those relationships will continue to bear fruit. Short-term profit is not nearly as important as long-term growth.

The richness of the past lies in memory. Learning about past mistakes and dramas helps ensure that we don't let them happen again. Remembering wonderful moments inspires us to repeat them. Historical memory could spare humanity from reliving its darkest times, but during times of turmoil and crisis, we often fail to heed these lessons from the past. Mental memory is also vital for each man. For the Tadié brothers, "It is memory that makes man."[18] Jean Cambier explains, "Memory renders perceptible the continuity of existence and establishes the awareness of the self."[19] You can enhance your memory by such strategies as paying conscious attention to details in order to remember them later, repeating and rehearsing, providing a context and finding associations, and so on.[20]

The importance of the present is captured in the famous adage *"carpe diem"* (seize the day). The present is where life takes place.

The future is when our dreams will hopefully materialize. The future gives meaning to our present actions. People and organizations want to grow and achieve their vision at last. The "Global Scorecard" (see chapter 12) is a tool for global coaches to use to support a far-reaching vision that embraces prosperity for everyone and on multiple fronts: ecological, social, economic, and so on. Global coaches do not resign themselves to seeing bad present situations persist. They want to make utopias happen and help improve the world.

Examples of the Dimension

Beyond its presence in our actions, the time dimension also surfaces in what we talk about. Some people evoke memories: childhood, college, past successes and failures, and so on. Some, living in the moment, may speak about present events and experiences. Others may prefer to dream about the future and discuss long-term projects.

To bridge cultural gaps, you need to be willing and able to adapt to your interlocutor's time orientation, and that will be reflected in your communication. For example, Trompenaars tells the anecdote of a Dutch manager who was frustrated by his unsuccessful attempts to organize a management-of-change seminar with Ethiopian managers. "[They] kept harking back to a distant and wealthy era in Ethiopian civilization." The breakthrough occurred when the Dutch manager started to study Ethiopian history books, learn about the company's past, and frame change initiatives as a way to "recreate some of the greatest glories of the past."[21] To the Ethiopians the future became more credible when it became a new occurrence of the past.

Leveraging Past, Present, and Future

The short-term and long-term orientations are not mutually exclusive. Effective leaders want short-term *and* long-term gains. But, as is true with the other dimensions, at times choices have to be made. Take training, for example. Your priority can be to develop specific technical competencies providing an immediate competitive advantage to your company. The alternative choice is to provide a broader education. To that end, major companies have started their "corporate universities" or similar endeavors. This second option makes less sense from a short-term perspective but is clearly the best choice to help people grow and build their capacity to contribute in the long term.

John Hennessy, president of Stanford University, advocates for "building an education that won't wear out":

> Stanford, sitting as it does in the center of Silicon Valley, is sometimes associated with a focus on the "new new thing" as opposed to areas of intellectual exploration that are older and more complex. It is a matter of great pride, of course, that we have been so deeply involved in the birth and development of the Valley. This pivotal role, however, should not obscure our belief that the humanities must remain at the center of a great university and at the core of its undergraduate program. As I begin my tenure as president, I want to reiterate that core principle and speak to the importance of creating an even higher profile for the humanities.[22]

"The interplay of the sciences and humanities" has been central from the beginning, in the minds of founders Leland and Jane Stanford. The commitment is to embrace history and information technology, ancient philosophy and modern biology. Making the most of the past and of the future is a key to explaining the institution's lasting greatness.

Applications and Advice

Employing various time perspectives can be a matter of credibility: if you present coaching as a new concept in France, you may not be taken seriously. There past history is seen as an important cultural heritage. It is more sensible to frame coaching as an approach that builds on the work of past philosophers, psychologists, business consultants, and others.

Without going far enough to consider Socrates a coach, we know from Plato that the great Greek philosopher was a master at helping others discover solutions through questioning. Rather than advocating his ideas, Socrates was using a process of inquiry to help his interlocutors develop their own ability to reflect. He would question them, building on their references and using their language. Over two thousand years ago a man was using what we think of as a basic technique of modern coaching![23]

Someone lacking a past orientation probably would not care about Socrates' contribution to coaching. However, failure to study the past deprives you of sources of wisdom and lessons from experience. Knowledge of the history of civilizations helps us to gain a clearer sense about permanent and universal human needs, such as the desire for love and power. It can show alternative life options people have invented to meet those aspirations.

Coaching is present oriented when you invite coachees to reflect on what makes them happy, on what matters here and now, and when you help them address immediate challenges.

If the ambition is to reach depth and foster meaningful actions, coaching also needs to envision long-term goals. Coaching is an opportunity for people to take a broader view on their life. A coach may ask, for instance, "How do you want to be remembered?"

A long-term bias also means more emphasis on sharing tools with coachees. Coaching moves beyond addressing present challenges. Coachees acquire a "toolbox" to deal autonomously with similar situations in the future. Coachees grow as people.

Coaching Tool: Timeline

Working with Time

Coaches help coachees engage in a long-term journey toward high performance and high fulfillment. The timeline consists of questions to help you step back and look at the big picture, the journey of your career and your life. It leverages past, present, and future orientations.

```
—————————————————————X—————————————————————————>
Past                    Present                   Future
```

Exercise

1. You can invite your coachees to consider the following questions.
   Remote past:
   - What are the important lessons you have learned from the past that can help address present challenges?

   Recent past:
   - Reflecting back on the last year (month, week, since our last meeting…), what have you done well? What success have you had? What is still an issue for you?

   Present:
   - List ten activities that make you happy (whether you do them currently or not). In other words, how do you charge your "battery?"
   - List ten energy drainers. How do you run down your battery?

Near future:

- What is your vision for your leadership over the next year or so? What kind of leader do you want to be in the context of current challenges and challenges that you anticipate in the short term?

Distant future:

- What is an accomplishment that you would like to be remembered for? What legacy do you want to leave behind? How do you want to be remembered?

2. Ask participants to project themselves into the future and imagine they have become a centenarian radiant with happiness and health. Have them, from that perspective, tell what happened to make this enviable result possible. What had their lifestyle been like? What had they achieved, professionally and privately?

3. Ask coachees "What would you do if you had only one year to live?" I have heard participants over and over talk about going on a long trip around the world with their family (or occasionally alone). And yet, many of them were currently not even coming close to spending any significant time vacationing with their loved ones.

The timeline obliges you to remember that life is passing by. What are you waiting for?

Chapter 6
How to Leverage Our Definitions of Identity and Purpose

How do you define your identity and what is your purpose in life?

Being/Doing—Individualistic/Collectivistic

Being: Stress living itself and the development of talents and relationships
Doing: Focus on accomplishments and visible achievements
Individualistic: Emphasize individual attributes and projects
Collectivistic: Emphasize affiliation with a group

> *Being human signifies, for each one of us, belonging to a*
> *class, a society, a country, a continent and a civilization.*[1]
> —Claude Lévi-Strauss

Who are you? Coaches need to be prepared for a range of responses to this essential question. The choice is culturally dependent and tends to fall along two primary axes: "being-doing" and "individualistic–collectivistic." By appreciating these variations, you enlarge your very sense of identity and understand that this is a multifaceted concept.

Being/Doing[2]

Doing: Doing is the dominant cultural orientation in mainstream American society. It demands the kind of activity that is focused on achievements that are measurable by external standards. "What do you do?" is often the first question an American asks of a new acquaintance. The doing-oriented person says, "Let's get going," "Let's do something about this problem." The Puritan work ethic is an outstanding example of the doing orientation, an ethic prevalent in Western management systems.

Being: A being orientation values the person, not the achievement. It is inward and introspective, placing greatest emphasis on rewards that are intrinsically meaningful to a person, regardless of how much or how little those rewards conform to the expectations of those around us.[3] A high quality of life is not only, or even primarily, measured by career advancement but by personal growth. Latin Americans, for example, tend to fall within this orientation.

Doing stresses tasks and visible achievements. Motivators include job performance and material rewards. Being emphasizes quality of life and growth. Fulfilling relationships and interesting and meaningful work procure job satisfaction and constitute important rewards, which are nonmaterial.

Different terms have been used to describe this polarity. Each pair illuminates various facets of a fundamental human reality.

Robert Blake and Jane Mouton talked about relationships/tasks. Paul Hershey and Ken Blanchard followed them, also distinguishing between task and relationship behaviors in their classic *situational leadership* model.[4] Task behaviors occur any time the leader provides help to complete an assignment. Relationship behaviors consist of making the follower feel valued and appreciated by providing positive reinforcement.[5]

Kluckhohn and Strodtbeck implicitly suggest the pair internal/external. For example, your purpose can be formulated as an internal feeling (be happy) or/and as an external accomplishment (make money). The internal and external terminology reveals the important point that when you work with the inner reality—personal growth and introspection—better performance in the external world is facilitated.

Failure to appreciate the being pole of the continuum can lead to the faulty assumption many managers have made: believing that by explaining the task, setting clear goals, and assigning deadlines, employees will feel compelled to act. The issue is always trust and relationship. If you have not established the relationship, the sense of urgency you are trying to convey will simply be deflected! This also implies that if you want your salespeople to develop business in a "being" culture, you need to give them even more resources, time, and money to build relationships that are a sine qua non condition to close deals.

Examples of the Dimension

Somewhat paradoxically, more being is usually necessary to ultimately get more doing. You cannot, for example, expect great success by bringing together talented individual football players and focusing group meetings solely on the technical/tactical aspects of the game. In 2000 the football team of Calais, an amateur team playing in the modest fourth division, reached the final of the Coupe de France. A formidable team spirit, close interpersonal relationships, and faith and commitment to winning—for the group, not just the individual—enabled them to beat four professional teams that were technically and physically superior.

Timothy Gallwey developed an approach based on inner skills, which he applied to tennis, golf, and, more recently, to work.[6] These skills, which include the ability to connect mind and body, to trust yourself and to focus your mind, are probably as important as technical-"doing" skills to achieve enjoyment, performance, and progress.

And as you will discover, the "Global Scorecard" includes by design internal and external targets, in contrast with traditional scorecards. The "Global Scorecard" honors both the being and doing poles of the cultural dimension.

Leveraging Doing and Being

Niall FitzGerald, Cochair of Unilever, insists that "to make the business grow, we—Unilever executives—need to make ourselves better human beings." Growing as people and as a business go together. The rhetoric is followed by tangible action. Several initiatives are offered to help executives develop. For example, one-on-one executive coaching has been made available for all senior leaders. It is a one-year process where regular meetings are arranged at mutually convenient times between the coach and the executive. The process is designed to serve the leader as well as the organization. The coaching encompasses being (striving for fulfillment and balance, developing leadership competencies, building constructive relationships) and doing (achieving business results and growth). In fact, the confidential coaching sessions constitute an opportunity to enhance and connect the two: taking better care of oneself to sustain one's business performance, nurturing relationships to help work projects be achieved smoothly, and becoming a better coach to unleash more potential and achieve greater business results. Top executives sometimes feel that coaching is great...for their subordinates. But at Unilever, Chairmen FitzGerald and Antony Burghmans lead by example. They invite feedback from their executives and have committed to continual improvement of their leadership by working with a coach.

Leveraging being and doing was also key in Baxter Renal UK's success. I interviewed each team member prior to our first retreat, insisting on the fact that the conversation was confidential and that my goal was to serve the team overall as well as each member individually.[7] Peter Leyland announced several purposes for the journey. In the being category, he wanted all members to enjoy themselves and to grow as leaders. He also wanted more trust, pleasure, and unity in the team. In the doing category, he envisioned further business growth despite an already dominant position in the market. As I coached the team over the years, we spent significant time developing leadership and team competencies. We also avoided cramming our retreats with endless sessions. We focused on the essentials and took the time to have fun together. (Our go-karting race in Silverstone, near the famous Formula One track, still brings back vivid memories.)

My colleague Sally Carr watched the Baxter team and noted, "People seemed open to others' views. There was no evidence of people distancing themselves because they were feeling powerless or sensing hidden agendas, and there was a lot of good humor, laughter, fun, and creativity."

The being/doing orientation was also a factor in another coaching situation. An executive I coached was complaining about feeling stressed out. He set the internal goal of being more serene, which he felt was achieved a few months later. Several avenues enabled him to feel less negative tension. He reconsidered some of his beliefs, learning, for example, to celebrate small successes rather than dismissing them as unimportant. He also learned to engage in "constructive politics,"[8] which allowed him to feel more in charge of his destiny, less like a victim.[9] The point is that he leveraged internal (or being) goals to achieve greater external (or doing) outcomes. For anyone knowing tennis, it is easy to appreciate how being tight prevents you from hitting good shots. Being loose and serene instead enables peak performance, which is true in the workplace as well. As a coach, you want to make sure your coachee reaches an internal state where he can do his best work. It would be a mistake to focus solely on the external and visible game.

Applications and Advice

In my experience, the best leaders and organizations understand the value of leveraging being and doing. In contrast, others tend to focus on one pole, typically the doing one.

Some executives will want you to facilitate business discussions (doing) but will be reluctant to engage in the "touchy-feely stuff" (being). They will insist on getting right down to business. But there is no miracle. Without the trust, mutual respect, and self-awareness—intangible benefits—a group cannot hope to reach peak performance, let alone sustain it. In fact, research reveals that the two major problems that can stall an executive's career are not doing issues but being shortcomings: problems with interpersonal relationships and difficulty building and leading a team.[10]

Coaches can err on the side of doing when they focus solely on external results. In this scenario, coaching becomes superficial when it gives in to pressure to deliver rapid results and quick fixes. Without the being pole, coaching loses its richness and identity, and ultimately its effectiveness. Coaches can, however, also err on the being side, focusing on personal growth but failing to articulate and work toward achieving external objectives. To my way of thinking, coaches need to work at both ends of the continuum and integrate them.

As a coach, I often facilitate the formulation of specific targets, an action plan, and enlist genuine commitments on concrete deliverables. A critical task is to ensure that the team does not settle for a low common denominator but that it will be satisfied with nothing less than making the most of every team member's talent. We will not settle for mere compliance or even buy-in. We want genuine passion for the plan. This level of commitment cannot be faked. It has to resonate with members' personal desires and values and with the intrinsic meaningfulness to each person.

Another implication for coaching is that coaches do not always need to do something to be effective coaches. They can simply be there. A senior executive told me he appreciated the opportunity to speak to someone who could listen and understand without judging, whom he could talk to without censoring himself, whom he could explore his inner thoughts with. Another executive commented about his experience of becoming more self-aware and about his delight with the insights he was able to generate.

Coaches need to develop this quality of *presence*, which Brian Hall elegantly defines in the following manner: "The ability to be with another person that comes from the inner self-knowledge that is so contagious that another person is able to ponder the depths of who he or she is with awareness and clarity."[11]

For sure, variations exist along a being–doing continuum; for example, *Take Time for Your Life*[12] emphasizes extreme self-care and quality of life, whereas *Coaching for Performance*[13] suggests great achievements, in business or sports, for example.

I defined coaching as the art of facilitating the unleashing of people's potential to reach meaningful, important objectives. Coaches help people grow—and grow results. I believe the extraordinary contribution of coaching comes from its integration of being and doing.

Individualistic/Collectivistic[14]

Individualistic: "The smallest unit of survival is the individual. People identify primarily with self, and the needs of the individual are satisfied before those of the group. Looking after and taking care of oneself, being self-sufficient guarantees the well-being of the group. Independence and self-reliance are stressed and greatly valued, and personal freedom is highly desired."[15]

Collectivistic: "The primary group, usually the immediate family, is the smallest unit of survival. One's identity is in large part a function of one's membership and role in a group (e.g., the family, the work team). The survival and success of the group ensures the well-being of the individual, so that by considering the needs and feelings of others, one protects oneself. Harmony and the interdependence of group members are stressed and valued."[16]

The individualistic/collectivistic dimension has practical business applications. For example, decision making can take more time in a collectivistic culture, where group decision may be the norm. But implementation is likely to go more smoothly because everybody has participated in the decision. Representation is likely to be plural in a collectivistic culture. A delegation will engage in the negotiation in contrast to individualistic cultures, where one person can have a mandate to make decisions alone on the spot.

Despite differences in cultural orientations, which sometimes lead us to adopt one pole and neglect the other, both the self and the group ultimately matter. It is interesting to note, for example, that when affiliation needs are not satisfactorily met, as is often the case in our individualistic Western society, a reversal can occur. People may join religious sects and surrender their selves in an extreme fashion. More frequently, they can identify themselves with the organization employing them for better (loyalty) or worse (abuse) to meet their affiliation needs. James Collins and Jerry Porras suggested that the most successful organizations have developed cult-like cultures.[17]

Examples of the Dimension

Individualistic people can grow by adopting collectivism. Western organizations became fascinated with teams to the extent of placing Japanese management practices on a pedestal two decades ago.

Collectivistic people can likewise grow by taking on some aspects of individualism. *The Wall Street Journal* Europe published a column titled "Japan's Decline Makes One Thing Rise: Individualism."[18] "When the 1990s began,

individuals didn't count for much in Japan.... Promises of lifetime employ-
ment and a tidy pension kept corporate soldiers in line, but years of stagnation
have planted deep doubts about all that." The article evokes the example of
Mr. Kuzuoka who, at the age of 57, has decided to "stand firmly on my own
and think for myself...." Mr. Kuzuoka has joined a group called "Entry-Level
Employees With Pride." Washed-up salarymen, they meet to discuss ways to
make more of their lives.

As is true with all the dimensions, these orientations are not black and
white. We are all individualistic and collectivistic at the same time, but to various relative degrees and in different manners. Moreover, the phenomenon is
dynamic, not static: the Japanese shift toward individualism described above
is an example.

In Europe, countries like France or the United Kingdom are careful about
giving up their individualistic sovereignty.[19] The countries feel rightly proud
about their cultures and would hate to see them diluted in a collective European entity. As the concept of leveraging "individualism" and "collectivism"
suggests, this does not have to happen. To move the European construction
forward, what is required is not necessarily less individualism but more collectivism. Europe needs a sense of purpose. What does Europe stand for, and
what would each country recognize as a rallying mission? A concept of human
rights and social justice, a commitment to respect the environment, a passion
for the arts and the sciences, and cultural intermixing could be a part of this
European identity.

Bengt Anderson contrasts the example of the Swedes with the Chinese and
Japanese:

> In both these cultures, the individual is subordinate to the
> group. The group of workmates and intimate friends provide
> a large part of a person's concept of self. The psychological
> dependency on the collective is extremely great. In the
> Swedish culture, on the other hand, the individual remains
> superior to the group. Swedes have a strong desire to remain
> independent and establish their own identities.

But, according to Anderson, the nature of Swedish individualism is particular:
"Swedes have a strong desire to be their own masters but not to be different....
Swedes often describe themselves as *en vanlig Svensson*, an average Swede.
They try to lie low, not say too much, and, above all, not show off." [20]

Leveraging Individualism and Collectivism

Baxter Renal serves as a strong example from coaching in a company that has been able to establish a culture that makes the most of individualism and collectivism. On the one hand, you have a collection of strong personalities. Many Baxter Renal executives I met were quite open about their personal ambitions. One woman appreciated the fact that she could work part-time, mostly from her home, and was not prepared to give that up. Many executives were eager learners, looking forward to raising their profile and moving to jobs with bigger responsibilities. Everyone was interested in the opportunity to grow personally. I did not meet people ready to sacrifice their own needs and individuality for a collective entity above themselves.

Yet, at the same time there was a strong sense of being a part of Baxter and of Baxter Renal UK in particular. One team member said, "I would never have thought of myself as a company person, yet here I am speaking highly of my company." I saw very little turnover; executives clearly felt they were part of Baxter. In fact, one unusual executive who had left Baxter soon after the first retreat in 1997 was back for the fifth retreat in 2001. What they liked about Baxter was a culture of ethics and excellence: "We understand the business we are in." "We strive to provide a better way for the patient versus just make more money." "I feel empowered." "There is little red tape." "We help one another." "It is a team of friends, not just colleagues." Paradoxically, the individualistic motives, "The company allows us to grow personally," "The company values diversity in personalities and backgrounds," contributed to holding the group together, creating strong collectivism. The role of the team leader, acting as an internal coach, and my role as the external coach was to keep emphasizing the common purpose and pointing out the synergies.

In another example, I remember coaching a Japanese manager. He loved the idea of giving himself permission to follow his own path. He was feeling stuck due to his dependence and perceived obligation to follow the journey his organization had designed for him and his colleagues. This was several years ago. As I indicated earlier in this chapter, individualism seems to have become even more attractive in Japan since then. Asian executives in Chubb,[21] influenced by Western leaders and trainers and by Australian colleagues, saw the importance of engaging in a personal leadership development journey. Dealing with outspoken Australians in particular, it became a necessity! The Asians allowed themselves to openly share personal opinions and to challenge constructively. They had to make their voices heard or suffer domination by their Australian peers. Australians, on the other hand, learned from the Asians to pay more attention to the group. They started to listen to verbal and nonverbal messages (see chapter 9), as a way of bringing everyone into the discussion and of patiently building consensus. They learned to view their personal journey in relation to the team journey, realizing that they were all in the same boat.

Applications and Advice

As global coaches, we need to resist the tendency to judge differences. To Maslow, affiliation needs may be less advanced than the self-actualization needs that top his pyramid of human needs. His model reveals an individualistic bias. From a collectivistic perspective, this statement is not true.

Traditional coaching has normally promoted self-actualization by reinforcing an individualistic orientation. Hopefully, this is not done at the expense of collectivism. Affiliation to multiple groups can be encouraged. Service to self and others can be simultaneously promoted.

In the case of team coaching, I have developed an approach that proactively seeks to leverage both poles in considering both the individual and the group dimensions. A somewhat paradoxical injunction I like to use with teams is to invite members at times to be selfish. The rationale is that individual commitment to the team is higher to the extent that individual needs are met in the team context. When I started using this injunction in the mid-1990s, I found it violated the common belief that good team members should banish personal agendas (despite the fact that only lip service to this rule existed because it was going against "human nature"). My goal was instead to legitimize individual desires and use them as engines for action. Consciously or unconsciously, members need to have good personal reasons to engage in collective action and be fully committed to the team success.

Conversely, good coaches also avoid "groupthink"[22] and peer pressure. A skillful facilitator might be tempted to use peer pressure to manipulate. Manipulation is a negative form of influencing, where you convince somebody to do something he does not really want to do. Being committed to serve each individual and the team overall requires avoiding manipulative shortcuts. In an individualistic culture this takes time. If time is not available, then a different process from coaching can be used. It is important for the team leader and team members to consciously decide what they hope to achieve and the level of participation that can be expected.[23] In a collectivistic culture, the notion of individual needs may be less pronounced and people may more readily come to consensus. In any event, the art of coaching consists here in exploring and integrating individual and collective needs to the right level.

Coaching Tool: Collages to Reveal Your Common Purpose[24]

The goal of this activity is to help you explore your purpose, from a being and a doing perspective. In addition, performed in a group it will help you leverage the individual and collective perspectives. For the activity itself, you will need to collect a large variety of magazines and pictures ahead of time: exotic travel, local photographs, depictions of fashion, sports, arts, children, women, men, and so on. You will also need large sheets of paper, scissors, and glue.

The activity revolves around the notion of desires, "the very essence of each person" (to paraphrase Spinoza). Desires are where the coaching assessment begins, as I have indicated in chapter 1. Coaching questions include

- What makes you happy? What do you enjoy? What do you love?
- What is truly important to you?

Incidentally, as a coach, I try to help people do more of what they desire and less of what they only do because they have to (see chapter 11 for a more elaborate discussion of the concept of desire).

In the case of teams, here is the situation:

Map of Team Members' Desires

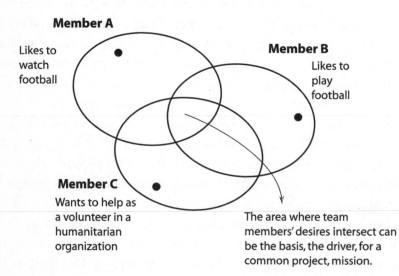

Member A
Likes to watch football

Member B
Likes to play football

Member C
Wants to help as a volunteer in a humanitarian organization

The area where team members' desires intersect can be the basis, the driver, for a common project, mission.

While we recognize that people have different desires and even encourage them to pursue their individual aspirations, we also know that the intersection of these desires is where the team can potentially meet and build from. The junction provides the basis, the drive to build a common project and mission for the team. We know that there will be a lot of energy available to make it happen because this area represents something all members truly want.

Exercise

Think of a team you are part of. It could be a group in your current organization, a project team with members from different organizations, or a network of independent people collaborating. Once you have identified this particular team, read the following questions:

- What attracts you to this team/organization/project/network?
- What do you find special about this team/organization/project/network?
- What about this team/organization/project/network can foster a passion for success (performance and fulfillment)?

Make sure the questions are clearly registered in your mind...and then forget about the questions. You will now create a collage.

- Keep in mind that this is not an artistic contest and that you don't have to come up with a breakthrough insight. Just enjoy the process.
- Find pictures that attract you and cut them out of the magazines or select them from your photo pile.
- Place the pictures on the sheet of paper in any way you want.
- When you are happy with the display, glue the pictures on the sheet.

You may limit yourself to about 20 to 30 minutes. Once the piece of art is completed, look at it, and just like in the postcard exercise (chapter 3), let the collage speak to you, in connection with the original questions.

You will want to record your insights in your learning journal. You may even take a Polaroid photograph of the collage and place it in the learning journal as well. What is great about collages is that you don't need to have any artistic skills to produce a pleasing result.

Then comes the part where you can share your collages in pairs or in small groups. Show your work and self-disclose. What do the images represent? What is the relationship of the collage with the initial questions? What about the overall disposition and movement? And the empty spaces, lights and shadows, and colors?

Let your colleagues ask probing questions and make comments such as "If this were my collage, it would mean ..." (you don't want to let them arrogantly imply they have figured out your motives).

An interesting phenomenon takes place when you share your collages. You naturally see connections and resemblances. This is similar to what happens when two people converse. Their gestures and postures tend to become the same. People find a similar wavelength. It also happens when walking with someone: if you gently pick up the pace or slow down, the other person is likely to simply follow without even noticing the difference.

The similarities you perceive in the collages are precisely the intersections you are looking for. In a large group, you can display the creations on a wall or craft a little art gallery. You can go back several times to these collages and find new insights and new connections. You can also proactively look for synergies by answering these two questions: "What opportunities for synergies do you see when you look at all the collages?" "What are the common themes that stand out?" Your art is a means for self-expression. It gives you a pleasant vehicle to talk about your passions and to let your common purpose emerge or solidify out of these conversations.

The room may feel like kindergarten. Let go of control! Connect with your inner Child,[25] where creativity, spontaneity, and vital energy reside. Your challenge will be to keep this sense of excitement alive as you embark on the team project.

Chapter 7
How to Leverage Organizational Arrangements

What structures and arrangements do you favor in your organization?

Hierarchy/Equality—Universalist/Particularist—Stability/Change—
Competitive/Collaborative

Hierarchy: Society and organizations must be socially stratified to function
 properly.

Equality: People are equals who often happen to play different roles.

Universalist: All cases should be treated in the same universal manner.
 Adopt common processes for consistency and economies of scale.

Particularist: Emphasize particular circumstances. Favor decentralization
 and tailored solutions.

Stability: Value a static and orderly environment. Encourage efficiency
 through systematic and disciplined work. Minimize change and
 ambiguity, perceived as disruptive.

Change: Value a dynamic and flexible environment. Promote effectiveness
 through adaptability and innovation. Avoid routine, perceived as
 boring.

Competitive: Promote success and progress through competitive
 stimulation.

Collaborative: Promote success and progress through mutual support,
 sharing of best practices and solidarity.

---

*Generally, management of many is the same as management
of few. It is a matter of organization.*[1]

—Sun Tzu

To make projects come true and to satisfy social instincts, people most often
come together and form systems called organizations. To coach people, you
need to appreciate the *organizations* they take part in. As one would expect,
these systems are very much influenced by culture.

The different parts can relate to one another in multiple ways. The word *organization* in fact refers either to these possible arrangements or to the overall system itself.[2]

The system exists at many levels. It can refer to a person, a group, or society. Most frequently however, we mean "companies" or "institutions" when we speak about organizations.

Literature certainly does not lack sophisticated descriptions of organizations, both static and dynamic. I can only mention a few here. Management guru Henry Mintzberg has classified organizations into seven types, which include the entrepreneurial, machine, and professional.[3] There is no one ideal form in absolute terms, only more suitable configurations for a given purpose (for example, innovative or efficient).

Using Mintzberg's classification, Geert Hofstede[4] has discussed how two cultural dimensions (i.e., his equivalents of "hierarchy–equality" and "stability–change") often generate specific types of organizations. Hofstede argues, "The structure and functioning of organizations are not determined by a universal rationality," being themselves culturally tainted.

Gareth Morgan has used metaphors to describe various facets of organizations. For example, he views them alternatively as machines, organisms, brains, political systems, or even "psychic prisons."[5]

In a global environment, Stephen Rhinesmith, building on Christopher Bartlett and Sumantra Ghoshal,[6] writes about domestic, exporter, international, multinational, global, and transnational organizations. These forms of corporations could either represent different stages of organizational development (OD) or alternatives whose suitability depends on the industry and type of business. Furthermore, all forms could coexist in one corporation.

Organizational consultants come in various sorts too: human resource advisers on job descriptions and classifications, business process reengineering specialists, management information systems experts, organizational structure professionals, and so on.

OD is a distinct discipline whose purpose is to "improve organizational performance and organizational functioning."[7] Originally viewed as an application of behavioral science knowledge, OD has grown to encompass a strategic perspective, organizational theory, and applications in international and cross-cultural environments. OD constitutes a good entry point to introduce coaching in organizations. Reciprocally, coaching is useful for OD in that it offers a process to unleash individual and team potential to promote organizational progress. Both OD and coaching draw from behavioral psychology and have gone beyond this discipline, notably by embracing a cultural perspective.

As I indicated in the "Visioning Model" in chapter 4, the organization (structure and work processes) is a key lever of progress. The lever includes bringing together multiple organizations, as is the case in mergers and acquisitions and in partnerships constituting a virtual organization. Coaches and leaders don't have to become organizational experts, but they need to acquire sufficient familiarity with the topic to appreciate how organizations enable or prevent the "unleashing of people's potential."

Global coaches appreciate how culture affects and unconsciously determines organizational decisions, something even many organizational experts often overlook. Raising cultural awareness and viewing culture as a process, something that can be changed, can help leadership make better organizational choices and thus positively affect performance and fulfillment.

Four key cultural dimensions stand out as common themes in organizational arrangements. I shall focus on these now.

Hierarchy/Equality[8]

Hierarchy: People in cultures at the high end of the hierarchy orientation "accept that some among them will have more power and influence than others. Those with power tend to emphasize it, to hold it close and not delegate or share it, and to distinguish themselves as much as possible from those who do not have power. They are, however, expected to accept the responsibilities that go with power, especially that of looking after those beneath them. Subordinates are not expected to take initiative and are closely supervised."

Equality: Those in cultures at the high end of the equality orientation often feel quite strongly that power inequalities are largely artificial and are not natural or fair. Those in positions of power tend to deemphasize it, to "minimize the differences between themselves and subordinates, and to delegate and share power to the extent possible." Decisions are made by consensus when possible, and subordinates are encouraged to take initiative and feel uncomfortable with close supervision.[9]

Of course, as is generally true with all the dimensions, every culture has parts of both orientations. Nevertheless, cultures do tend to be more one than the other.

In hierarchical cultures, such as China, people assume that society and organizations must be socially stratified in order to function properly.

Confucius believed in strict hierarchical structures: ruler/subject, father/son, older brother/younger brother, husband/wife, senior friend/junior friend. "A young man, at home, must love and respect his parents. Outside his home, he must respect those who are older or of higher rank than himself."[10]

The two orientations, hierarchy and equality, although important in all aspects of society, manifest themselves particularly in the workplace. Organizationally, hierarchies tend to result in more centralized structures, equality, in flatter and decentralized structures.

Whereas a hierarchical orientation can lend itself to the making of unilateral decisions and efficiency in dealing with a crisis situation, an equality orientation will naturally cause managers to foster teamwork and an individual sense of autonomy and responsibility. If the ambition is for people to use their full creative potential and be innovative, a rigid hierarchical orientation is likely to constitute a serious obstacle.

Another aspect of hierarchies has implications for leadership development: the reluctance to carry out 360-degree feedback surveys and to give feedback to superiors.[11]

Examples of the Dimension

A characteristic of hierarchies is that one needs appropriate relationships and connections to put plans in place. Political activities become a necessity.[12] I conducted leadership training in France with two different companies in different sectors. In both cases, I remember being struck by the amount of informal political conversation. With humorous French sarcasm, participants portrayed the key leaders in their organizations, commenting on their agendas and peculiar traits.

Jackie Chang, human resources manager of Chubb Insurance North Asia, pointed out that the Chinese still tend to respect and follow hierarchical superiors, regardless of their behaviors. If their superiors are inept, Chinese workers will feel frustrated but will remain loyal and will not confront their bosses. If their superiors spend time and appear with them in public, they will feel honored. They will appreciate the fact that everybody can see they enjoy a special relationship with their bosses and will want to "pay double to them," meaning working even harder to serve them.[13]

In contrast, I remember Israeli fellow students[14] at Stanford University openly challenging our professors.[15] Never mind the fact the faculty was world-class, forget the age difference, the students seemed unimpressed with their professors' ranks and would say, "Your reasoning is wrong!" They would then spontaneously go to the blackboard and, chalk now in hand, would show the professor the "right way." Equally surprising to me was the fact that these professors did not seem offended!

The United States believes strongly in equality—at least equality of opportunity and at least in theory. Assuming equality as a superior form of leadership, however, can backfire. A manager who was on an expatriate assignment from the United States had to manage a group in Belgium. She relied on open-ended questions and group consensus. Her deeply engrained assumption was that people are all equals; therefore she had no right to give orders and make unilateral decisions. As it turns out, she alienated people and lost their respect. They did not want to waste time in meetings trying to reach consensus for every issue. They wanted her to be more decisive, give orders, and confront people when necessary.

When I speak of the U.S. form of equality, I am not talking about equality of revenues or social conditions. Sanford Weill of Citigroup and Jack Welch of General Electric made over $100 million in 2000, while the median household annual income was $42,680 and the minimum hourly wage $5.15.[16] I am referring to equality of rights, which has been a long battle resulting in anti-discrimination laws against unequal treatment based on gender, race, or age differences. I am also referring to the value of equal opportunity. In the U.S., people tolerate CEO compensations that would be considered outrageous anywhere else, partly because many success stories perpetuate the "American dream," that is, making it to the top is potentially available to anyone.

People who prefer equality still need to deal with the reality that hierarchies exist in many parts of the world. Despite modern management theories, hierarchy *and* control sometimes deliver results efficiently. Robert De Niro in Martin Scorsese's *Casino* builds the most successful casino by choosing control over trust.

Leveraging Hierarchy and Equality

Leveraging hierarchy and equality often means that managers engage in political activities in order to obtain the necessary support and resources (i.e., viewing their organizations as a hierarchy), while sharing power and promoting participation within their teams (i.e., demonstrating an orientation for equality).

The following example is taken from my article "Constructive Politics: Essential to Leadership."[17] I explain the underlying "Constructive Politics" below.

> When I work with executives, I seldom find that they have given any deliberate attention to the sources of power. So I typically brainstorm with them about what constitutes power. This helps them become aware of what they have overlooked and consider what actions they could take to gain influence.

> One executive complained about the lack of resources allocated by top management to his research and development (R&D) division. He was cynical about their poor understanding of the strategic importance of R&D. At the same time, the president of the corporation was concerned that the division did not have real team spirit. He expected the division to articulate an overall vision of its contribution to the organization, not to mention a sound business plan.

> In order to respond to these expectations, the R&D team had two retreats, over five days, to build trust and respect and then to design a strategic plan for itself. The plan started from a customer perspective and offered an integrated R&D approach that would serve customer needs better than any company in the market had ever done.

> I described constructive politics to the team; they thereby became aware of external networking as a way to garner support from key customers so that they could then "sell" the plan inside the company. Before the retreat, these engineers had never thought of such political action as a part of their job, but they realized they had to do this in order to gain the backing of top management. Their political action, far from being destructive, brought win–win–win–win results: for the company as a whole, which improved its business; for the R&D division, which established a better relationship to the rest of the company; for customers, who got better service; and for team members, who made it possible for themselves to do more relevant and interesting engineering work.

Applications and Advice

The coaching relationship assumes equality.[18] As a coach, you help the coachee access his own potential, learn from his experience, and reflect on his desires. This assumes the coachee has considerable potential, has gone through unique experiences (not necessarily similar to yours), and has legitimate desires. If you were his superior, on the other hand, you might doubt the value of his potential, the richness of his experiences, and the legitimacy of his desires.

Because coaching assumes equality, coaches might be ill equipped to help coachees deal with a hierarchical manifestation, namely politics. The political perspective is a useful angle coaches can learn to adopt. It is this political perspective I will address next, in some detail, because I have found it to be of great value in my coaching experience.

Constructive Politics

Coaches can help coachees systematically examine their sources of power and power dynamics. The notion of constructive politics is consistent with the basic values of coaching. In fact, I have defined *politics* as "an activity that builds and maintains your power so that you can achieve your goals." Accordingly, *power* can be understood as "the ability to achieve your meaningful, important goals." Politics is a process. Power is potential and it comes from many sources. In "Constructive Politics," I refer to the following sources of power: external networks, internal allies, knowledge, credibility, availability of choices, formal authority, interpersonal skills, and intrapersonal skills. Politics becomes constructive when it also works in the service of others. You attempt to understand the hopes, needs, and dreams of people and to creatively seek common ground between their goals and yours. You want to be open to their wishes while staying true to your own, looking for synergies or for innovative win–win situations. It may also be that one of your goals is helping them achieve theirs.

I have found that a good way to understand the interaction of the two dimensions of constructive politics, which are power and service,[19] is to think of four basic political types, which can be arranged in a two-by-two matrix (see table page 124): the Individual Achiever, the Idealist, the Prince, and the Enlightened Builder. The four political types can be used to help you assess your situation and set developmental goals with respect to developing constructive politics. As power gives impact and leverage, service can guide your actions.

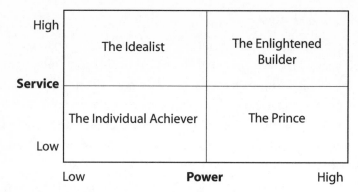

The *Individual Achiever*. With a low service orientation and not much power, the individual achiever is seen as self-centered. This type can have a high technical competence and be very successful at some activities—think of a lone rock climber who can negotiate a long vertical ascent. If the conditions are right—with a protective boss or in a situation with few interdependencies—the individual achiever will likely not feel powerless or feel the need to engage in politics. In an interdependent situation, however, he or she may be very frustrated by an inability to focus on and productively engage in the technical work.

The Idealist. The idealist has a genuine desire to serve others but is low on power. Often seen as a crusader, this type may succeed through perseverance but is often frustrated by bureaucratic obstacles. The tendency of the idealist is to resent politics, often because he or she is avoiding conflict. The idealist may also, because of the focus on others, devalue self-affirming activities that relate to personal goals. In some cases, this results in blaming others for failure and unconsciously playing the victim.

The Prince. The prince, as described in the classic work by Machiavelli, has a lot of power but is largely committed to, or is understood as being largely committed to, self-advancement. Although often seen negatively, this type of person can make things happen and achieve objectives. However, the prince runs a high risk of alienating people, which in the long run can erode power.

The Enlightened Builder. With a desire to serve others and well-developed power, the enlightened builder is the type that is most likely to be described as a "leader." This type can use politics to help people identify and respond to the challenges necessary to achieving the organization's mission. The enlightened builder has personal goals and accepts that other people do too, but he uses the energy that comes from these in the service of people in general.[20]

I refer you to the article for more information on how to use the matrix as an assessment and developmental tool. Moreover, the coaching tool at the end of this chapter will show you a systematic approach to building internal alliances.

Universalist/Particularist[21]

How do you know something is true? On what basis do you consider something fair?

Universalist: There are certain absolutes that apply across the board, regardless of circumstances or the particular situation. Fons Trompenaars explains, "The universalistic approach is roughly: 'What is good and right can be defined and always applies.'"[22] Storti adds, "What is right will always be right. To be fair is to treat everyone alike and not make exceptions for family or friends."[23]

Particularist: "In particularistic cultures, far greater attention is given to the obligations of relationships and unique circumstances. For example, instead of assuming that one good way must always be followed, the particularistic reasoning is that friendship has special obligations and hence may come first. Less attention is given to abstract societal codes."[24] What is true and fair in one situation might be wrong in another.

From the universalist pole, treating all cases in the same manner will guarantee fairness. From the particularist pole, treating each case on its special merit is the right approach.

In universalist cultures, the same broad criteria will be applied to all members of a given role or status. Common processes, policies, and systems will be developed and expected to be applied everywhere. In particularist cultures, specific criteria are applied to individuals or sub-groups on the basis of their particular situation. People prefer systems tailored to their needs and resist abiding by universalist processes and policies when these do not make sense in their particular circumstances.

Examples of the Dimension

I remember training leaders internationally from a large automotive manufacturer. Managers in the United States would insist on becoming more global, which in their minds meant common platforms, universal designs, and sales worldwide. Europeans on the other hand would advocate particular solutions and would explain that "one size fits all" did not equate with globalizing from their perspective.

In my experience, this is the most important cultural dimension U.S. multinationals can become aware of. I have heard endless debates between American senior managers insisting that the same rules, processes, and policies apply everywhere and French middle managers trying to explain why that does not make sense in France. Research suggests that the United States, as a national culture, scores very high on universalism.[25] Americans who have not developed cultural sensitivity can become very judgmental about particularists who "just don't get it." Likewise, when the French managers are not open to the economies of scale and the consistency universalism can bring, polarization occurs.

Contracting is another frequent source of frustration between universalist and particularist cultures. Universalists insist on detailed and written contracts to capture the nature of a business agreement. This usually means spending hours sending letters back and forth to contractually cover all possible scenarios. Particularists prefer to rely on trust and goodwill to deal with special situations when they arise.[26]

Trompenaars makes the following link with Christian religions:

> Universalists are more common in Protestant cultures where the congregation relates to God by obedience to His written laws. There are no human intermediaries between God and His adherents, no one with the discretion to hear particular confessions, forgive sins, or make special allowances. Predominantly Catholic cultures retained these features of religion, which are more relational and particularist. People can break commandments and still find compassion for their unique circumstances.[27]

Trompenaars also tells the anecdote of a Venezuelan country manager who had misused the Hay (after the name of its designer Colonel Hay) job classification system for his own ends. Rather than relying on objective criteria to evaluate and rank possible candidates for a promotion, he decided himself who should get the job, then ensured by tinkering a posteriori with the Hay forms that the candidate he had chosen appeared as the best using Hay's universalist process. When confronted with this maneuver the manager replied, "Who decides on the promotion of *my* subordinates, Colonel Hay or me?" Cross-cultural differences are too complex to remain unmanaged. In this case, lip service was paid to Hay's universalist approach. But alienation or even sabotage may also happen when mutual respect and understanding are not developed.

Many other examples of the dimension could be given, but let me just mention that Japan, interestingly, is on the particularist side. In art and gardening, for example, "a dynamic harmony is created from myriad differences with no tree, leaf, flower, or stone like any other."[28]

Leveraging Universalism and Particularism

Unilever exemplifies the approach of leveraging common technologies and processes with particular consumer habits.[29] Common brands such as Lipton are offered as long as they meet local needs, but the company does not hesitate to develop tailored solutions whenever it means better serving particular customer tastes and traditions. In fact, over the years, Unilever has acquired local brands to become stronger in select markets. Recently, the acquisitions of Slim-Fast, Ben & Jerry's, and Amora Maille have built up Unilever's position in functional foods, premium ice cream, and culinary products. These businesses are rapidly integrated while retaining their unique identity. In Mexico, leading international brands Cornetto and Magnum are sold alongside Mordisko, a "local jewel" (a Unilever term to refer to special, particular brands). In China an understanding of the local consumer enabled Unilever to launch Zhonghua, Chinese herbal toothpaste. In 2000 all the Unilever employees in Indonesia—from offices, factories, and warehouses—spent a day meeting consumers at shops and supermarkets around the country. There, they gained firsthand insight into retailing and consumer behavior and preferences.

Because it values particularism, Unilever fosters the dynamism of a small business. It also allows managers and employees to feel empowered, which would not be the case if their role was limited to implementing universal solutions devised by central headquarters. To leverage particularism and universalism, Unilever holds multiple meetings and creates numerous communication opportunities. Several leaders described Unilever as a "networked organization": the web of personal relationships allows the sharing of best practices, minimizes the risk of wasting time reinventing the wheel, and allows the creation of global solutions wherever possible.

This philosophy is apparent in the first half of Unilever's corporate purpose:

> Our purpose in Unilever is to meet the everyday needs of
> people everywhere—to anticipate the aspirations of our

consumers and customers and to respond creatively and competitively with branded products and services which raise the quality of life.

Our deep roots in local cultures and markets around the world are our unparalleled inheritance and the foundation for our future growth.

We will bring our wealth of knowledge and international expertise to the service of local consumers—a truly multi-local multinational.

Applications and Advice

A major implication for coaching is the risk of overlooking cultural particularism. Too often, unfortunately and despite good intentions, models are presented without any hint of the underlying implicit cultural assumptions and without the necessary care one needs to exercise when trying to implement the models across cultures.

These monocultural models are still useful as long as cultural limitations are properly understood. For example, a recipe that works in the United States will not necessarily function in France, and vice versa. Of course, models that explicitly integrate the cultural dimension or that hold true across cultures will be preferred in a global environment, though they will not necessarily have universal validity, in an absolute sense. According to logic, one particular exception is sufficient indeed to invalidate a supposedly universal law. But practically, it makes sense to devise models that can be broadly applied in a cross-cultural environment. These are *generally* rather than *universally* valid, as is the case for most models in this book.

For a coach, leveraging universalism and particularism in practice means adopting a consistent yet flexible approach. The danger would be to fall instead into the negative flipsides: uniformity or incoherence. Working with an international network of professional coaches, I find these criteria to be critical for success. My goal is indeed to tap into the richness of diverse talents. Therefore I don't want to impose rigid methods and rules that would stifle my colleagues' creativity. On the other hand, I do want to offer my clients the benefit of a consistent approach. To have the best of both worlds, universalism and particularism, I carefully choose partners and make sure we agree on a common coaching philosophy and process. Then I let them and in fact encourage them to be themselves, to use their unique gifts, and to coach in their own ways. I find it enriching when we can learn from our differences while building on our similarities.

Blending universalism and particularism is of equal importance to building synergistic teams and learning organizations. Information that feeds the learning organization becomes useful knowledge when its universal/particular context is properly understood.

Stability/Change[30]

As the modern cliché goes, change is the sole constant these days. Everything changes; that is what does not change!

Stability: Cultures that are high on the stability end of the dimension are skeptical or even anxious about change that is too substantial or turbulent. Considering that immobility is rarely a viable option, such cultures will favor some change but only to the extent that it is incremental and within the current "paradigm"; in other words, the environment is still stable and orderly. "Familiar risks are acceptable but ambiguous situations and unfamiliar risks are often feared. Rules, because they generally control behavior and change, are welcome. Generally, where rules or guidelines exist, change is orderly and predictable."

Change: Cultures that are high on the change end of the dimension welcome changes that are significant, nonlinear, innovative, and turbulent. "What is different causes curiosity, not anxiety. Ambiguous situations and unfamiliar risks cause little or no discomfort. Rules are to be limited to those that are absolutely necessary. Unusual or innovative ideas and flexibility are encouraged."[31]

If change is the sole constant, coaching is quite naturally destined to steer the change process (and usually to speed it up, which brings us back to chapter 5) or to help cope with change.

In reality, despite the current dominant rhetoric, stability is still very much present and necessary. Throughout history, progress has occurred through *evolutions* and *revolutions*. Apart from setbacks, periods of gradual enhancement in a stable environment have coexisted with times of radical transformation. Calm waters turn into turbulent rapids and back again to tranquility. Immobility, however, was never a long-term viable option in a world that keeps moving forward. For organizations, the best scenario for continuous development alternates improving existing work processes (total quality management) and designing new and better-suited ones (reengineering).

It is very disruptive and demoralizing when you get a new boss or are restructuring every other month. It is equally frustrating and unproductive when your company holds on to business processes that have become obsolete. One needs to find the right rhythm between evolution and revolution, working both efficiently (doing things right) and effectively (doing the right things).

Examples of the Dimension

Baxter values innovation and change. One consequence is the high internal mobility of executives. If an employee does well, the company culture encourages him or her to seize new opportunities and be promoted quickly. Peter Leyland realized he needed to balance this tendency with stability in order for his unit to at least harvest the human talent available. Since he could not coerce managers into staying, he had to create an environment where they would *want* to spend a few years. Together with them, he created a vision that was appealing, a project that was challenging, and a climate that was exciting. As a result, team members made a significant contribution to the company. More members were promoted than for an average Baxter team, plus they were equipped with a strong learning experience.

Although Baxter Renal UK initially emphasized articulating a vision, devising a strategy and building excitement and unity around the project, in 1999 the challenge was to avoid letting the initial enthusiasm drift as the team was making it all happen. A key theme for the fourth retreat, therefore, was to appreciate the beauty of implementation. It was necessary to restore the nobility of stability in a culture where change alone was deemed attractive. Suggesting that stability is critical and can be exciting too was an important step.

If you think of top athletes and artists, you observe that excellence only comes through consistent, disciplined, and long-term dedicated work. It can also be rewarding and even fun to repeatedly execute the same routine and gradually improve, and not just for top athletes and artists. As much as I like innovative enterprises, I look forward to my tennis practice with a coach. The content does not change much, but I still enjoy hitting the ball and repeating the same tennis movements, and gradually I get better (though there is still a long way to go!).

Leveraging Stability and Change

In "The Making of a Corporate Athlete," Jim Loehr and Tony Schwartz indicate that the capacity to mobilize energy on demand is the foundation of what they call the Ideal Performance State (the capacity to bring talents and skills to full ignition and to sustain high performance over time). They argue that effective energy management involves "the rhythmic movement between energy expenditure (stress) and energy renewal (recovery), which (they) term *oscillation*." They explain that "the real enemy of high performance is not stress.... Rather, the problem is the absence of disciplined, intermittent recovery. Chronic stress without recovery depletes energy reserves, leads to burnout and breakdown, and ultimately undermines performance."[32]

James Collins and Jerry Porras' research indicated that the most successful companies, those "built to last," leverage stability and change; they "preserve the core and stimulate progress."[33] Even though their research focused on U.S. companies, in Europe Unilever would certainly have qualified. The commitment to grow ("passion for growth") by challenging the status quo is only matched by the continued adherence to the fundamental values of "meeting everyday needs of people everywhere" and being a "truly multi-local multinational."

Likewise, Chubb Insurance keeps innovating to offer specialized solutions to clients as opposed to commodity insurance products. But that positioning has not changed over the years. Also permanent are the values of honesty, integrity, respect, and commitment to continuous improvement, which have enabled Chubb to consistently achieve the ideal its founder, Thomas Caldecot Chubb, expressed in the nineteenth century: "Ours is an organization that is as eager to have a good reputation as 'Chubb & Son, the employer' as it is to have a good reputation as 'Chubb & Son, the underwriter.'"[34]

Applications and Advice

Global coaching does not merely help with change. It also challenges you to strike the right balance between change and stability.

The Kirton Adaptation-Innovation Inventory[35] contrasts people who tend to challenge the paradigm (Innovators) with those who exert their creativity within the confines of the existing system (Adaptors). Coaches should ideally be able to act as both Adaptors and Innovators, regardless of their own preference. Some coachees prefer a very structured approach. Others like open-ended procedures. Some will rigorously follow your X-step model (i.e., a linear model consisting of X sequential steps). Some will want the general idea and will devise their own innovative ways to apply it. Some hate ambiguity: instructions need to be detailed and precise. Others love it: ambiguity gives room for creativity. The art of coaching is to adapt your style to the situation, which intentionally does not exclude stretching a coachee outside his comfort zone.

To coach an organization, that is, to unleash its human potential to achieve important, meaningful objectives, you must typically break down the intervention into smaller-scale actions. You work with select individuals and teams. What is important is to build a critical mass of "progress agents" while considering at least two factors. First, identify those who hold the power positions,[36] realizing that these people don't necessarily occupy the higher positions in the formal hierarchy. Second, you should take into account people's readiness to venture outside their comfort zone and embrace new ideas. Only a few will be the "entrepreneurs" who take the initiative and the "opinion leaders" that the majority listens to in order to determine if the initiative is worthy. "Followers" allow the critical mass to be reached. "Late acceptors" will go along once there is enough evidence that the project will be successful. A few "laggards" will still cling to the old habits despite the evidence that the innovations make sense. In organizations, external coaching efforts are typically aimed at senior managers and high potentials. Together, they often have both the power and the influence to promote change. Furthermore, they can themselves act as coaches and build more momentum.

Global coaches do *not* assume that people who "resist" change are less enlightened than those who seek change. In fact, these coaches reframe altogether the notion of "resistance to change" into a "preference for stability," which has merits, too. Not every change is for the better. A restructuring could make sense to shareholders and select executives but may not be to the advantage of certain categories of employees and customers. Why would you expect them to support the changes?

Global coaches are eager to learn about the merits of stability and change for various stakeholders, and to help determine the best synergies among all parties' interests. Paradoxically, this attitude of respect and readiness to take a different cultural perspective will do more to "break resistance to change" than will any patronizing message that "you should change."

Another way of looking at the stability/change dimension is through Henry Mintzberg's work. Bureaucracies ("machine organizations") value stability and are best suited to operate in a settled environment. Innovative enterprises (Mintzberg's "innovative organizations"), on the other hand, thrive on change.[37] The structure itself may not be straightforward enough to modify. However, if your mind is open to the differences and is eager to leverage them, then it becomes easier to create organizations that make the most of both polarities. People don't necessarily have to be entrenched in their cultural orientations. In a bureaucratic organization, you can, for example, let specific entities operate under different norms, cutting any red tape and encouraging innovation. In an innovative enterprise, you can install systematic processes wherever it makes sense without generating a rebellion.

Competitive/Collaborative[38]

Competitive: In competitive cultures, the workplace is the stage of a permanent contest between individuals, teams, or divisions. The drive for winning, and the fear of losing, motivate people to devote their best efforts. Establishing one's supremacy could be at the expense of others, because only "the best" are destined to succeed.

Collaborative: In collaborative cultures, the emphasis is on working together. A sense of solidarity unites people, inspiring them to help each other and to share information and best practices, in order to succeed together.

It is worth noting that what motivates you, competition or collaboration, could very well alienate a colleague with the opposite orientation.

In the business world, competition is the name of the game. But achieving competitive advantage does not necessarily imply fostering a competitive culture inside your organization. In fact, promoting internal collaboration could be an effective approach. Preserving some degree of collaboration is always necessary anyway, due to the interdependencies inherent to organizational life.

Competition is frequently the reality, notably in U.S. multinational corporations. For example, a common practice is to rank executives according to their performance. The appraisal is usually tied to financial rewards and promotion opportunities. The top tier can expect to move *up* (where the fewer positions are reserved for "the best"), while the bottom tier's prospects will be to move *out* or, at the very least, to quickly improve performance.

To some extent, competition is inevitable in the workplace. There may be more candidates than attractive job opportunities and financial resources. However, competition, just like politics, does not have to be mean and destructive. Unless the implications of losing are dramatic, competition, viewed as a game, can even be fun! The key is to avoid attaching too much ego to the game. On the other hand, if you let your sense of self-worth be determined by your winning record, you may develop a strong drive to compete, and you may achieve a lot. But you also run the risk of losing self-confidence despite outward appearances, as you won't humanely be able to win every battle. Of course, if the stakes are high and if the winner takes all, it will be difficult to regard competition as a game and maintain a friendly atmosphere.

Examples of the Dimension

In 2000 my wife was working for a company called Ariane II, which was elected "Belgian Company of the Year" in 1998. I attended their annual meeting and noted that rather than presenting sales figures and ranking the performance of each sales executive (typical in a competitive culture), the sales manager chose to share humorous anecdotes and idiosyncrasies about each of his team members. In Ariane II's collaborative culture, sales executives were going out of their way to help each other, filling in for each other when necessary. They enjoyed working together and many of them had developed friendships outside work. Interestingly, they still had individual responsibility and accountability, but this had not prevented a high level of cooperation.

On the other hand, to replace Juan Antonio Samaranch as head of the International Olympic Committee, Jacques Rogge had to compete with several candidates. In July 2001, Rogge won. He immediately tried to foster a spirit of collaboration with the other candidates who had competed for the top job. Rogge said, humbly, that unlike at the Olympic Games, there were no losers here. I am not sure Richard Pound, who had long had ambitions for Samaranch's role, felt the same way![39]

Professional groups too can exemplify collaborative and competitive cultures. In the Belgian Polytechnical School, engineering students collaborate, readily exchanging notes and tips, helping each other succeed. This culture continues in the professional association of engineers. People call each other "comrades," like in the old communist party, even if engineers are undoubtedly prime contributors to the capitalist system!

In contrast a competitive spirit seems to prevail among other professions, such as business consulting and advertising. Less sharing takes place between members, and being the best acts as a powerful motivator.

This dimension also influences corporate growth strategies. Competition is obviously dominant in the market economy. However, a spirit of collaboration can foster successful alliances.

Much has been written about the success of Nissan and Renault's alliance. Under Carlos Ghosn's leadership, "a thumping loss of ¥684 billion ($6.1 billion) in the year ending March 2000 has been turned into a profit of ¥331 billion for the past fiscal year. Nissan has, as Mr. Ghosn says, moved from the emergency room to the recovery room." Through the alliance, each company can benefit while retaining its identity, which Mr. Ghosn sees as the basis of motivation. "By 2010, Renaults and Nissans will be made of essentially the same building blocks, even though they will look different. This platform-sharing is expected to bring huge savings." Mr. Ghosn also "sees Renault-Nissan as a global group, with Renault the European core and Nissan the pole for Asia and America."[40]

Leveraging Competition and Collaboration

The European Union is an example of leveraging competition and collaboration. The European construction may seem to go slowly. The issues are still multiple: presenting a united and credible defense that is able to take swift action when necessary, harmonizing fiscal laws and social regulations, finding the right governance and balance of powers between nations, and so on. But the fact is that by uniting, Europeans have enjoyed an unprecedented level of peace in the last fifty-five years. Germany and France had three major wars within the previous seventy years. The English fought with the French, the French with the Dutch, the Dutch with the Spaniards, and so on. With unification the old enemies have become allies. And what about the Deutsche Mark, French Franc, and other monetary national symbols? All gone! The Euro has become a reality.

Europe is leveraging competition and collaboration to come together. Leaders keep making comparisons between countries: "Look at what our neighbors have achieved!" It is easier for your public to accept the sacrifices that reducing the public deficit entails if you can show that other European countries are doing the same. The competition, however, in this form of a healthy emulation, occurs together with collaboration. Students spend semesters in other European countries, learning from different people and places. Best practices are exchanged in all areas: science, engineering, medicine, and so on.

But more fundamentally, the European Union exemplifies the leveraging of two doctrines: (1) liberalism, competition in a market economy, and (2) socialism, collaboration through state intervention and social regulations. Politically, the old socialists from the 1970s were at odds with the liberals. The communists were still very influential in several European countries, and both were wary of the capitalists. Today the socialists have embraced the market economy, and far from ruining it, they have shown a capacity to manage it.

The Economist, not exactly a left-wing journal, endorsed Tony Blair in 2001. In the same year, Lionel Jospin and Gerhard Schroeder, both social-ists, were respected leaders governing France and Germany. The right wing, too—not considering its nationalistic and racist extremists—appeared more occupied with social concerns. Most European liberals realize that the market's "invisible hand" cannot take care of everything. Privatizing railroads certainly did not make for a superior public service, for example.

The "third way" in politics represents an approach that in essence attempts to leverage liberalism and socialism, embracing the best while limiting the excesses of each. This synergy, I believe, has enabled Europe to get this far in the political union.

In the business world, achieving competitive advantage is sometimes, paradoxically, best attained through collaboration with competitors. I am not referring here to collusion. Secret price agreements among competitors violate the rules of the market game and are detrimental to end consumers. On the contrary, Baxter Renal UK decided to offer third-party haemodialysis products to complete its own home haemodialysis portfolio and offer the best therapeutic solution to home patients. As a result, competitors such as Gambro also became Baxter's partners, taking advantage of Baxter Renal UK's unique logistics and distribution infrastructure to the benefit of the end users, the patients.

Applications and Advice

Coaches have to consider both competition and collaboration as possibilities. The following example illustrates this point.

I was coaching the president of a vast territory of an international cor-poration.[41] He was finding it difficult to motivate the executives in charge of regions (each consisting of either several midsized countries or one large country) to collaborate to serve the whole territory. Taking a competitive cul-tural perspective, I challenged the assumption that they should collaborate in the first place.

The president indicated that each executive was responsible for a relatively independent entity. Autonomy made a lot of sense, as there were limited opportunities for synergies between the regions. The cohesion was good among the executives when they met, and they were all in line with the gen-eral direction of the company.

The president realized that the best approach was to let the executives focus on maximizing performance in their own regions. In fact a dose of competitive stimulation between the regions was probably the best way to unleash potential and achieve success. Extensive travel and communication to enable more collaboration would have only distracted the executives from concentrating on their priorities.

On the other hand, the president recognized that collaboration had to be reinforced among his team of direct reports located at the company's headquarters. They were the "engine" for the whole territory, acting as strategists and liaison points between the regions. They had to become more united and speak with one voice. The president was willing to adapt his style, without any cultural totem or taboo, relying both on competition and collaboration to achieve success.

Collaboration seems to characterize the coaching profession today. While it would be naïve to think that competition is totally absent, I have noticed, for example, that members of the International Coach Federation view fellow members more as colleagues than as competitors. Generally speaking, at conferences, for instance, many presenters share best practices freely, providing the level of detail that allows you to put the information to use! The cultural orientations of coaches and strategic circumstances foster this situation. Independent coaches and small coaching companies enjoy bringing their expertise into the open and helping colleagues. Moreover, collaboration fosters a positive reputation and serves to attract potential clients and partners.[42]

The coaching "industry" overall is in a growing market. The issue is not to get a bigger slice of a limited pie. It is rather to promote a new discipline with high quality and ethics. This can only be achieved through collaboration. The nature of coaching work also favors this orientation: as a coach, you want to share your tools and models so that your client becomes a real partner in the discussion. You also want to promote the client's autonomy: it is not considered ethical to create a dependency, where you play the role of the "Rescuer" and your client becomes the "Victim."[43]

It is a rare profession in that respect; coaches collaborate with their clients so they can become better coaches themselves. There is yet another element. To handle large projects, coaches tend to form ad hoc project teams; learning from one another and ensuring consistency in the approach is essential. Collaboration is necessary to make it all happen.

Moreover, coaching serves multiple stakeholders. This is obvious in team coaching, where the coach's agenda is to help every member live more productive and fulfilling lives individually and collectively. But it is also true in one-on-one coaching, where the coach helps the coachee leverage his potential rather than beat others. Surely, the effect can and probably will be that the coachee gets ahead. But the motive is a constructive one: serving self *and* others.

How far can coaching go in embracing collaboration and competition? Collaboration, as I have shown, is aligned with coaching. But what about competition? In my view, there is a limit. Coaching is appropriate with some internal competition, when competing is stimulating and healthy. But if coaching becomes an instrument to serve some at the expense of others, its impact becomes neutral at best and is probably destructive rather than constructive. Such an outcome is not compatible with global coaching, which strives, even in small ways, to improve the world.

Coaching Tool: Building Alliances

Coaches help people achieve their important, meaningful objectives. In organizations, interdependencies imply that coachees need others to reach their goals. This is one of the reasons why I suggest earlier in the chapter that coachees engage in constructive politics. One of the sources of power mentioned in the constructive politics section is the internal alliances coachees can forge.

The task of building internal alliances is best approached in a systematic fashion. Assuming you are coaching yourself, this is how you can proceed.

1. **Identify your key stakeholders**

   Copy in your learning journal the latest organization
   chart with names and positions of key stakeholders (e.g.,
   executives having a say in determining the company's
   direction and allocation of resources, which may directly or
   indirectly influence your work).

2. **Assess your proximity to each key stakeholder**

   Make your assessment from a *strategic* standpoint and from a
   relational standpoint.

I suggest you build a simple "stakeholders' assessment table," based on the following template:

Key stakeholder (name, position)	Strategic alignment	Relational closeness	Strategic positions	Desires (drivers)
e.g., John Smith, Senior VP Marketing	(a)	(b)	(c)	(d)

You create a row for each key stakeholder. The assessment starts with quick *quantitative* measures:

   a. + if your strategic view is aligned; – if you disagree; 0 otherwise (neutral)

   b. + if you feel close; – if you feel antipathy; 0 neutral

As you systematically reflect on key stakeholders, you may notice that you have little knowledge about some of them. In that case, a "?" will replace the "+," "–" or "0."

You could further break down (a) into several sub-categories, each subcategory corresponding to one of your key projects (the same stakeholder may indeed share your views on one project and disagree with you on another). Alternatively, you could create a separate stakeholders' assessment table for each key project.

You could further break down (b) into two subcategories: *social* level and *personal* level. Social level has to do with sharing hobbies (either in conversations or in actual activities), common interests, and so forth. Personal level refers to more intimate exchanges where both of you feel confident to openly share feelings and views.

Next, I invite you to add *qualitative* remarks:

   c. The stakeholder's strategic positions/views on issues that impact your work

   d. The stakeholder's desires (or personal drivers): sources of motivation, values, areas of interest (including hobbies)

3. **Get to know your key stakeholders and find synergies**

Scan your table for instances of "?." For each one, your objective is to make contact. The purpose is to eliminate the question marks by establishing a relationship with the key stakeholder and by acquiring a sense of his strategic view. Your first goal is to understand the stakeholder's agenda and motives.

Once you are acquainted with the person and his strategic view, your goal is to find synergies, win–win scenarios. Prepare, for example, an "elevator speech"[44] that focuses on the intersection between both of your agendas.

4. **Deal with challenging situations.**

For challenging situations arising from incompatibilities at a strategic or relational level (or both), I suggest that you make a note in your learning journal. If you and the person have had a personal interaction, please try to capture in writing the specifics of that interaction.

You can review your notes later alone or with a coach, referring to Appendices 1 and 2 (Transactional Analysis and Neuro-Linguistic Programming) and chapter 9 ("How to Leverage Communication Patterns"). You can explore various options to build a relationship that is as constructive as possible. In case of "irreconcilable differences," you can examine actions that can reduce the negative effects.

Let me conclude with the following remarks. First, I encourage you to tailor the "stakeholders' assessment table" to fit your needs. For example, referring to the discussion on "stability/change" you could mention the stakeholder's read-iness level for each of your projects: from "entrepreneur" to "opinion leader," "follower," "late adopter," and "laggard." You could also include people who are part of your extended organization, including partnering organizations. You could apply the method for your external network.[45]

Second, keep in mind that when your agenda is fundamentally aligned with your organization's purpose and values, building these alliances allows you to serve your organization and achieve more impact. This will positively affect its people, clients, and society at large (assuming your organization strives to serve society—see more in chapter 12).

Chapter 8
How to Leverage Our Notions of Territory and Boundaries

How do you delineate your physical and psychological territory?

Protective/Sharing

Protective: Protect yourself by keeping personal life and feelings private (mental boundaries), and by minimizing intrusions in your physical space (physical boundaries).

Sharing: Build closer relationships by sharing your psychological and physical domains.

> ...*but near him thy angel,*
> *Becomes a fear, as being o'erpower'd; therefore*
> *Make space enough between you.*[1]
>
> —William Shakespeare

Protective/Sharing

Protective: In protective cultures, people are keen to protect their physical and mental territory. Erecting boundaries around their physical space and keeping people at a distance reduces the risk of intrusions, which are perceived as threatening or at least annoying. In the workplace, people prefer to keep their personal life and feelings private; intimate and authentic exchanges are avoided. People assume they are less vulnerable when little is known about them personally.

Sharing: In sharing cultures people long for an open environment in which closer relationships can be built. In the workplace, people discuss personal subjects as well as business matters. This intimacy allows them to feel more comfortable with one another. On the other hand, the absence of sharing is perceived as threatening, since it leaves people clueless about who their colleagues really are. Likewise, physical boundaries and distance are seen as obstacles to being together.

Edward T. Hall explored the cultural differences for what is considered an appropriate *physical distance* between individuals.[2] *Intimacy distance* is the space we allow to be entered only by people with whom we feel we have an intimate relationship. *Personal distance* is the range within which we have personal conversations with another individual, even if we are in a group. *Social distance* refers to when we talk to several people at once, and *public distance* is when the audience becomes undifferentiated.

Psychological space refers to the amount of privacy/sharing expected about personal life and feelings. I use the word *territory* to designate both external and internal (psychological) spaces.

Psychological space is related to Talcott Parsons' diffuse/specific dimension.[3] In *diffuse* cultures individuals relate to one another on many levels. For example, the conversation shifts from business topics to family and more personal subjects. Relationships cannot be conceivably built if areas remain compartmentalized. In *specific* cultures, such as Germany and the United States, boundaries keep business conversations, for example, solely focused on business. Superficial smalltalk is the only "distraction" allowed and is supposed to be brief.[4] But beyond the distraction, the idea is to protect oneself by avoiding being dragged into intimate subjects.

In this chapter, I shall devote most of my attention to these psychological aspects.

Examples of the Dimension

Referring to Hall's work, what is considered appropriate personal distance in the Middle East or Southern Europe may equate to intimate distance in the United States or Northern Europe, hence creating a feeling of intrusion. He is "too close" and we find ourselves backing away, only to discover that he keeps (probably unconsciously) reducing the distance so that it's right for him.

Physical layouts, such as found in office space, are also linked to this dimension. Is the space open or is it partitioned? A classic mistake is to assume that open space will necessarily be conducive to better communication and productivity. The opposite can be true, where people complain about the lack of privacy and the noise, which make it difficult to concentrate. Ideally, the space layout should be engineered taking into account the tasks at hand and the cultural preferences for performing them.

As an example of protecting one's psychological space, let me mention the French actress Catherine Deneuve, who never discloses anything to journalists about her private life. In contrast, former French TV-host Michel Polac published his private journal and felt comfortable sharing his most private personal stories and thoughts.[5]

In the workplace, *self-disclosing* and *exchanging feedback* exemplify sharing practices, which will improve leadership and team effectiveness. On the other hand, developing assertiveness allows people to protect themselves, when they struggle to set up and maintain personal boundaries. In the rest of this chapter, I elaborate on these practices.

Leveraging Protective and Sharing

Leveraging protective and sharing orientations starts by challenging the assumption that you have to keep your personal life and feelings private in order to protect yourself. Instead, you can have the best of both cultural worlds: share *while* protecting yourself, and even, paradoxically, share *to* protect yourself.

By sharing, I mean self-disclosing in particular. You let others know how you feel, what makes you happy, what frustrates you. You reveal your hopes and dreams. This gives others the opportunity to help you and to recognize similar needs, hopes, and challenges that they face. Self-disclosing can unite you.

Of course, there is the risk that some people will take advantage of your openness. A colleague who views you as a competitor may be tempted to harm you, mentioning your words of frustration as evidence of your lack of commitment to the company.

Therefore, it is imperative that you establish a safe and constructive environment. You have to build a climate of trust, mutual respect, and willingness to help each other. This happens gradually and your goal is to create a *virtuous circle*: more sharing, which fosters relationships built on trust, which diminishes the need to protect yourself with privacy, which allows more sharing, and on around the circle. You share more and enjoy better protection, being confident that you can trust colleagues who genuinely respect you and want to help you. When you have established the right climate, leveraging protective and sharing orientations is indeed possible.

I am obviously not suggesting you go to the extreme of disclosing everything. Even in sharing cultures, people still have to preserve some healthy privacy (which the French call *"son jardin secret"* — one's secret garden).

Exchanging feedback is another form of sharing, which can be intimidating because it implies self-questioning. But when done appropriately, the sharing will increase your confidence level, resulting in better self-protection. Once again, you can make the most of protective and sharing orientations.

Feedback constitutes information destined to make someone more effective. Feedback describes the behavior itself and its impact or outcome, which can be positive (making the person more effective), negative (making the person less effective), or neutral.

For example, the behavior could be that you interrupted a person five times. The impact on the person being interrupted could be negative (e.g., he felt frustrated) or positive (e.g., he welcomed the diversion). The impact on the group's project may have been effective (his interruptions added new ideas) or ineffective (the meeting ended up being much longer than necessary).

Positive feedback will encourage the recipient to repeat behaviors that make him effective. Negative feedback gives him a chance to stop making the same mistakes. In both instances, feedback allows the recipient to become more effective, which in turn will often boost his self-confidence.

The key is to exchange feedback in a productive fashion. In the next section, you will learn how to do that. But first, let me mention a model that captures the two activities we have discussed. The "Johari Window," after the names of its authors Jo Luft and Harry Ingram (on page 145), provides a useful visual representation.

When you self-disclose and ask for feedback, you are in essence expanding your "arena," by removing some of the "mask" and "blind spots."

Blind spots are like spinach in your teeth. You see people laugh and you think that it is because you are funny. You really don't know what others are laughing at! More interestingly, blind spots represent strengths and weaknesses you are not aware of, which means you can neither capitalize on the strengths nor correct the weaknesses. The mask is what you don't reveal to others.

I described earlier how, through self-disclosing and feedback, you can promote a virtuous circle characterized by increased confidence, candidness, and safety. Expanding the "arena" allows you to tap into the fourth region, namely "potential creativity" or "synergy." You may discover talents neither your observers nor you even suspected existed.

I invite you to practice putting the Johari Window to use, and experience its benefits for yourself in fostering both individual and team development. The exercise at the end of this chapter gives you a structured way to do this.

Johari Window

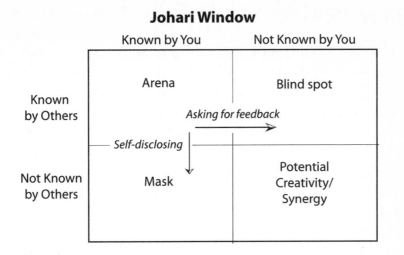

Applications and Advice

To briefly evoke physical territoriality, let me simply suggest that coaches need to pay attention to finding the most comfortable distance between themselves and their coachees.

Coaching over the phone, for example, which we saw prevailing in the United States, may not provide enough intimacy in sharing cultures. Likewise, in face-to-face coaching several options might be provided, letting coachees choose their seats and therefore their distance from the coach.

Moving back to psychological space, keep in mind that while self-disclosing is critical for building closer relationships within a team or with the coach, it cannot be demanded. Coaches need to foster a safe climate, which is non-judgmental and constructive, so that people less inclined to open up will feel secure enough to do so. Paradoxically, by respecting people's preferences and not putting them on the spot, more self-disclosure will usually take place.

Coaches obviously need to challenge their own assumptions. Several psychotherapists I know who now coach reviewed the idea that they should not talk about themselves with clients. In fact, when done appropriately, sharing personal experiences and learnings can bring people closer by conveying a sense that we are all humans facing similar challenges, and that a coach one day can be a coachee the next.

Now I will elaborate on how to exchange feedback (a beneficial sharing practice), and how to protect your territory (a useful protective practice). These illustrate the merits of both poles on the protective–sharing cultural dimension.

Exchanging Feedback[6]

The first thing to realize is that feedback is different from giving advice, judging, or interpreting. When you give feedback, you do not say, for example, "You should not interrupt people." You say instead, "When you interrupted me, this is how I felt or this is the impact I perceived in others." The difference may seem subtle. However, the first approach is more likely to put your interlocutor on the defensive.[7] Feedback is different from psychological interpretation as well. Using the same example, you do not say, "Your father probably provided you with a role model of being overbearing." Playing the amateur psychologist is likely to foster defensiveness. Furthermore, it is worth recognizing that even an expert psychologist cannot usually claim to know you better than you know yourself. There may be unique circumstances that explain your behaviors and that the psychologist could not possibly know. With feedback, we avoid this analysis altogether. We assume you had good reasons for behaving as you did. And we concentrate on the impact of that behavior, so that you can decide whether you want to continue or stop that particular behavior.

Here are some tips for exchanging feedback in a safe and constructive manner, together with remarks about other cultural dimensions to be considered.

When *giving* feedback, remember the following suggestions:

1. Describe the context, the behavior, and its impact.[8]

    Be precise when you describe the behavior, referring to "low-context" information (the words said) as well as "high-context" content (how the words were said: posture, gestures, tone of voice, etc.). See discussion of these orientations in chapter 9.

2. Focus on what is changeable.

    Do not say, "You are too tall or too short." One could choose different heels and shoes, but there is not much else one can do to change one's height.

3. Refrain from giving advice, proffering judgments, or proposing a psychological interpretation.

    All of the above may be valuable in a different context. But they are not feedback. Furthermore, they tend to put people on the defensive rather than inviting them to take ownership and responsibility.

4. Be honest.

   People benefit more and usually expect candid and honest feedback. Avoid over-protecting them.[9] Admittedly, the injunction to give candid and honest feedback reflects a cultural bias toward directness (see chapter 9, direct/indirect communication). If the person either giving or receiving the feedback prefers indirectness, someone must go outside his comfort zone. Handling of this sort of situation has to be that much more sensitive and careful. Building confidence and ensuring there is mutual respect and appreciation are prerequisites before sharing difficult feedback. Sticking to giving feedback (see numbers 1 and 3), insisting on the fact that you are not judging, and conducting delicate conversations between four eyes whenever in doubt will help to maintain harmony and avoid loss of face.

   Moreover, using an indirect approach (see chapter 9) may in some situations constitute an altogether advantageous alternative to the direct approach.

   When exchanging feedback, intercultural sensitivity requires you to also deal with other cultural dimensions at play:

   - hierarchy/equality (e.g., giving feedback to a "superior" may feel inappropriate);
   - being/doing (e.g., feedback should refer to what a person does [doing] and not to who the person is [being]; however, constructive feedback will have the effect of helping a person to grow [being]);
   - individualistic/collectivistic (e.g., singling out a group member for feedback, even positive, may feel awkward and embarrassing in a collectivistic culture).

5. Balance negative feedback with positive feedback over time.

   People tend to remember negative feedback more than positive. One rule of thumb says that 80 percent positive, 20 percent negative will be remembered as 50 percent positive, 50 percent negative! So be sure to also catch people doing things right.

When *receiving* feedback, bear in mind these tips:

1. Consider the feedback a gift.

   Remember that the person giving you feedback is taking a risk. His goal is to help you. Even if you do not believe his intention is positive, you are better off assuming it is, because such belief is more conducive to a constructive exchange. Encourage more feedback by thanking your feedback-giver.

2. Seek to understand, not to agree, justify, or defend.

   You have good reasons to behave the way you do. The purpose of the feedback exchange is not to discuss those reasons but to understand the impact of your behavior. You can debate an opinion, but when it comes to appreciating the impact of your behavior, all you can do is understand how others have perceived it.

3. Listen, ask probing questions, and reformulate.

   To understand, the best tactic is to listen actively. You may also ask probing questions and reformulate what has been said. Reformulation allows you to think, digest a possible emotional blow, ensure you have understood what was said, and reinforce a sense of connection with your feedback-giver.

Protecting Our Territory

Joe[10] was describing his nightmare of e-mail overload. He did not see any escape. He had "tried it all." The habitual advice of sorting what is important from what is not was of little help. In 60 to 70 percent of the cases, Joe could readily tell if the message was important or not. That was the easy part. But in the other cases, Joe had to first read carefully, reflect, and do some research, only to figure out if the matter was indeed important and required further investigation and action. So, for over 30 percent of his daily 40 e-mails, an average of half an hour was necessary to merely assess the importance. After 6 hours of work (i.e., 30% x 40 x $\frac{1}{2}$), Joe's productive work could begin: he would at last be solving problems! Needless to say, he was working very long hours. A dry sense of humor helped him to relieve some of the stress: "I have a very long list of number one priorities!"

The intrusions precipitated by modern technology are real. Requests come from all over the globe and can catch you anywhere, on your portable PC, mobile phone, and so on.

Erecting boundaries is vital. Over and above performance and fulfillment, it is first and foremost a question of staying sane. Many authors give tips on how to set those limits. But Eric Berne's Transactional Analysis, in my opinion, remains the best reference. TA reminds us that we have other options than being the Victim.[11] Joe's perfectionism (Be perfect)[12] and desire to please everyone (Be nice) fostered the role he unconsciously played.

Any suggestion to help him leave the rut was met by a "yes, but…" or "I have tried this, but it does not work because…." Joe had first to realize that he was contributing to the difficult situation and that he also had options to turn it around. He had to be prepared, however, to revisit his deeply engrained beliefs ("You have to be perfect," "You have to be nice"). The key was to give himself permission to set boundaries: there is only so much one can do.

The lessons from a "protective" cultural perspective are in the form of creative ways to protect your territory: physical space, time, and psychological privacy.

You can set rules, adhere to them, and invite others to respect them as well. Take e-mail, for example. Unless it is absolutely critical to do so, don't commit to a duty of responding within twenty-four hours. Such a norm is a sure way to become enslaved. And if you don't keep up, you feel guilty for failing to honor your promise. Do you really have to schlep your portable PC around, struggle with incompatible plugs and poor connections in hotels to retrieve e-mails when you travel for a few days? Why not take the time to reflect and relax? You can leave an automatic reply message stating when you will be back, with instructions in case there is really something urgent nobody else can take care of during your absence. Establishing and reinforcing an e-mail code of conduct are also critical: short, clear messages that minimize the "cc" often used as an umbrella strategy that ends up frustrating the "cc" recipients; using alternative modes of communication when appropriate; and avoiding abuses of "urgent" flags.[13]

Incidentally, company access to those messages is another issue with cultural variations: some organizations believe they are entitled to monitor all e-mails ("sharing orientation") while others consider that this would violate rights of privacy ("protective orientation").

You have the right to protect your territory and you respect the same right for others. In other words, you need to adopt the "I'm OK—You're OK" position; that is, you have to be *assertive*.[14] Back in the 1980s, in Silicon Valley, most of the engineers I came across were working very hard. One colleague, however, set a limit: he was not prepared to work on weekends. He was very committed and passionate about his job, but he told our boss that the weekend was sacred and devoted to his family. Back then, his stance was really going against the cultural grain and required some guts. The boss was not pleased, but since he didn't want to fire my colleague, he learned to accept the limit.

Fifteen years later in Europe, another manager I know used to call one of his staff at any time—during the evenings and on weekends. This same manager would not even have entertained the idea of calling his other staff at these times. The manager sensed the staff members' "not OK–OK" position in the first case. The woman in question was committed to doing a "perfect" job and had not given herself permission to set boundaries. She almost invited the exploitation[15] by adopting the Victim role: "I have to be perfect to feel worthy, and since it is mission impossible, I feel bad. It is so unfair!"[16] In the cases of his other staff members, the OK–OK position meant the employees were protecting their territories. They felt serene about erecting boundaries.

If the other party is not prepared to respect your space, you have one last option and that is to leave. Feeling "I'm OK" means that I am not prepared to put up with abuse. It is when you feel "I'm not OK" that you tolerate mistreatment, believing that after all, you only get what you deserve, which does not amount to much.[17] Do not be afraid to calmly stand up for your rights. But as a leader, take care and show respect so that people don't have to keep fighting to protect their space.

Coach Cheryl Richardson writes,

> Based on my experience, weak boundaries are the root of
> 80 percent of the problems I've observed among people
> who are struggling to live more authentic lives. When we
> allow others to step over our boundaries because we fear
> confrontation or the consequences of putting our own needs
> first, we end up feeling angry, frustrated, and resentful. A
> strong boundary is like an energy field or "psychic barrier"
> that protects your body, mind and spirit.[18]

Feeling angry is actually useful. Observe what happens if you come close to a cat with her kittens. She hisses, bares her teeth, and becomes threatening.

Her anger is a protection mechanism. TA describes the "racket" phenomenon, which takes place when the anger mechanism doesn't work. We feel an emotion that is not adequate. For example, crying and being sad will help you to mourn a loss but won't enable you to stand up for your territory. To overcome the racket you have to give yourself permission to feel angry when your space is violated. It is a vital emotional skill, and it doesn't mean you have to behave aggressively. Helen Palmer said, "Anger is a wake-up call toward self-remembering."[19] To protect yourself, you cannot always be nice to others, acting as they wish.

It should be apparent by now that the two constraining messages, "Be perfect" and "Be nice," tend to result in weak boundaries. Let me highlight possible antidotes that come in the form of permissions.

1. "Be perfect."

What about "Be effective" instead? Do you really need 100 percent when 95 percent will do adequately with half the effort? And do you focus on what is really important?

Permissions:

- I don't need to know it all and be the best in everything.
- I can make mistakes. Others can as well.
- I focus on the essentials.
- I don't always need to be thorough.
- I don't need to have all the facts. I can trust my intuition, too.

2. "Be nice."

What about "Take care of yourself," too?

Permissions:

- I set my own objectives and priorities and communicate them.
- I say no calmly without feeling guilty.
- I do something every day that I enjoy.
- I am nice to myself.

Coaching Tool: Feedback and Self-Disclosure

Exercise

Enhancing awareness through feedback and self-disclosure is the purpose of this exercise. The medium is videotaping a group discussion and then reviewing the behaviors on the tape.

In other words, you will explore the virtues of a sharing orientation. The protective orientation is acknowledged as well. The following rules will ensure that a safe environment is created. You choose what you are prepared to share and you decide if you want to receive feedback. This means that if you want to give feedback to someone, you will first need to ask permission.

Instructions for the Coach

Set up the camera so that everyone's face is visible. The ideal group size is six to eight people. The topic of the meeting should be somewhat controversial for the group. The goal is to observe team dynamics in a challenging situation where some disagreement and confrontation are expected.

Once you have a thirty-minute segment, invite participants to observe the video and share comments.

As the coach, you will then

- brief the group on how to give and receive feedback,
- invite the group to observe nonverbal behaviors (changes in posture, gestures, tone of voice) as well as verbal contributions while they watch the video,
- encourage them to pause the video frequently to let anyone who wishes ask for feedback or self-disclose about how they were feeling or what they were thinking at that moment,
- challenge them to speak only to exchange feedback and self-disclose, not rediscuss the content itself,
- warn them against the tendency to passively watch the tape, without taking the risk of speaking up, and
- give people permission to try new behaviors and make mistakes. The purpose is not to judge or evaluate anyone. Frame the experience as a laboratory, not as an assessment center.

Comments for Participants

Seeing yourself in action is a useful way to raise individual and collective awareness. You may suddenly realize that you kept interrupting people, spoke with a low voice, and did not see the nonverbal cues from people who expressed disagreement, discomfort, or frustration. You can also appreciate the value of praise, the positive impact of providing a synthesis for the group. The feedback and self-disclosure remove blind spots and masks, enabling effectiveness and trust. As a leader and as a team, you can decide on the strong behavioral points you want to keep, and the weak ones you want to discard.

Chapter 9
How to Leverage Communication Patterns

How do you communicate with people?

High Context/Low Context—Direct/Indirect—Affective/Neutral—
Formal/Informal

High Context: Rely on implicit communication. Appreciate the meaning of gestures, posture, voice, and context.

Low Context: Rely on explicit communication. Favor clear and detailed instructions.

Direct: In a conflict or with a tough message to deliver, get your point across clearly even at the risk of offending or hurting.

Indirect: In a conflict or with a tough message to deliver, maintain a cordial relationship at the risk of misunderstanding.

Affective: Display emotions and warmth when communicating. Establish and maintain personal and social connections.

Neutral: Stress conciseness, precision, and detachment when communicating.

Formal: Observe strict protocols and rituals.

Informal: Favor familiarity and spontaneity.

> *Coaching is an advanced form of communication, in which people are authentic and totally present. I dream we could say the truth with grace and love, respect and compassion. Then coaching could become something of the past.*[1]
>
> —Cheryl Richardson

Coaching is communication. And perhaps communication can be coaching. Every interaction can be constructive, helping our interlocutor be more fulfilled and/or effective. Every exchange can foster joy and diminish pain.

The purpose of communication is to bring together, to build unity from diversity.

Coaches can only claim to communicate in the most noble and mature fashion when they appreciate and leverage various cultural alternatives.

High Context/Low Context

High Context: In high-context cultures, communication of meaning is transmitted not just in words;[2] it also relies heavily on group understanding of voice tone, body language, facial expressions, eye contact, speech patterns, and use of silence. In what you say, the words you choose play a relatively small part in the communication. The overall context conveys a lot of information. People often refer, for example, to what is not said, the way something is said, and where it is said.

Low Context: In low-context cultures most of the meaning is "invested in the explicit code,"[3] that is, words. In such cultures people require a lot of background information before they commit to something. They usually miss much, if not most, of the subtle nonverbal signals in an interaction. In low-context business interaction, nothing is taken seriously unless it is written and signed.

High-context cultures dispense with giving detailed instructions. People discuss the main points and the recipient is expected to come up with the details through knowing the overall context. Often the recipient already knows at least some of the details anyway because information is usually freely circulated. In other words, everyone knows quite a lot about everyone and everything else.

In contrast low-context cultures provide ample details; for example, complete job descriptions, thorough inventory of competencies, and all their visible manifestations. High-context communicators may not even bother to read those details, but low-context communicators are likely to be frustrated if they have to fill in the blanks when only the big picture is provided.

If your purpose is to ensure that people reliably implement your decisions, the strategy you choose to make this happen depends on your orientation. In high-context cultures communication is a way to form and develop relationships. Relying on relationships and trust will in turn ensure proper implementation. In low-context cultures, the purpose of communication is to exchange information. To that end, words are the only elements that matter. Detailed instructions are the strategy to guarantee correct implementation.

Gestures, posture, and tone of voice reveal vast amounts of high-context information. *Gestuology*, the study of gestures, uncovers feelings and intentions. The "dilatation–retraction" law suggests that

> when someone "espouses" a situation, adheres to an
> idea or to a person, has confidence in himself and in his
> environment, or exudes a strong energy, his gestures tend
> to open up, become more expansive, and move away from
> his body. Conversely, if he feels some doubts about his ideas
> or his person, if he is suspicious about his surroundings, or
> lacks energy, gestures will retract, sink, and shut down. He
> will adopt retreat postures, and favor barrier gestures that
> filter information (judged as too novel or destabilizing).[4]

Reading books on gestuology like the excellent *Les Gestes Vérité*[5] (*The Truth Gestures*) can really help low-context communicators develop an appreciation for the wealth of information embedded in gestures, posture, and movements.

Facial expressions can be very revealing, even something as "innocent" as a smile. In "How to spot a liar," *Time* magazine argues that careful observation (and the assistance of new software) can help you find out if someone is telling the truth. Photographs A and B feature the same person smiling. The impression is different somehow. "An authentic smile, A, is usually characterized by crinkly eyes and a generally relaxed expression. A lying smile, B, reveals itself in subtle ways, notably eye wrinkles that are more crow's feet than laugh lines."[6] Of course, a smile can also mean different things culturally. A Japanese or Chinese smile may convey embarrassment, discomfort, or even anger.

The voice is also worth paying attention to; the same words with varying intensity and tone will have different meaning. A strong and low voice will convey earthy concreteness, while a high pitch may be heard as aerial theory.

The pitfall would be to confuse indices with reality. If someone yawns, it does not mean he is not interested in what you say. He may simply be very tired. Moreover, gestures often have various meanings in different cultures, so they need to be treated as question marks rather than evidence.

While anyone who pays attention can become attuned to all these high-context cues, people in high-context cultures (in Asia and South America, for example) tend to invest time getting to know one another. This allows them to understand the broader context, in which all current manifestations (verbal and nonverbal) take place. As a result, they know what to expect, what signals to look for, and how to interpret subtle facial expressions. Fewer words need to be said.

The high-context–low-context dimension affects the type of *communication media* that will be favored. The choice may or may not be consistent with the fact that certain media are more conducive to certain types of communication. Ranking them from high context to low context, we have:

High-Context—Low-Context Dimension

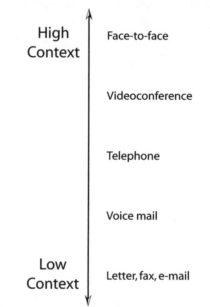

For example, in the United States, coaching is often conducted over the phone. The phone may be viewed as a sufficiently high-level context medium in a culture where the orientation is toward low context.

Remote teams should be particularly concerned with this cultural dimension. CCL has compiled research on what they refer to as "geographically dispersed teams" (GDT).[7] Most of the current research findings are quite predictable but still useful to keep in mind. For example, the loss of "human moment" described as an "authentic psychological encounter that is difficult to achieve without face-to-face meetings" tends to increase dissatisfaction. Or

> dispersion seems to result in less social interaction among teams; this lack of interaction may result in team members having inaccurate perceptions of other team members and of the task. This reduced social activity may result from the inability of communication technologies to effectively and efficiently transmit social context cues (such as tone of voice, facial gestures, or body language), making it difficult for team members to bond.[8]

Examples of the Dimension

In high-context cultures, people assume the existence of implicit messages. These may be sent unintentionally. Jackie Chang from Chubb Insurance told me of the case of a Chinese manager she describes as one of their key performers. This manager felt his supervisor neglected him because he was not receiving much attention and was not praised for his good work. "He felt that he was working so hard but didn't get the respect and recognition he deserved." This resulted in a misunderstanding. "This manager was heavily hurt and didn't feel comfortable with his work environment." Through Jackie Chang's mediation, the manager learned to interpret his superior's behavior in light of his low-context orientation: there were no hidden implicit messages. As it turns out, the superior was quite pleased with the manager's performance. He simply had failed to give positive feedback and did not realize that in this high-context culture, no feedback was tantamount to negative feedback. The low-context manager wasn't aware that the absence of message is a message; sometimes it means good news, but in this instance it was supposed to mean the opposite.

In low-context cultures, coaches may believe they always have to be explicit to avoid misunderstanding. I remember attending a seminar on consulting skills in the United States in 1999. The recurrent advice was to make everything explicit in communication: "So we agree that…," "What you are saying is…." We even received a little card with a specific sequence of steps to follow[9] to ensure that the consulting communication process would move swiftly and unambiguously. If you encountered client resistance, the advice was to name the resistance to help the client open up. You would say, for example, "You seem to avoid taking responsibility." While this advice could sometimes indeed be useful, the consultant did not seem to realize that it was not universally applicable. Some coaching schools make exactly the same mistake, which is a serious problem in high-context cultures.

The United States and Germany are generally considered relatively low-context cultures.[10] Contracts with numerous explicit clauses are a normal way to conduct business.[11] In higher-context cultures, such as Mexico or France, these contracts may be viewed as frustrating and even insulting. A simpler agreement is preferred. Relationship and trust allow parties to build faith in the spirit of the agreement and to have confidence that mutually beneficial solutions can always be found for unusual situations that might arise.

Examples of low-context managers and executives blundering because they forgot the importance of face-to-face contact to establish connection are plentiful. I remember, for example, a company president getting carried away with videoconferencing. He thought he had found the perfect solution to cut down travel expenses and meet with everybody worldwide without having to move out of his office. The "real" meeting with candid exchanges would usually take place once the TV screen had been switched off. The president had not yet established personal relationships with these people. Had that been the case, it would probably have been a different story and videoconferencing could have constituted an optimal solution to maintain contact. It was, however, definitely a mistake to use the medium as a first contact.

Leveraging High Context and Low Context

Leveraging high-context and low-context communication means *relying on both implicit and explicit communication*. To improve communication, you have to pay careful attention to the words (low context) while also considering all the nonverbal cues (high context).

At Chubb Asia Pacific, a Western executive expressed his frustration to me. His Asian colleagues would say yes to his requests but then not take any action. He complained, "How many times do I have to ask them? Each time they say yes, I think they will do it at last. And they don't! I cannot rely on them. I have become very upset; sometimes, I just want to shake them up!" During our leadership development seminar, we videotaped a group meeting, and, in one instance, the executive asked his colleagues, "Are we all on board with this decision?" At that point, one Korean twitched his upper lip, while smiling and leaning gently backward. The Westerner did not look at his Korean colleague and, hearing no objection, wrongly assumed consensus had been achieved.

Reviewing the video gave the Korean the opportunity to self-disclose what had really happened for him. Having limited command of English, he was still trying to understand the rationale for the solution proposed by the Western executive. Since the Korean man did not want to break the group's harmony and was somewhat uncomfortable to speak in English anyway, he did not offer his alternative and valuable perspective. The Korean executive was not yet on board with the decision. For the attentive observer, he had given several cues about his reservations: the lip movement, the artificial smile, and a subtle movement of the body backward. To his credit, the Western executive decided from then on to pay better attention to all the information, implicit as well as explicit, rather than blaming his Asian colleagues. He knew this would make him a far more effective leader.

Everything you do conveys a message. Leveraging high-context and low-context cultures implies that what you say (low context) is consistent with the symbols inevitably associated with your actions (high context). When there is alignment, your message becomes stronger. Otherwise, confusion and suspicion arise.

Peter Leyland from Baxter carefully chose unusual venues to hold team retreats. The castles and manors transformed into hotels exuded a sense of magic and majesty. Each place was unique just as the team members were. You can imagine that saying to the team "You are very special" while holding the meeting in some unstylish commodity hotel by the airport somehow rings hollow. However, the hotels were not the most luxurious and expensive either; this would have sent the wrong message, too, inappropriately encouraging spending company money lavishly. Peter was sensitive and able to communicate through symbols. In other words, he ensured the context would support the rhetoric.

Leveraging high context and low context also means making the most of communication media, understanding that various technologies are all potentially useful, while appreciating that none is a panacea. IBM serves as a good example of a company destined for low-context communication—the Internet is at the heart of IBM's e-business strategy—but that understands the value of face-to-face communication. European sales executives, for example, are trained during their first nineteen weeks. In 2001, eight of those weeks were spent at the IBM International Education Centre in La Hulpe. Sophisticated online education complements the actual meetings, allowing the combination of real work with formal training.

Applications and Advice

Coaches need to carefully choose media consistent with their goal and the coachee's culture. Although I do some coaching over the phone in Europe and find it a valuable alternative to traveling long distances, in most cases my coaching takes place face-to-face. In a high-context culture, the telephone does not quite qualify as a medium for important dialogues.

E-mail and the Internet are a great help to coaches who want to exchange files, share information, and perform surveys. Still, they are no substitute for high-context communication. Implicit messages simply cannot be conveyed via a low-context medium. People are likely to get the wrong message, miscommunication is prone to occur, and in the end trust can potentially be eroded rather than built.

As far as remote teams are concerned, the most effective ones I have seen and been a part of all tend to combine high-context with low-context communication. They will not expect people to waste their time putting up with another plane delay or car traffic jam; many meetings are held over the telephone. Somebody just needs to organize a "bridge": all members call a dedicated number at an agreed-upon time. The team tries to accommodate time differences: the executive in New York will call at 8 A.M., while his colleague in Singapore dials the same number at 8 P.M. The phone meeting is followed by e-mail correspondence, where files are exchanged. Smaller group conversations are also planned.

At the beginning and at regular intervals (preferably yearly at a minimum), team members spend a few days together. The high-context bonding allows the "relationship batteries" to recharge. Lower-context communication media can then take over for another period during which time relationships can be maintained, work performed, and information passed on. The team should discuss its communication protocols and gradually develop optimal norms, which leverage the benefits of high- and low-context forms. It should keep reevaluating those norms, taking into account new technological possibilities and project circumstances.

Developing high-context sensitivity requires training. You need to open up and learn to take in contextual cues you have ignored and overlooked in the past. A useful exercise is to videotape real meetings or role plays. The coach can guide coachees when they watch the tape. He can point out such nonverbals as posture, gestures, movements, and tone of voice. Gestuology books and simple common sense provide useful help in learning how to interpret nonverbal communication cues. But you can never be totally sure why, for example, somebody stood back or folded his arms. When there is a climate of trust and openness, you can ask people to share what was actually going on for them. Bringing people's attention to the wealth of high-context information available is, in my experience, an effective way to help people be more attuned to implicit forms of communication.

Coaches can always benefit from expanding their own repertoire. Silence, for example, which is a high-context form of communication by definition, can be a powerful coaching technique. Silence is a time to think, a way to keep options open, or a tactic to save face. Don't feel rushed to fill it!

Direct/Indirect

Direct: In direct cultures, people tend to spell things out, "say it like it is," say exactly what they mean rather than hint or imply. Others' feelings are not hurt by bluntness; they appreciate it because nothing is left to guessing. Straight-forwardness is a virtue.

Indirect: In indirect cultures, people prefer to imply things rather than say them straight out, which may (in fact, usually does) lead to a severe loss of face. Because loss of face and harmony are both primary in indirect cultures, confrontation is avoided at all costs. Preserving the relationship is of utmost importance.

This dimension refers specifically to difficult situations, when you are in a conflict or when you have to deliver a tough message.

Richard Mead summarizes the direct/indirect tradeoff: "There is a tradeoff between directness, which gets your purpose across but can create resentment and hence be less persuasive, and indirectness, which maintains a cordial relationship but at the risk of misunderstanding."[12]

In direct cultures, like the United States, straightforwardness is sometimes confused with honesty. From this perspective, coaches are supposed to speak directly, and this is interpreted as a sign of honesty.

Communicating straightforwardly is…straightforward: you simply say what you mean. So I will not elaborate on direct communication strategies. The point is that directness is not a panacea; it is worth examining indirect forms of communication.

Indirect communication strategies include the following:
- Mediation: a third person is used as a go-between
- Refraction: statements intended for person A are made to person B while person A is present
- Metaphors: analogies are used to deliver the message
- Hints: subtle suggestions are made

Examples of the Dimension

In chapter 2, I contrasted the British indirect style with Swedish directness. We saw how Mark Philips learned to stop beating about the bush, and how communicating directly made him more effective. This is an area where Brits and U.S. nationals tend to differ. Sometimes, Brits could be more direct and Americans more indirect.

Asian cultures are known for their indirectness. In contrast, and alongside the United States, the Dutch culture is generally perceived as direct. Those from indirect cultures may experience the direct style as pushy and insincere, which can be a disadvantage in sales and marketing.

One of my favorite examples of the indirect approach occurs in the movie *The Godfather, Part II*. Michael Corleone, played by Al Pacino, is on trial. A witness is about to publicly accuse him of mafia activities. But Michael Corleone's men have managed to bring the witness's brother with them to observe the trial. That is all. The witness immediately gets the indirect message: "If you speak, your brother gets in trouble." The judges cannot believe it when he (the witness) goes on to exonerate the mafia boss.

A manager felt one of his employees was dressing a bit too casually, coming into the office with ragged pants. This bright woman, fresh out of business school, would not think twice about taking off her shoes in the middle of a team meeting. And what's more, she wasn't wearing socks! While the overall atmosphere at the company was friendly and relaxed, the manager wanted the new executive to appreciate that the dress code was different from the university campus. He spoke to his executive secretary, who was also the informal team confidante. Coming from her, the message would be softened and there would be no loss of face.

The secretary, a mature woman, added a second degree of indirectness in the form of a hint. One day, the young executive came into the office wearing an elegant dress. The secretary said, "You look so pretty in that classy outfit. It suits you much better than your usual clothes." The young woman inquired, "Have you heard any remarks about the way I dress?" The older woman replied, "No, but I have the sense that something will be said one of these days." This was enough for the young woman to get the message and adhere to the dress code. Mediation plus a hint still allowed the message to be understood, while ensuring that nobody lost face or felt the slightest embarrassment.

For the same reason, we sometimes use indirectness in our family. If I want to pass on a delicate message to my mother-in-law, I may use my wife as a messenger. Likewise, my wife considers me as the intermediary for delicate communications with my mother. Our mothers are comfortable with direct communication from their children, but not necessarily from their children-in-law. Indirectness allows harmony to be preserved in the extended family.

I have seen refraction brought into play to confront a boss who was constantly darting into the office and interrupting the work in progress. In a hierarchical and indirect culture, challenging the manager directly would have probably damaged the relationship. An opportunity for an indirect approach arose when a colleague came by during one of the occasions. As he too was about to invite himself into the office, the employee politely but vigorously notified him, "I am sorry I have to say this, but it is hard for me to concentrate and work effectively if I am interrupted. That is why my door is closed for two hours. You probably did not see the note on my door, but I would appreciate it if you could come back later unless there is something that cannot wait for two hours." The manager, for whom the message was really destined, did not make any comment but subsequently appeared to intrude less often. The remark about the "Please do not disturb" sign on the door allowed both the other employee and the manager to save face. Positive intention was assumed: "You probably did not see my note" rather than "You don't even think about the disturbance you create."

Leveraging Direct and Indirect

Leveraging directness and indirectness means blending the two communication patterns, retaining what is best about each. The merit of directness is clarity (you say what you mean), while the downside is that it can be perceived as offensive. By contrast, the virtue of indirectness is its underlying sensitivity (you don't want to hurt a person's feelings), while the danger lies in its potential evasiveness, leading to possible misunderstandings.

To leverage the two orientations, I suggest being clear and firm with the content while being careful and sensitive with the form; in other words, direct on the substance and indirect on the process (as much as is necessary to avoid loss of face). Unfortunately, sometimes people do the opposite, using what is worst about each orientation: direct and even aggressive in the mode of delivery but vague concerning the message itself. For example, a boss will shout at his subordinates without really telling them specifically what they have done wrong. The subordinates will end up being frustrated and confused. In this case, the lever effect amplifies the problem instead of multiplying the benefits.

Applications and Advice

It should be apparent by now that the feedback exchange model presented in chapter 8 is culturally biased toward direct communication. The assumption is that you describe behaviors and candidly talk about their impact. This does not exclude, however, the possibility of using indirectness. You can in fact choose some indirect strategies initially and gradually switch to directness if necessary, as I will explain.

From a monocultural direct perspective, indirect approaches could be perceived as unassertive and cowardly. Yes, indirectness could be ill inspired by a "not OK–OK" outlook. Global coaches, however, also appreciate the potential benefits of indirectness and learn to

- be direct without being aggressive (by being assertive, "OK–OK"),
- use various indirect communication forms, and
- choose a communication approach based on its merits in the particular situation.

Indirect communication allows you to maintain ambiguity purposefully. If you have a delicate message to pass on, you may want to first test the waters. You drop a hint to check if the other party is receptive. If he ignores it or expresses negative judgment, there is still time to retract. You are not on record as having made a damaging remark. On the other hand, a smile in response to your hint may indicate that the terrain is favorable. You can gradually move to more clarity and directness as the trust builds between you. Lovers, politicians, and business negotiators fancy these tactics.

I know coaches who hold bluntness as a virtue: "Be straightforward!" "Practice tough love." "Maintain eye contact." Challenging coachees directly becomes a sign of courage and honesty. This approach may well backfire across cultures.

The truth is you can confront a coachee without being blunt. But if you decide to behave counter-culturally, be reasonably sure your coachee understands that you are attempting to pull him outside his comfort zone.

Indeed, you don't want your directness to be confused with aggressiveness. Temper or explain your direct (OK–OK) approach, then use some indirect strategies. A coachee, a German manager, had to explain the difference to her French colleague so that he would not misinterpret her behavior. He learned to stop being upset by imaginary animosity while she cut the edge by using indirect communication.

Becoming comfortable with directness is also necessary. In the Western corporate world, straightforwardness is a virtue. A lack of directness may be considered a lack of character.

Affective/Neutral[13]

Affective: People from affective cultures are less concerned with the precision of communication than with the establishment and maintenance of personal and social relationships. Displaying emotions and warmth is valued. Emotions are persuasive in affective cultures and are often used (and considered valid) in arguments. Being cold and objective is the greater flaw. A wise and respected person speaks from the heart.

Neutral: Objectivity, facts, logic, and a cool head are valued in a neutral culture. Emotional pleas or expressions of feelings carry little weight and are considered "soft." People in a neutral culture become impatient when feelings get in the way of clear thinking.

In affective cultures, the expression of emotions can be raised to the level of art. It is important to present ideas aesthetically. The use of poetry is an example. In neutral cultures, there is little interest in the beauty of a well-crafted sentence. "Don't give me metaphors and cut the frills. Just give me the bullet points."

Again, aesthetics can be seen as elevating or as futile. Bullet points can be viewed as lack of class and refinement or, alternatively, as pragmatic and to the point.

Examples of the Dimension

Ang Lee's film, *Crouching Tiger, Hidden Dragon*, transports viewers to Ancient China. Li Mu Bai, the film's hero, is in love with Yu Shu Lien but waits until the last moment to express his feelings. In his culture, purity is the ideal and implies detachment rather than indulging in passions. Meditation allows one to reach this state of detachment. But as Li Mu Bai is about to die, he decides to declare his love, even at the risk of "being damned." His act can be interpreted as moving from "culture as a given" to "culture as a process" (see chapter 2). In this instance, the hero ends up regretting his "neutral" orientation. Li Mu Bai eventually embraces the "affective" pole. Some people, of course, have traveled in the other direction, finding fulfillment in detachment. *Coaching Across Cultures* does not oblige you to choose one form over the other; it invites you to leverage both.

Leveraging Affective and Neutral

Leveraging affective and neutral orientations was effectively demonstrated by the British and Italian executives already mentioned in chapter 5. For example, the Italians' ample gestures and outward display of emotion did not trigger suspicion, dry humor, and rejection in the British managers. Instead, I noticed that these globally attuned managers welcomed the Italians' affectivity as a sign of passion and engagement. What is more, these managers became more comfortable in spontaneously expressing their own feelings in a professional context, which to some felt liberating. They did not give up their cultural sense of detachment, which still served them well in being able to step back and calmly evaluate options. Instead, they enriched it with an ability to connect more effectively with people at an emotional level. This proved essential in gaining the trust of their Latin colleagues and in subsequently tackling the tasks at hand. It must be noted that for managers using a coaching style, "emotional intelligence"[14] is crucial, because establishing a trusting relationship is indeed a necessary condition for productive coaching. With a similar attitude, the Italians learned lessons from their British colleagues.

My motto regarding leveraging the affective/neutral dimension is "cool head and warm heart."

This duality has classically existed in the art of persuasion.[15] You convince the head but you persuade the heart. Over two thousand years ago, the Greeks were already distinguishing *logos* (reason) and *pathos* (emotion).

Fénelon wrote, "Cicero was right to say that you can never separate philosophy and eloquence. For the talent to persuade without science and without wisdom is pernicious; and wisdom, without the art to persuade, is not capable of winning men over, and of bringing virtue in their hearts."[16]

In some respects the Myers-Briggs Type Indicator represents a synergy of both poles. Carl Jung's book *Psychological Types*[17] reveals the author's vast knowledge of human history through numerous stories. However, it is very difficult for the layperson to understand the richness of the stories' practical implications in day-to-day life. Katherine Briggs and her daughter Isabel Briggs Myers, however, turned Jung's theory into a practical instrument, which has become the most commonly used of its kind.

Applications and Advice

Neutrality can be used on purpose when efficiency and clarity become essential. But the X-steps models[18] and "bullet point" approach may lack the sophistication and spontaneity required in affective cultures.

It is easy to become judgmental and view managers who are too emotional as incompetent and lacking self-control, but that would be an ethnocentric view. Powerful communication must integrate both forms. Top-notch global coaches strive to have a cool head and a warm heart.

The neutral pole reminds you to clearly show the evidence and present the argument precisely. People will learn the facts and will be convinced. The affective orientation allows you to move people and surprise them with images. They will be touched. As a communicator, you need to find the right combination of logos and pathos. This is an art because the ideal mix is rarely the same. But whatever your inclination, to be an effective coach you have to communicate both with the head and with the heart, and encourage your coachees to do so too.

Using Poetry in Coaching

Poetry could be viewed as "touchy-feely" and inappropriate for coaches in a business context. In the following anecdote, I want to show how poems can sometimes enhance the coaching process. This exemplifies how affectivity can enhance neutrality.

Good poets know a great deal about beauty and passion. This knowledge can be valuable in the corporate world, where people often struggle to find meaning in their work and where managers wonder how to foster genuine commitment.

Professional coach Ellen Wingard had a client who had reached the top position she had always wanted. Now she was finding herself very frustrated. She hated the prevalent politicking, absence of feedback, and lack of camaraderie. Yet, she was staying. Apparently, she was under the seduction of this opportunity to hold a high-status function.

Ellen asked her, "What is going on that keeps you in that seduction?" Then she made a suggestion in the form of the following poem by Robert Frost, which fostered a breakthrough insight in her client.

> Yield who will to their separation,
> My object in living is to unite my vocation with my avocation,
> as my two eyes make one in sight.
> For only where love and need are one
> And work is play for mortal stakes
> is the deed ever done, for heaven and the future's sake.

The poem invited her to choose the path of genuineness, where she could be true to her desires,[19] "uniting her vocation with her avocation." The poem depicts a vision where "work is play," where efforts become effortless, because "love and need are one." Life does not have to be painful. It can be joyful if you strive for unity, as your "two eyes make one in sight."

In poetry, words are carefully chosen and demand to be savored. Precision, sophistication, and authenticity help make the shift away from the banal, where all meaning gets lost. Poetry moves us beyond the usual business language of efficiency, performance, and so on. Poetry enlarges our perspective and speaks to our souls.

Through poetry, you may rediscover the fire inside you and learn to nurture the flame. You will learn to honor your desire to "live a life you can truly call your own."[20] And when you shine, your clients, families, and friends will also benefit.

Rather than dismissing poetry, metaphors, and stories, coaches should learn to complement the detached and factual business language with these alternative forms of language, more conducive to engage the hearts and the souls.

Formal/Informal

Formal: In highly formal cultures such as Japanese, formal codes of conduct, titles and honorifics, and polite forms of speech are apparent. People are adept at gauging the degree of formality required by the situation and the status of those they are interacting with. Language plays an important role in formal cultures. Romance languages, for example, distinguish between formal and informal pronouns for *you*. Other languages have far more elaborate systems of pronouns and honorifics. Formality extends beyond language to areas of dress, stance, seating behaviors, and other nonverbal expressions.[21] More generally, formal cultures observe strict protocols and rituals and follow specific rules of etiquette.[22]

Informal: Informal cultures, of which the United States is a prime example, believe informality is essential for sincere communication. Those in informal cultures feel uncomfortable with deference, titles, and rigid status categories. They prefer to treat people the same, at least on the surface. English long ago lost the distinction between formal and informal pronouns.[23] Informal cultures see formalities, social conventions, and customs as unnecessary and prefer casual, relaxed, and spontaneous conduct.[24]

While a formal code of conduct may appear cold, reserved, and disruptive to any real communication, "...it allows for smooth and predictable communication while avoiding risks of awkward and embarrassing encounters."[25]

In contrast, "while informality may appear brash and impudent by imposing an intimacy that has not yet developed,"[26] it can contribute to establishing spontaneous and friendly relationships.

All societies seem to allow for both formality and informality in specific relationships. Social context is the determinant. Societies where formality prevails recognize occasions where informality is called for. Societies where informality dominates still pay deference to judges and high-ranking political officials.

Examples of the Dimension

> In formal cultures, businessmen show sincerity and seriousness by observing strict protocols and rituals such as dress, greetings, business card exchange, forms of address or gift giving.... More emphasis is placed on the maintenance of image and status.
>
> This orientation is also embedded in language. English is really the only language that does not differentiate between formal and informal forms of address (for example, *tu/vous* in French, *tu/usted* in Spanish, and *du/Sie* in German). In many Asian languages, there are multiple forms of address with varying degrees of formality.[27]

Choosing between various forms of address is not necessarily straight forward. You face stumbling blocks at both ends. The formal approach (*vous*) may convey a distance, a barrier, and a feeling of superiority or inferiority. The informal approach (*tu*) could be perceived as too familiar. The idea is "You are my boss, not my friend. Don't pretend we are all equals: you have different status, make more money, and not all our objectives are the same."

The language itself, once adopted, influences the relationship: more spontaneous and familiar with *tu*, more reserved and distant with *usted*.[28]

In countries where language distinguishes formality and informality of relationships, assume formality first. In business settings, the relationship starts with a *Sie* and at some point, when trust and familiarity get established (which can take minutes, days, or years sometimes), someone will initiate a switch to *du*, asking if that is appropriate in case there is any doubt.

In French, the response *"Nous n'avons pas trait les vaches ensemble"* (literally: "We have not milked cows together") means "You have no reason to be so familiar with me" and is a clear signal that you have used *tu* when you should have stuck with *vous*!

The older or hierarchically superior employee is the one who should initiate the use of the familiar pronoun. You should use the same form of address with a couple of friends or spouses: if you say tu to one, and vous to the other, the latter will feel vexed, and so on.

As with any cultural phenomenon, customs depend on the social context. An individual may use vous and "Mr. President" during an official meeting, then address the same person a few hours later on the golf course with tu and on a first-name basis.

In Japanese, -san at the end of the last name is a polite form of address. If you say "Morita-san," Mr. Morita is likely to feel much more comfortable during the business meeting than if you had called him by his first name.

In Asia, exchanging business cards is a serious and formal ritual. You should hold your card with both hands and bow during the exchange. The intent is to show respect, but through an informal cultural lens, the ceremony can be perceived as strict. Conversely, Americans will sometimes simply toss their business cards on the table. Spontaneity is the underlying value, but the gesture can be perceived as too casual.

I remember watching a debate on Belgian television between a right-wing minister and a "green" deputy. The contrast in their appearance alone was striking and amusing. The minister, somewhat austere, was wearing a classic dark suit and tie, his hair carefully trimmed and combed. The ecologist, very laid-back, had no tie and a shirt with half the bottom hanging loosely over his pants. His long hair was wild and unruly. Both men were literally wearing their values on their sleeves: discipline and respect for tradition on one hand, spontaneity and informality on the other. Unfortunately, they did not seem to show much respect for these differences. The minister could not help patronizing the younger deputy. Meanwhile the deputy, in the rebel role, was sarcastic with the minister, whom he perceived as old-fashioned and rigid.

Leveraging Formality and Informality

Leveraging formality and informality means mastering the art of using informal and formal pronouns. You see the opening and seize the opportunity to become more familiar and closer to someone. You also understand when it is best to observe strict protocols and when keeping a distance will actually strengthen the relationship.

More fundamentally, leveraging formal and informal orientations is achieved when you synthesize their underlying positive values, which are ethics and spontaneity. Let me explain this notion.

The observance of protocols and rituals, that is formality, is taught to youngsters at an early age. André Comte-Sponville[29] views politeness as the first virtue, which he claims is not quite a virtue yet. Politeness resembles ethics, but unlike ethics, it only deals with the protocols, with the surface. Hopefully by repeating the rituals, by practicing politeness (e.g., *say* thank you), you will become ethical (e.g., *mean* thank you). In other words, you will genuinely strive to do what is right from a moral standpoint. If formality/politeness leads to real respect and ethics, that is great. The form itself then becomes secondary: even if you do not strictly follow the etiquette, people are likely to forgive you when they appreciate that you sincerely respect them. But conversely, politeness should not become a substitute for ethics, as it unfortunately sometimes is. If you show respect on the surface and feel contempt inside, you are being hypocritical and dishonest. You may end up alienating the other person once the truth comes out.

Leveraging formal and informal orientations means being strict on the *ethics* while reasonably flexible with the *etiquette* (to the extent you don't offend people), rather than strict on the etiquette but loose on the ethics.

Rituals can get you into the habit of regularly reflecting on what is important. For example, you may pray before eating to remember to appreciate eating a decent meal. Too many people on this planet still do not have that chance. To feel grateful and to express gratitude is a good thing, whether or not you believe there is a God to hear your prayer. However, simply saying the words out of habit without meditating on their content defeats the very purpose of the prayer ritual. It may be better instead to dispense with the prayer but feel grateful for the food and take action to stop the hunger among starving populations.

Rituals can paradoxically reinforce spontaneity. I have seen Asian workers meet and sing together before starting the day. The formal ritual increases affiliation and bonding, which enables more spontaneity and informality (for example, at night in the bar). This is another virtuous circle, composed of formality and informality, one reinforcing the other, to foster both respect and camaraderie.

Laughing clubs, initiated by Dr. Madan Kataria in India, are spreading across the globe. These are in essence clubs where laughter begins by being ritualized and artificial. The magic is that after a while, the formal laughter turns into real, informal laughter; people start to laugh in a spontaneous and natural way. Laughing is fun. It is also healthful and makes you more creative and productive and less fearful, sad, angry, or apathetic.

Applications and Advice

Coaches should not assume that informality always makes communication easier. In reality, both orientations can have the effect of excluding or enabling communication. Informality (for example, the use of first names) can make formal people feel more uncomfortable.

At another level, the lessons from the formal/informal dimension could be summarized in the following manner:

- Learn the local rituals and protocols, but more importantly meditate on their underlying meaning. Respect the etiquette, but, more significantly, observe the ethics. You can be looser on the etiquette if you are stricter on the ethics.
- Use rituals to systematically foster healthy habits such as exchanging feedback and expressing gratitude, and thrive on the paradox that more formality could lead to more spontaneity.

Coaching Tool: Coaching Videotaped Role Plays[30]

Coaching versus Influencing

As a *coach*, your intent is to help people achieve *their* goals, to realize what matters to them.

As their leader, you will seek the intersection between their goals and yours and hopefully identify some common ground where both parties' needs are met in the process. But the starting point is the other person's agenda, not yours.

As an *influencer*, you try to persuade and convince people to do what is on *your* agenda. You don't manipulate them, however; that is, cajoling them to do something that they really don't want to do or that is not in their best interest. Influencing with integrity means, as in coaching, that you try to find common ground between the others' agendas and yours. But what is different, again, is that the process is driven by your agenda, not theirs. It is fair to acknowledge that some influencing always takes place in the coaching arena. The coach probably cannot be fully neutral and should not be. In this book, for instance, I am suggesting certain values (e.g., diversity as a source of richness) and categories of objectives (e.g., "Global Scorecard"). However, despite the inevitable influencing (even unconscious), coaches differ from influencers in that coaches start with the coachee's agenda, genuinely helping him to do what he considers best for him and for the people he touches.

If you set out to coach in the following exercise and end up influencing instead, you are likely to foster frustration and resentment that will be visible even in the role play. On the other hand, if you do not position the discussion

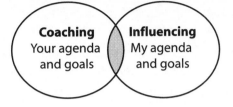

as coaching, you don't build an expectation that your primary goal is to serve the other person.

Role-Play Exercise

Objective. The purpose of this exercise is to help participants leverage their collaborators' potential to reach specific targets in challenging situations. The situation could involve dealing with a colleague whose performance or attitude is not up to standard, or it could relate to an already solid contributor. In this latter case, the goal is to help unleash even more potential to achieve greater success. Your goal in the end is to help participants identify new choices in the form of alternative communication strategies and development ideas.[31]

Description. This activity can best be done with 2 to 5 people. You can also benefit from having an external coach manage the process, facilitate the debriefing, and provide on-the-spot coaching. As a coach, I usually let participants devise their own scenarios.

The role plays focus on interpersonal communication. Interpersonal interactions, verbal and nonverbal, can be viewed as a chess game, where each move from one player allows for a variety of possible responses from the other. This analogy suggests that although you may already have an effective way of handling a delicate situation, there may be even better options. One role-play segment—role play and debriefing—lasts about 30 minutes.

Preparation. Place two chairs facing each other at a small table. This is where the role plays will take place, each involving two actors. The other participants will observe. You need a video camera to film the scene and a video plus monitor to play it back to the group. Ask participants (preferably in advance) to think of a challenging situation they would like to role play, one where they think they could benefit from others' ideas and perspectives on how to handle the communication more effectively. Alternatively, you can propose prewritten scenarios to participants. These scenarios capture typical situations participants encounter in their organizations.

The situations do not have to be limited to coaching. I find it useful, for instance, to allow for coaching *and* influencing situations. One reason is that participants often confuse coaching with influencing anyway. I explain the difference and later on invite them to reflect on whether they approached the interaction from a coaching or an influencing perspective.

Process. The exercise involves the following steps:

1. Ask each participant to choose and write down a challenging situation and briefly describe (1) the situation, (2) actor A (who he is, what he is trying to do), and (3) actor B (who he is, how he behaves). Actor A plays the part of the coach handling a challenging situation, and actor B is the one being coached.

   For example, B loves to immerse himself in technical details, tending to micromanage. Although he is a hard-working employee, several members of his staff complain that he is controlling and robs them of a sense of empowerment. The morale on his team is poor and performance suffers. B does not seem to acknowledge his leadership responsibility or the negative impact of his management style. A is B's manager. He would like to see B deal with this issue and improve his leadership ability. It is A's intent to genuinely help B determine his best choice forward: growing as a leader, making the technical–managerial transition, or realizing that his passion is technical and finding a more appropriate job.

2. Collect the scenarios and choose one for the first role play. Write a few words on a flip chart to summarize the scenario.

3. Ask participants to volunteer for roles. Tell the rest of the group they will observe. Each participant typically plays twice, once as A and once as B, to experience how it feels from each side. It is all right to mix up direct reports, peers, bosses, clients, and so forth.

4. Pull actor B aside and tell him to offer some resistance to A's attempt to work with him. In other words, B does not make it too easy for A. (The amount of resistance typically varies, and A never knows for sure what is coming.) However, instruct B to respond realistically and therefore favorably when A handles the interaction effectively.

5. Tell the participants to observe actor A and, along with the external coach, prepare to give him feedback and suggestions during the debrief-

ing. They should write down their observations during the role play and organize their observations around three questions: (1) What was effective in how A communicated? (2) What was less effective? And (3) What could A do to be more effective?

6. Start the role play and the video recorder. Stop the role play after 7 minutes.

Debriefing

I use the following format to structure the debriefing, referring to the questions mentioned above, and I invite you to try it as well.

Ask A, "What did you do effectively?" Then ask the same question to B and to the observers. Urge participants to resist the tendency to respond with negative criticism in order to help them develop a habit of appreciating the positive instead of taking it for granted. Coaches like to build on strengths. Add comments on what you thought worked well and perhaps share a model that captures what was effective about what A did. The model makes it possible to replicate and generalize effective communication patterns.

Next, ask A, "What was not (so) effective?" and "What could you have done differently?" After A has finished answering, turn to B and later to the observers with the same questions. And again, point out a pitfall you observed, drawing from your knowledge in communication theory, and discuss strategies to overcome the difficulties.

Insist on the fact that this is merely a role play, not a real situation, to preempt any criticism that this exercise is artificial. You will find that participants are invariably surprised by the lessons that can be learned. After all, the situations are realistic because the participants chose them (incidentally, this is one of the reasons why I prefer to let participants devise their own scenarios). You will also tell participants upfront that a typical coaching discussion lasts more than 7 minutes. You will remind participants that the intention is not to recreate the exact same situation, nor is it to judge the actors' performance. The role play has a developmental purpose. Encourage the actors to try new behaviors and to make plenty of mistakes! In the 7 minutes many transactions take place, and several opportunities for constructive communication are either grabbed or lost. Words, voice, posture, and gestures reveal rich insights.

As a coach, you will want to point out to the group the connections with psychological preferences and cultural orientations. Relate communication theories when possible (Transactional Analysis, NLP, etc.) to the actual experience: "Were you in the OK–OK position?" "What behaviors suggested that you moved to the OK–not OK position?" "What was the impact on the other person?"

You may or may not decide to watch the video. It is particularly useful to view the video when the actors displayed interesting nonverbal behaviors that they were not even aware of: barrier gestures that impeded the communication, open postures that favored contact, and so on.

Finish the exercise by asking participants to articulate what they learned and to summarize what they need to work on to become better coaches.

Before the first role play, you could offer John Whitmore's GROW model[32] to help participants prepare for the exercise.

> **Goal**: Know what you want to accomplish in the interaction.
>
> **Reality**: Start with a reality check (What is the other person's situation?).
>
> **Options**: Imagine and discuss options (rather than just sticking with one idea).
>
> **Will**: Close the discussion with precise agreements and commitments.

Chapter 10
How to Leverage Modes of Thinking

How do you think?

Deductive/Inductive—Analytical/Systemic

Deductive: Emphasize concepts, theories, and general principles. Then, through logical reasoning, derive practical applications and solutions.

Inductive: Start with experiences, concrete situations, and cases. Then, using intuition, formulate general models and theories.

Analytical: Separate a whole into its constituent elements. Dissect a problem into smaller chunks.

Systemic: Assemble the parts into a cohesive whole. Explore connections between elements and focus on the entire system.

> *To reach the truth, you need once in your life to get rid of habitual ways of thinking and rebuild the whole system of knowledge.*
>
> —René Descartes

The seventeenth-century French philosopher's advice is still pertinent. We are so busy thinking that we risk forgetting to reflect on how we actually think. There may be more than one truth, and we probably need to re-evaluate our thinking more than once.

As global coaches, we ignite our thinking when we learn the best from diverse cultural modes.

Deductive/Inductive

Deductive: The style of thinking that derives from ideas and theories is called "deductive." Once concepts or theories are firmly established, they are applied in particular cases. Europeans and Latin Americans tend to be deductive, or abstract, in their thinking style. Such thinkers are "likely to have more

confidence in their theories than in the raw data of empirical observation."
They don't feel compelled to amass facts and statistics. One or two connections between their concepts and the empirical world are plenty. "They prefer
to generalize from one concept to another. They place their trust in the power
of thought."[1]

Deduction has dominated Occidental thinking since Aristotle. In 1620,
however, Francis Bacon, a British philosopher and politician, showed the
limits of deduction and advocated induction to promote scientific progress.
Bacon's method emphasizes observation of natural phenomena, systematic
collection of these observations, and finally induction itself by generalizing
from the observed facts.[2]

I would say that irrelevance is the risk of deduction, when thinking loses
sight of the real world it is supposed to serve or at least describe, and theory
becomes an end in itself.

Modes of Thinking

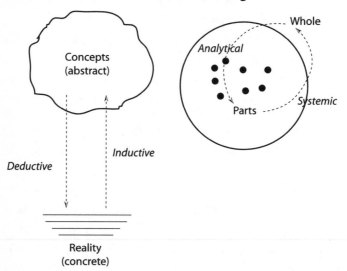

Inductive: The style of thinking that derives from analysis of data is known as
"inductive." In Western science, models and hypotheses based on empirical
observation are representative of the inductive style. Inductive thinkers, like
Americans, tend to "distrust theory and generalizations, which they might
label 'impractical,' 'unrealistic,' or 'too abstract.'"[3] They feel far more comfortable compiling facts and statistics to reach their conclusions.

Induction relies not only on facts but also on intuition, which is a "form of
immediate knowing that does not appeal to reasoning."[4] The knowing comes

as a flash. You have probably all experienced intuitive flashes, which tend to occur when you relax and let your logical thinking brain take a break. Interestingly, the etymology—*intueri* in Latin means "looking carefully"—suggests that careful observation is what enables intuition to generate valuable knowledge.

Induction starts with experiences, cases, and scenarios. Out of these, you formulate theories. Theories are aimed at helping you pragmatically engage with the world. The case study method rendered popular by Harvard Business School is an example of induction.

Simplism is induction's danger, when thinking clings so close to the experience that it can only generate a narrow and simplistic model of reality.

In Europe, thinking tends to be deductive. The very nature of deductive thinking is such that it does not lend itself to simple summaries and quick tips. What is missed in conciseness and simplicity, though, is gained in the sophistication needed to deal with a complex reality.

Deductive thinkers may find induction lacking in substance. For example, they may feel frustrated by the case study method. To paraphrase a famous commercial, they may say "Where is the beef?" meaning where is the overall principle, the general theory.

Inductive thinkers may be equally frustrated with deduction. They would ask the same question, but this time meaning where is the application, where can we put this to use.

Examples of the Dimension

I remember my electromagnetic class in the Brussels Polytechnical School. Our professor would need several sticks of chalk to fill the blackboard with complex mathematical calculations. The thinking process was clearly deductive to the extent that real-life applications were almost completely left out of the lectures. But afterward, we students did have separate hands-on sessions in the lab, during which the professor's assistants would help us apply the theory in concrete situations.

Our thinking materializes in problem solving but also in daily communication. An American used to induction may become impatient with a Frenchman starting a negotiation with significant time devoted to explaining the overall philosophy and stating the guiding principles at length. Likewise, a Frenchman can dismiss certain American models as too simplistic, too American, too naïve. The French believe that reality is more complex than such models and that you cannot simply generalize from limited experience. In their view, a more sophisticated conceptual thinking, that is, deduction, is called for.

To contrast deduction and induction, I think it is instructive to examine how these modes of thinking can be applied to foster happiness. After all, professional coaches should help people to live more happily. Let me compare André Comte-Sponville's French deductive method with Cheryl Richardson's American inductive technique. Depending on your own orientation, you might be tempted to dismiss Sponville's way as obtuse or Richardson's as simplistic. Instead, I challenge you to focus on the potential merits of both approaches.

Comte-Sponville's *Le bonheur, désespérément*[5] (*happiness without hope*) is a remarkable book on philosophy. Comte-Sponville carefully defines the concepts, starting with philosophy itself, which he adapts from Epicure: "Philosophy is a discursive practice (it proceeds 'through discourses and reasoning'), which has life as object, reason as mean, and happiness as goal…. Philosophy helps to think better, to live better." The sage loves happiness but prefers truth above anything. He cannot be happy with illusions. He prefers a sad truth to a false joy.

Through subtle, thorough, and clear reasoning (deduction) and with illustrative examples, Comte-Sponville shows how hope gets in the way of happiness. Hope is to desire something we do not have. We don't know whether it will be satisfied or not, and its satisfaction is out of our control. "Hoping is to desire without enjoying, without knowing (if it will be realized or not), without power (to make it happen)."

In other words, hope conveys a lack of power and appreciation for what you have. How many more promotions, how much more money before you allow yourself to feel happy? If I only had this or that, I would be happy! Unless you are going through something really terrible, you can choose to be happy right now. You can enjoy what you currently have and take action to change what you can!

The sage does not dream of pies in the sky but matches his desires with reality. He finds happiness by seizing the present and building the future.

Cheryl Richardson publishes a newsletter, which she sends weekly over e-mail. Each note is about one or two pages long. While the topic varies, the format is usually the same.

Cheryl tells a personal anecdote about an experience she had in the past week. With a simple yet elegant style, she shares her feelings and the lessons she learned from the experience. She then offers her readers a lesson in the form of coaching tips and finishes with suggested actions. One newsletter went something like this: Cheryl was overwhelmed with e-mails she had to reply to, domestic chores that had to be carried out, and so on. But the sun was shining, inviting her to enjoy life outside. She realized that many people could wait another day for her reply and that the dishes did not have to be cleaned up right away. She gave herself permission to take care of herself by enjoying a sunny afternoon and this is what made her happy in that moment. Each newsletter typically ends with tips (e.g., Enjoy life now!) and a "take action challenge" (e.g., "Do something fun at least two times this week"[6]). This sort of reminder is another way, inductive rather than deductive, to help people live happier lives.

Leveraging Deductive and Inductive

At Stanford University I attended a class by Professor Ronald Newbold Bracewell called "The Fourier Transform and Its Applications" as part of my program for the master of sciences in electrical engineering. The presentation felt almost like a dance between theory and reality. The professor was looking for an elegant way to formulate the theory and would not hesitate to take certain shortcuts. These were based on a careful examination of physical phenomena that would rule out certain options, thereby simplifying the mathematics. The theory was clearly enlightening our understanding of reality. But likewise, our attention to real physical manifestations ranging from electromagnetics to acoustics and optics informed our ability to intuitively grasp and create theories. Professor Bracewell was in fact brilliantly leveraging deduction and induction, liberating powerful thinking.

Coaches, too, can enhance their practice by proactively combining deduction and induction. You can help coachees make changes and venture into new territories. An intellectual understanding of leadership and communication, for example, can never replace experience and practice. I remember a coachee who told me he had read a book and had attended a class on Transactional Analysis. Although he had found the material interesting, he realized he had not suspected its practical power. As a coach, I showed him how several aspects of the models specifically applied to many of his challenges. I indicated the new and concrete communication options TA revealed. He gradually replaced psychological games with more productive communication. The application was essential, but theory proved to be important too, in that the coachee was now better equipped to decode and deal with a wide range of interpersonal communication situations.

Inductive cultures, by definition, start with experiences from which lessons are derived. Experiential activities (e.g., games that stimulate your reflection) are naturally a favorite form of learning. However, coaches who prefer deduction can also benefit from using experiential activities. These provoke insights and help raise an awareness that goes deeper than mere intellectual understanding. Experts and academicians sometimes fall into the trap of using concepts and rhetoric as a substitute for personal change. With deduction, particularly, the danger is to remain at the abstract level.[7] Michael Maccoby illustrates a similar phenomenon:

> Generally speaking, narcissistic leaders set very little store
> by mentoring. They seldom mentor others, and when they
> do they typically want their protégés to be pale reflections
> of themselves. Even those narcissists like Jack Welch who
> are held up as strong mentors are usually more interested in
> instructing than in coaching.[8]

Incidentally, Maccoby neglects to differentiate between mentoring and coaching (see chapter 1 for the distinction), but that is not the point here.

Experiential activities oblige you to examine how you behave. The coach will ask questions such as these: What happened in this activity? What did you do effectively? What could you have done differently? What have you learned that applies to your real situation? Filming people in action while they are solving a problem or communicating, and then watching the tape, can be useful too. Coachees can see themselves and become even more conscious of their behaviors and their impact. Other inductive methods include artistic activities, which I mentioned earlier, for example graffiti, postcards, or collages.

Deduction and theories are still important as long as connections are made explicitly with the real situations. In inductive cultures theory is usually kept to a minimum, which also explains why coaching takes less time. I believe richness is missed in the process, as is perhaps more importantly an enhanced ability to deal with complexity and ambiguity. The latter is critical, particularly at senior levels of management. This may explain why senior executives I work with in Europe are ready to invest significant time in the process and are not satisfied if the deductive component is reduced to its simplest expression.

Applications and Advice

To summarize, the lessons for coaches are twofold:

- You should learn to utilize deduction and induction. Deduction, in addition to being more suitable when dealing with cultures like France, celebrates the power of (conceptual) thought. Induction, preferred by Anglo-Saxons, forces you to stay close to the real experience.

- You should promote a "dance" between concepts and reality, one enriching the other to form a virtuous circle of powerful thinking. You want to remain anchored in reality and practical, while allowing yourself to take a high view so that you can see reality from a different perspective and promote innovative solutions to complex challenges. Coachees put these solutions into practice (coaching is indeed action oriented), resulting in new learning that allows you to refine your concepts, hence increasing your ability to propose effective solutions.

Analytical/Systemic

Analytical: Analysis breaks a whole into parts. Analytical thinking tackles problems by decomposing them.

Systemic: Systemic or "holistic" thinking brings the parts together into a cohesive whole. Emphasis is on connections between the parts and on the entire system.

Analytical thinking is often complemented with *linear* thinking, which proposes to link the chunks in chains of cause and effect. The term *linear* refers to this sequence, or line, which is by essence mono-dimensional—mathematicians contrast lines with surfaces (two-dimensional) and volumes (three-dimensional). Linear thinking is helpful in dealing with simple situations or with specific parts of a larger issue, but it is insufficient to deal with complex, multidimensional problems.

Peter Senge notes that analytical thinking has been favored in the United States (the same could also probably be said about Europe) and advocates the development of systems thinking. "From a very early age, we are taught to break apart problems, to fragment the world. This apparently makes complex tasks and subjects more manageable, but we pay a hidden, enormous price. We can no longer see the consequences of our actions; we lose our intrinsic sense of connection to a larger whole."[9]

Both types of thinking are valuable. Analytical thinking is very useful in that dividing and creating categories makes problems more manageable and allows for specialization. Systemic thinking lets one visualize connections in order to apprehend complex patterns that cannot be appropriately described when the whole has been broken down into separate parts. On the other hand, systems may be more difficult to grasp, to get one's head around. Again, what is called for is an ability to juggle the two types of thinking, looking at reality from both angles.

Examples of the Dimension

The "Balanced Scorecard" (see chapter 12) exemplifies analytical-linear thinking: "Every measure selected for a Balanced Scorecard should be an element in a chain of cause-and-effect relationships that communicates the meaning of the business unit's strategy to the organization."[10]

Systemic thinking is present in Peter Senge's work. Senge has developed archetypes to help visualize various systemic phenomena that would be missed with an analytical lens. Understanding the systemic dynamics at play can help to break vicious circles before it is too late. "Fixes that fail" constitutes an example. The dynamic is described below together with a suggested remedy.

Fixes that Fail

Description: A fix, effective in the short term, has unforeseen, long-term consequences that may require even more use of the same fix.

Example: Cutting back maintenance schedules to save costs, which eventually leads to more breakdowns and higher costs, creating still more cost-cutting pressures.

Management principle: Maintain focus on the long term. Disregard short-term "fix," if feasible, or use it only to "buy time" while working on long-term remedy.[11]

In some cases, lack of analytical thinking is what prevents success. An executive I worked with had a long-term vision and was able to readily see the big picture. But project management was his Achilles' heel. He had a hard time laying out steps to translate his vision into action. This resulted in over-commitments, last-minute rushes, and in some cases breakdowns. What prevented him from breaking down projects into distinct and clearly defined parts was a psychological preference[12] together with a cultural orientation for systemic thinking. His deeply rooted belief was that analytical thinking was somehow trivial and limiting. To make progress, he first had to change his attitude vis-à-vis analytical thinking.

Leveraging Analytical and Systemic

Leveraging systemic and analytical thinking occurs when you examine an entire system (rather than adopting a narrow view) and when you break down the whole into smaller parts, which allows you to be thorough. Metaphorically, you want to think about the forest *and* the trees, about the whole ecosystem *and* the individual species.

For example, Sandra Vandermerwe's marketing approach considers the whole customer experience (systemic thinking). Rather than strive to gain market share by delivering superior products and services, Vandermerwe urges executives to expand their market and look at the entire "customer-activity cycle" (i.e., all activities involved in the customer experience), which is broken into "pre, during, and post" phases (analytical thinking). In the travel industry for example, these phases might include: "first, deciding where to go and how, booking flights and getting to the airport; second, taking the trip, getting to and experiencing the destination; and finally, leaving the destination, finding transport, coming home and paying the bills." She claims her method can help managers assess opportunities for providing new kinds of value to customers at each critical experience. For example, "Virgin Atlantic joined with limousine companies to develop a plan to take business-class passengers to many airports free of charge, check them in, and issue an invitation to Virgin's Clubhouse lounge." Vandermerwe argues that this approach maximizes revenues by increasing customers' "breadth of spending," while inciting customers to remain clients since their needs are met in an integrated fashion.[13]

The professional coach does not intend to replace a strategist or a marketer, but he could still very well, and in fact should, challenge his coachees' thinking on strategic and marketing issues, especially when they fail to either look at the whole system or break it into manageable parts.

The same type of thinking can be applied to coaching in general. For example, my company's mission involves "helping leaders, teams, and organizations to unleash their human potential to achieve high performance together with high fulfillment." Analytical thinking implies breaking the mission statement into categories, while systemic thinking allows for the integration of the parts, with an eye on the overall mission. The services "Rosinski & Company" provides are not limited to executive coaching and team coaching. High positive impact is what matters and leadership development is usually achieved through a tailored combination of consulting, training, and coaching, and together with a global network of specialists.

As another example, your systemic thinking can allow your coachees to think beyond achieving their immediate business objectives and reflect on the impact on the broader system (i.e., our society and our planet). Peter Hindle talks about his company, Procter & Gamble, promoting a "good life today and a better life tomorrow for everyone." But in order to make this rallying cry operational, analytical thinking comes in, breaking down the goal into four areas: "human and environmental safety, regulatory compliance, resource use and waste management, and addressing social concerns."[14]

The "Global Scorecard," by design, leverages the two forms of thinking for goal setting. Analytically, objectives are broken down into four categories to provide focus: self, family and friends, organization, and community and world. Systemically, interconnections between the categories indicate possible synergies, and the global perspective prevents losing sight of what is truly important.

Applications and Advice

Coaches provide invaluable assistance when they help coachees think differently about their issues. Finding alternative ways to formulate a problem is comparable to discovering new doorways into a building; there may be easier, more accessible ways in.

For example, interviewing senior executives as a first step in an executive team coaching intervention revealed, among other findings, the need to frame short-term tactical decisions in the context of a consistent long-term vision and strategy. Acting without reference to the vision and long-term strategy created an impression of confusion and a loss of confidence, according to some interviewees. For example, expenses had been cut in areas critically supporting the overall strategy (another issue was actually the need to more precisely articulate the strategy), while necessary decisions had been delayed. This was starting to erode credibility and foster a vicious circle of downward performance and demotivation. After our first session, the team was actively working on building, agreeing on, and communicating a clear strategy for the rest of the organization. The goal was to strive for consistency, making decisions congruent with the shared vision and strategy.

At a conference, one of my participants from Hong Kong insisted on the fact that coaching is not just a management skill. To flourish, it also requires a developmental culture and consistent human resources systems in the company (e.g., a reward system that favors managers who actively develop their subordinates). Her comment illustrates complementing an analytical view (i.e., developing coaching skills) with a systemic perspective (i.e., fostering an environment in which coaching can blossom).

Leveraging analytical and systemic thinking is undoubtedly still too rare. It is powerful but certainly challenging. It is particularly noteworthy, therefore, that in the seventeenth century, French mathematician, physicist, and religious philosopher Blaise Pascal was already advocating such a synthesis, which was also an ideal. He declared, "I consider [it] impossible to know the parts without knowing the whole, and to know the whole without particularly knowing the parts."[15]

Coaching Tool: Creative Problem Solving

Creativity is the "faculty to find original ideas, different approaches, when confronted with a problem or challenge that resists habitual solutions."[16]

Think of such a challenge you currently face. The usual approaches have led you nowhere. You are ready to take a different angle. A good place to start is by thinking differently about your challenge. First, consider how you have been thinking about it. Then, try something different, including applying the thinking orientations presented in this chapter and other possible solutions that you may have overlooked.

The creativity techniques presented next make the most of various modes of thinking. This presentation assumes you are coaching yourself, but you can certainly use these techniques to coach others. These creativity techniques include the creative process, tools, and methods.

The Creative Process

The creative process is a set of fundamental steps we follow naturally to develop a creative solution to a given challenge. Four sequential steps are usually identified in the creative process.

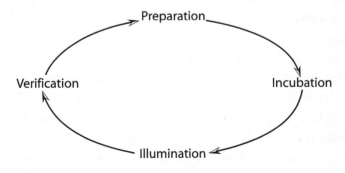

Preparation is the moment when you become interested in trying something new and gather the information that is necessary for thinking "outside the box," as the cliché goes.

Incubation is the vital gestation period when your mind works toward the objective without conscious effort.

Illumination is the moment when a key connection and insight occur.

Verification is the final step, where you verify the idea through the test of logical reasoning and practical feasibility.

For example, this sequence happens initially during the coaching process when the coachee's challenge is to articulate a list of key target objectives. The assessment step is a form of preparation. The coachee gathers data systematically about his stakeholders' expectations, collects feedback about his current performance, and meditates on his desires, strengths, and weaknesses. When the assessment is thorough, insights will typically follow after an incubation period. The coachee's target objectives emerge almost naturally. Intuition rather than logic generates the synthesis, the illumination. Somehow what he should aim for becomes clear for the coachee. Finally, before committing himself, the coachee verifies that the objectives are indeed important, meaningful, and realistic.

A good way to master the creative process is to become conscious of the various modes of thinking and to practice thinking from these different orientations. A strong creative process leverages all modes of thinking.

For example, systemic thinking will allow your preparation to take into account the big picture. Inductive thinking will favor illuminations. Analytical and deductive thinking will be handy for the verification.

Tools

Creativity tools can stimulate the creative process, allowing you to generate more depth (in-the-box ideas) and breadth (out-of-the-box ideas) and speeding up the natural thinking process (fostering quicker illumination).

The following tools can help you in the incubation and illumination phases.

Associations. You foster free associations with the studied object (or concept). Brainstorming is Alex Osborn's classic technique. In the initial *divergent* phase, you suspend judgment and stimulate all mental associations, starting with the initial object or concept, which can be anything: transportation, margarine, health, and so on. Make a list of all thoughts or ideas that come to you during the brainstorming phase. In the second, *convergent* phase, you review your list and search for ideas that could actually be useful.

Brainstorming can be enhanced using "inductive lists": you stimulate more associations with injunctions such as Sydney Shore's CREATIVITY (C: 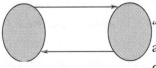 Combine; R: Reverse; E: Enlarge [magnify]; A: Adapt; T: Tinier [minimize]; I: Instead of [substitute]; V: Viewpoint Change; I: In other way [rearrange]; T: To other uses; Y: Yes! Yes!).

For example, if your challenge is to find new ways to help people increase performance and fulfillment, the list could stimulate the following ideas:

C—combine coaching and training—offer a leadership development seminar (which covers basic notions and strives to enhance self-awareness) and follow it up with one-on-one coaching (to put insights into action and achieve objectives)

R—let your approach be driven by clients' challenges rather than by your predetermined agenda or content—that is, coaching as opposed to teaching

E—enlarge performance and fulfillment by learning lessons from different cultures

T—strive to achieve "more with/from less" (e.g., more impact with less effort by focusing your energy on what matters the most; more value for customers with less raw material, creating less waste)

V—get into the habit of viewing every challenge from alternative cultural perspectives

Y—catch people doing things right and build on the positive

It is also worth mentioning "mental maps" here,[17] which are graphic tree-like representations of associations.

Combinations. Combinations of two variables help you identify new possibilities. The "discovery matrix" lets you represent those combinations (for example: capabilities in one column, client needs in the other one), and hopefully discover new opportunities.

Analogies. An analogy refers to a "resemblance established by the imagination between two or more objects of thinking that are essentially different."[18]

For example, to explore the object "engineer" or "manager," you can draw analogies with, for instance, a "sports champion" (If the engineer were a sports champion, it would mean that…). Then, keep the useful comparisons for the convergent phase.

The analogous objects should be sufficiently distinct from the original without being too far out. They should relate to a topic that you know (or can learn about) and like.

I helped a group find ways to improve their total quality procedures. Participants generated useful ideas from the following analogous objects: Formula 1, theater program, encyclopedia, greenhouse, and so on. They came up with these objects after being presented with a long list of possible analogical domains (biology, sports, mythology, etc.).

The next question was "If quality procedures (i.e., studied object) were a Formula 1 car (i.e., analogous object) what would this entail?" For example, there is always a back-up car and likewise you need back-up solutions in case a machine breaks down. In Formula 1, engineers constantly work at improving the car's performance to maintain and improve its competitiveness while complying with evolving regulations. Likewise, improving quality procedures has to be an on-going process. Safety concerns are essential in Formula 1. Likewise, quality procedures should guarantee maximum safety in your factories, for the consumers,...

In fact, participants list numerous analogies and should not censor themselves (notably so that the flow of ideas is not interrupted). In the end, you ask, "But quality procedures are not a Formula 1 car, so what does that imply?" This obliges participants to concentrate on specific solutions while eliminating ideas that may be irrelevant.

Artistic Techniques. Artistic techniques such as painting, sculpture, cinema, poetry, music, and the arts in general allow you to set in motion different parts of your brain. You look at reality from a different perspective when you paint a sunset, for instance.

In this book, you have also been exposed to coaching tools using postcards and collages.[19]

Methods

Let me simply mention that methods have been developed to facilitate the entire creative process by making use of one or several creativity tools. William Gordon's "synectics,"[19] which is a classic, and my own "analogical method"[20] rely primarily on analogies. It is beyond our scope to discuss these methods here but the Center for Studies in Creativity (Buffalo State College), for example, is a good source of information.

* * * * * * *

In summary, try to consciously make use of different thinking modes and follow the outlined creative process to address your problem or challenge. Learn more about creativity tools and methods to enhance the process.

Do not hesitate to question the formulation of your problem. Don't simply try to solve the problem as it is presented. The statement of the problem itself could be what's holding you back. Creativity starts by exploring the problem, modifying or adapting its enunciation, finding the adequate formulation.

For example, engineers and scientists still use Newton's laws of physics today, because they are very acceptable for normal speeds, which are way below the speed of light. Yet, when Einstein sought to understand why the speed of light is a constant regardless of the observer's position, he challenged the classical premises by pretending that time does not have an absolute measure. This audacious hypothesis was confirmed later by comparing the hours on a clock placed on a special vessel after a trip at high speed with those on a watch that had remained on earth. Einstein's new framework led to a breakthrough. "Relativity" was born, which, in turn, would be followed by more breakthroughs in physics throughout the twentieth century. But back in the nineteenth century, many scientists believed the study of physics was nearly complete. As physicist Alastair Rae remarked, "By the end of the nineteenth century, it seemed that the basic fundamental principles governing the behavior of the physical universe were known."[21] How wrong that perception was.

Part III
Facilitating the High-Performance and High-Fulfillment Journey

Heroes reside in us, and it is our role as coaches to facilitate these heroes' journeys.

In virtually all the religions and mythologies of the world, Joseph Campbell found that the journey follows a similar pattern:

> ...whether presented in the vast, almost oceanic images of the Orient, in the vigorous narratives of the Greeks, or in the majestic legends of the Bible, the adventure of the hero normally follows the pattern... a separation from the world, a penetration to some source of power, and a life-enhancing return. The whole of the Orient has been blessed by the boon brought back by Gautama Buddha—his wonderful teaching of the Good Law—just as the Occident has been by the Decalogue of Moses.... Prometheus ascended to the heavens, stole fire from the gods, and descended. Jason sailed through the Clashing Rocks into a sea of marvels, circumvented the dragon that guarded the Golden Fleece, and returned with the fleece and the power to wrest his rightful throne from a usurper.[1]

Let's face it, the heroes are not just mythical figures you admire; we as coaches and those who are coached are the heroes. The leaders are not solely the senior executives and politicians we follow; we are the leaders.

Carol Pearson, in *Awakening the Heroes Within*, writes,

> This is a time in human history when heroism is greatly needed. Like heroes of old, we aid in restoring life, health, and fecundity to the kingdom as a side benefit of taking our own journeys, finding our own destinies, and giving our unique gifts. It is as if the world were a giant puzzle and each of us who takes a journey returns with one piece. Collectively, as we contribute our part, the kingdom is transformed.[2]

Before you engage coachees, you will have to embark on your *own* journey. You will need to find the courage and muster the will to achieve your own objectives, doing all you can to make your dreams come true. You will have to be true to yourself, unleash your potential, and bring your contribution to society. On this journey toward performance and fulfillment, the first dragons you will have to slay will be inside; you will need to confront the fears, beliefs, and weaknesses that are holding you back. But you will also meet your heroes within: the talents and strengths that will be your resources to win those bat-tles. You will learn to cherish the journey itself and not only the destination.

Here in Part III, I invite you the coach, or the aspiring coach, to be the coachee. To advance on your journey, you may choose to work with another person (working with a good coach will likely help you to be a better coach) and/or be your own coach. This said, I also understand that many of you who read this book are already well advanced on your own journey; if so, you will be ready to use the process described in Part III in your coaching as you wish.

For Peter Leyland the journey began with a wake-up call. He received disappointing 360-degree feedback on his leadership behaviors. He had been pressuring people to achieve business results but had failed to build a trusting and empowering environment. He engaged in a leadership development journey. His colleagues were surprised and skeptical at first. But over the years, he demonstrated his commitment to serve Baxter clients and employees alike, helping his team be the best it could, enabling both productivity and satisfaction.

For Lou Gerstner, the journey was one of reinstilling confidence, ambition, and passion into an IBM that had become moribund.

Niall FitzGerald's and Antony Burgmans' journey was about growing people to grow results, tapping into the cultural diversity that constitutes the very fabric of Unilever.

At Chubb the motto became "beyond expectations." The heroes would work over the long haul to fulfill Thomas Caldecot Chubb's aspiration: "Ours is an organization that is as eager to have a good reputation as 'Chubb & Son, the employer' as it is to have a good reputation as 'Chubb & Son, the underwriter'."[3]

Coaches have traditionally provided tools and frameworks to facilitate the process, but to engage wholeheartedly in the journey, you will need to find deep meaning and noble purpose in your work. This is where *Coaching Across Cultures* comes into play, by allowing you to consider a larger context. Yes, achieving 20 percent return on investment, 35 percent growth in market share, and a number 1 position are important and part of the goal. I have found, though, that most often, even with hard-line business executives, these objectives alone are insufficient to elicit the best efforts. Invariably, it all arises: the question of their legacy, their impact on society at large, the reason for being. Inevitably, their fulfillment comes to the fore, as they find that their success cannot be measured solely by external achievements.

Global coaching invites you as coach to connect your own personal voyage with the journey of your executive, team, organization, and the world. Part III is about putting into practice the insights and tools you have gained in Parts I and II. Having acquired a habit of learning from different cultures, you will be better equipped to overcome challenges along the way. Leveraging diverse views, you will think more creatively, communicate more effectively, and guide those you coach more sensitively. Part III provides a framework that allows first you and then your coachees to engage systematically on a high-performance, high-fulfillment path.

Chapter 11 is where the journey begins. In the assessment, the radar screen is large to accommodate a global perspective. Chapter 12 proposes a new tool, The "Global Scorecard." Its scope goes beyond traditional scorecards, such as the "Balanced Scorecard." Improving overall social, ecological, and economic conditions is a part of this larger focus. As would be expected, the excellent companies depicted in this book are actively committed to making the world a better place. Chapter 13 describes the journey itself during which actions take place and learning occurs. The various roles of the coach are also discussed.

As you read Part III, I ask you to keep in mind that multiple journeys may be occurring: that of the leader or team you coach, those they supervise, and, perhaps most important, your own. The journey is never complete; there is always room for growth and learning. Your goal is to help potential (in those you coach and your own) unfold in a synergistic fashion.

Chapter 11
Conduct Your Assessment

Global Coaching Process

Step 1: Conduct your Assessment

Coachee's Self-Assessment

- Desires — Sources of motivation / Values
- Strengths
- Weaknesses
- Present situation — Successes, Satisfactions / Challenges, Frustrations
- Preferences — Psychological preferences / Cultural orientations

Organization's Stakeholders

Current Level ———— (gaps) Expectations

- Competencies
- Performance

Family and Friends   Community and World

Current Situation ———— Wishes
                    (gaps)

- Love
- Friendship
- Citizenship

Step 2: Articulate Target Objectives—Global Scorecard

Genuine
Leverage
Outcomes
Balance
Assessment
Limited

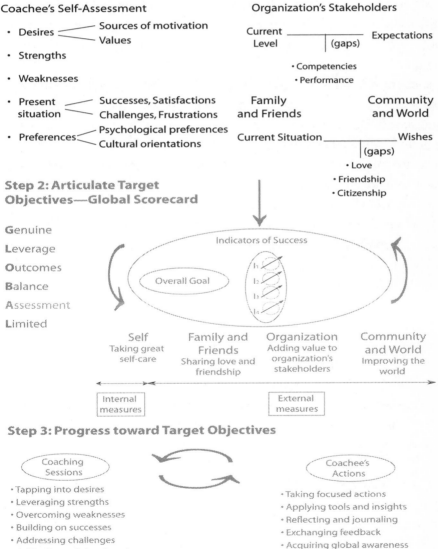

Indicators of Success

Overall Goal

Self
Taking great self-care

Family and Friends
Sharing love and friendship

Organization
Adding value to organization's stakeholders

Community and World
Improving the world

Internal measures | External measures

Step 3: Progress toward Target Objectives

Coaching Sessions

- Tapping into desires
- Leveraging strengths
- Overcoming weaknesses
- Building on successes
- Addressing challenges
- Achieving real-time learning

Coachee's Actions

- Taking focused actions
- Applying tools and insights
- Reflecting and journaling
- Exchanging feedback
- Acquiring global awareness
- Leveraging cultural differences

When I begin the coaching journey, I start by asking my coachees to take a step back. This is the time where I ask them to pause and honestly face the present situation; I ask them these questions: What is going well and what is not? What energizes you and what is draining you? I also invite them to explore crucial parts of their inner reality, starting with personal desires: What do you want and what do you value?

Candidly and courageously, they assess their strengths and weaknesses to ensure that they are exploiting the former to the fullest and avoiding the latter becoming obstacles to success.

I ask coachees to consider their preferences, both psychological and cultural, and how these impact thinking processes, feelings, and behaviors. We identify orientations they may have overlooked and discern opportunities for leveraging.

I encourage them to bring others into the picture and systematically find out their perceptions and expectations. In the case of executive coaching, the organization typically conveys those expectations in two ways: performance (doing) and competencies (being).

It is also important for coachees to honor important people outside of the immediate work environment. I usually start by asking them questions about family and friends: "How much have you taken them for granted?" "How much energy do you invest in nurturing these relationships that are probably your most important ones?" "What are their wishes in terms of love and friendship?" Then I ask them to reflect on their communities and the world at large: "How much do you owe your community for being where you are today?" and "What can you give back, as an active citizen, to do your part?"

As I start the systematic assessment with coachees, I suggest that as they go through the process, they record their insights and refine their ideas in their learning journal. I caution them that they will not be able to please everybody, so they should not set up unrealistic expectations that they will be able to do so. They can commit, however, to take various viewpoints into account. I remind them that they must take care of themselves first so that they will be in a position to give their best to others. Then they can search for creative win–win scenarios to meet others' expectations.

Even though I shall primarily describe a situation where the coachee is an individual, the method can be generalized and applied to teams and organizations.

Coachee's Self-Assessment

The assessment includes four interconnected areas: desires, strengths and weaknesses, present situation, and preferences.

Desires

The assessment starts with desires. This notion may have been overlooked in traditional business education and corporate culture, where a "rational" view has led us to think of organizations as machines and people as cogs. In 1993, Michael Hammer and James Champy published a book called *Reengineering the Corporation*,[1] which promised breakthrough increases in performance, but, predictably, the "revolution" turned out not to be straightforward to implement. Two years later Champy recognized in a subsequent book that "the only way we're going to deliver on the full promise of reengineering is to start reengineering management—by reengineering ourselves."[2] I am not sure that you will want to "reengineer" your coachees or yourself, but the second book has at least the merit of acknowledging the primordial human factor. We cannot understand the human factor if we ignore human desires, even though desires have been denied in the mechanistic management culture, where people are "assets," "capital," or "resources" (e.g., human resources department) to be deployed to maximize profit and achieve business objectives.

The idea of placing people's desires first is hardly new or faddish. It is anchored in human and philosophical tradition. In the seventeenth century, Baruch Spinoza, the famous Dutch philosopher, affirmed that "Desire is the very essence of man."[3] With the word *desire*, Spinoza was referring not only to our impulses and appetites but also to efforts and volitions. Indeed, desires give us the determination to act. But as the Dutch philosopher himself pointed out, desires come in different forms.

When I say that coaches should help people clarify what they desire, I refer specifically to authentic desires that ultimately foster joy and reduce pain when satisfied. These can legitimately serve as special guides.

Simply stated, you will begin by asking questions such as the following:

- What makes you happy?
- What do you enjoy?
- What do you love?
- What is *truly* important to you?

I usually invite coachees to jot down the answers to those questions in their learning journal.

I differentiate between sources of motivation and values. If I use Transactional Analysis vocabulary (see Appendix 1), I explain that sources of motivation relate to the Child, while values refer to the Parent. In other words, sources of motivation have to do with a spontaneous emotion (What brings you happiness, joy, love?), whereas values represent ideals (What is truly important?).

Sometimes I review questions in the "Timeline" exercise (see chapter 5). The time perspective is important because if one simply focuses on the here and now (present orientation), he may miss the impulse emanating from a long-term life project (future orientation).

As I indicated in chapter 1, desires are essential because they house energy and passion. Remember the difference between *wanting* to do something and *having* to do something. As André Comte-Sponville once said, "When love is present, one does not have to worry about duty."

As a coach, I try to help people do more of what they desire and less of what they only do because they have to. Cheryl Richardson, coach and author of *Take Time for Your Life*, calls this "extreme self-care." It should not be confused with selfishness. Coaches must take care of themselves if they want to effectively and lastingly serve people. In the process, they will foster joy for themselves and for others.[4]

In the case of a team, let me mention again that I believe you can best serve the overall team to the extent to which you are able to serve each member individually. Genuine commitment is found when team and individual objectives intersect. This creates a congruence or resonance, which is the basis of true synergy. The intersection is the basis or driver for a common project, vision, and mission. We know there will be a lot of energy to pursue this common agenda because, by definition, this is what team members all truly desire. This is where unity can form and counteract forces that polarize the team. As a coach, you will want to spend time with each team member in a confidential, one-on-one manner to obtain, among other things, a feel for those desires and for areas of potential synergy before working with the team as a whole.

The reality of coaching is complex. Should coaches help people realize all their desires? I indicated that coaches help people be true to themselves and achieve authentic desires. Authentic desires should fundamentally serve coachees and their stakeholders. Desires that would imply, for example, crime or damaging drug addiction do not qualify.

Even the desire to win needs to be balanced with the desire to live. If one is so obsessed with the destination (winning), he may forget to enjoy the journey, playing his part, improving, and doing the best possible.

Moreover, in some cultures, like the Buddhist culture, growth involves *not* desiring. You may be attracted to a beautiful woman, desire to seduce her and make love to her. But giving in to your impulses, apart from moral considerations influenced by culture, may jeopardize a happy marriage and may not be worth it. Learning to be happy by enjoying what you have, rather than being miserable longing for what you don't have, could be a good recipe for happiness. Alternatively, you could work to make new goals and dreams happen (driven by a desire for something you want and don't have yet), while at the same time enjoying what you already have (driven by a desire for something you have already). In reality, desiring not to desire is also a desire! Spinoza's affirmation that desire is the very essence of man has universal validity. You as a coach can provide invaluable help clarifying and prioritizing desires. You can help coachees to find synergies (several desires aligned, which reinforce each other as drivers) and to make tradeoff choices between desires (in the case of polarized and competing desires).

Strengths and Weaknesses

The assessment also involves identifying the qualities, competencies, or skills necessary to succeed. Once the list is established, it is a matter of identifying coachees' strengths and weaknesses.

For example, leadership development may be the primary focus of executive coaching. Your organization may have established a list of leadership competencies, as IBM and Unilever have done (see chapter 1).

I tell coachees they will benefit from feedback given by others, either directly or through a 360-degree feedback instrument (review chapter 8 for guidelines on how to exchange feedback). I emphasize that they will need to own the assessment. Colleagues may tell a coachee that they don't see him as being original and farsighted. Once he has understood their perception and the situations that have led them to that impression, his goal is to reflect on the following: (1) Do I agree or not? (2) What do I need to do differently (if anything)? For example, your coachee may conclude that he is original but simply needs to share his creative thoughts more with others.

Goran Ivanisevic received a wild card to play in the 2001 Wimbledon tennis tournament. Coming into the championship, he was ranked 125th in the world. Coincidentally, the bets were also a mere 1 to 125 that he would win the title. People simply did not believe he had the capacity to claim a grand slam victory. Goran was good for the jester role, with memorable dialogues between his good, bad, and third self. However, he believed in his talent and ended up winning. Any 360-degree feedback undertaken before the event would not have shown Ivanisevic's true strength.

But in the case of leadership, 360-degree feedback is usually beneficial.[5] Our observers cannot possibly really know us objectively, but for practical purposes it does not actually matter. Indeed people act toward us based not on who we are but on the *perceptions* they have of us. If they find us friendly, they are more likely be at ease in our presence.

Perceptions depend on the observer's filters. For example, someone can see people as manipulative while someone else may assume positive intentions. In addition, perceptions are typically created through certain events. For example, you may have lost your temper once, so the person in your presence at that time may continue to think of you as a generally aggressive person based on that one instance. The important point is that perceptions are reality. More accurately, the perceptions others have of you constitute the external reality you need to be aware of before you can effectively set developmental goals.

I advise coachees to contrast those external perceptions with the impressions they have of themselves. This analysis may help in refining their assessment of personal strengths and weaknesses.

Research suggests that the most effective leaders are self-aware,[6] which tends to be the case when the perceptions of others are aligned with the leaders' own perceptions. On the other hand, if one often overestimates oneself, this may be a sign of self-confidence, but it may also reveal blind spots. Your coachee may be fooling himself, thinking he is doing a fine job at empowering people while his staff complain about his difficulty letting go of control. If coachees tend to underestimate themselves, it may be that they have overly high standards, which they can never live up to, resulting in a lack of self-confidence. When I coach someone, I always have to be subtle and careful when interpreting 360-degree feedback. I conduct the feedback session in the form of a dialogue—after all, the coachee is the best expert on himself. In any event, there is a high value in contrasting external and internal perceptions to develop a more accurate assessment of strengths and weaknesses.

The remark also applies to teams and organizations: systematically soliciting external feedback will generate a more valid assessment, which eventually needs to be owned by the coachees. They can obtain feedback using standard team surveys, climate surveys, and client evaluations. With standard surveys, you and your coachees obviously avoid the need to design them and can furthermore benefit from benchmark comparisons with normative samples. With your help, your coachees can also develop their own tailor-made versions.

Present Situation

Coaching applies to your coachee's concrete situation. This is what he has to deal with at the present time. It is his starting point for moving forward. Therefore ask, "What are your successes?" "What are your challenges?" "What is satisfying?" "What is frustrating?"

You notice that I am getting at what *is*, not what *should be*. The person you are coaching may have the "perfect" job and "should" therefore be happy, but that is not how it works. Encourage him to acknowledge his feelings. The job may seem wonderful but he may hate it, or it could appear insignificant but he may love it.

You can also ask your coachee to connect his present situation with a list of desires: "To what extent are you honoring your sources of motivation and your values?"

Linking the present situation with strengths and weaknesses yields other key questions: "How much do you utilize your strengths?" "What talents do you currently underutilize?" "What weaknesses, left unmanaged, are contributing to your frustration?"

Preferences

Understanding preferences, both psychological preferences and cultural orientations, sheds lights on the other parts of the assessment. Again, this is true whether the coachee is an individual, a team, or an entire organization.

The most popular instrument today to measure psychological preferences is the Myers-Briggs Type Indicator (MBTI), based on Carl Jung's psychological types. A personality type is characterized by a certain set of preferences[7] (see table on page 204), for example, ENFP (Extraversion, Intuition, Feeling, Perceiving). There are four dimensions, sixteen possible combinations, hence sixteen personality types.

Energising	Extraversion Preference for drawing energy from the outside world of people, activities, or things	Introversion Preference for drawing energy from the internal world of ideas, emotions, or impressions
Attending	Sensing Preference for taking in information through the five senses and noticing what is actual	Intuition Preference for taking in information through a "sixth sense" and noticing what might be
Deciding	Thinking Preference for organising and structuring information to decide in a logical, objective way	Feeling Preference for organising and structuring information to decide in a personal, values-oriented way
Living	Judging Preference for living a planned and organised life	Perceiving Preference for living a spontaneous and flexible life

One application of MBTI is problem solving. Confronted with a problem, people with an intuitive preference (Intuitors) tend to have a hunch about the solution. More importantly, they will tend to trust their intuition. A posteriori, they will search for facts and evidence to support their idea and develop a case for it.

People with a sensing preference (Sensors) may also intuit a solution, but typically, they will not readily trust it. They tend to approach the problem logically and sequentially: gathering facts, applying logical reasoning, and devising a solution. If it does not work, Sensors will go back to the facts, which they see as the basics they can trust.

These differences can generate frustration and misunderstanding. Sensors may view Intuitors as lacking rigor, as dreamers presenting bizarre ideas without substantiating them with facts. Intuitors may consider Sensors as slow to see new possibilities and as lacking imagination. Through coaching, people can learn to see the positive contribution each personality type can bring. Intuitors may naturally come up with the innovative ideas and original thinking necessary to create constructive *revolutions*. Sensors can naturally provide the thorough research, the reality checks, and the pragmatism necessary to succeed. They bring the positive *evolutions*.

The MBTI gives an indication about preferences but *not about abilities*. Interpreting his MBTI profile with the assessment of strengths and weaknesses will give the person you coach information about both the preferences and

Myers-Briggs and Problem Solving
Intuitors versus Sensors

Typical Process

Intuitors

1. ⎯⎯⎯⎯⎯⎯⎯→   ⟩⟨

    have a hunch   Solution
    about a solution

2.   X
    X   X   gather facts and
    X   X   evidence to support
        X   the hunch
    data

Sensors

1. X X
    X X X   gather facts and data
    X X X
    X X
    data

2. ⎯→ ⎯→ ⎯→ ⎯→   ⟩⟨

    analyze facts and data logically and   Solution
    sequentially to reach a solution

If Typical Process Does Not Work

Intuitors

1. trust their intuition

2. search for other facts and evidence
   to support their intuition

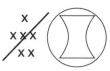

Sensors

1. discard the solution

2. start over, going back to the facts
   and using logical analysis

the abilities. For example, if he has a Sensing preference, he can develop a better appreciation for the feedback he may receive from Intuitors. By their standards, he may not be seen as an innovator. And likewise, if he prefers Intuition, it will be less surprising to him when Sensors do not view him as being quite as thorough as they expect. On the other hand, preferences are, as I just said, different from abilities. And it could be that even with a Sensing preference, your coachee is perceived as being capable of thinking intuitively. If this is the case, it means that he has demonstrated an ability to venture outside his comfort zone (see chapter 2).

Preferences also connect with desires: an Extravert is more likely to enjoy being with lots of people, and an Introvert will prefer solitude or the company of a few friends. Becoming aware of one's preferences illuminates the nature of one's desires. For example, a person may be very at ease with people but still long for quiet moments. Maybe that person did not realize he had an Introvert preference and had learned to behave like an Extravert over the years. The awareness allows him to legitimize the need to make space for some solitude, enabling him to recharge his batteries.

Sensing, Intuition, Thinking, and Feeling represent the four psychic functions. The concept of preference refers to those functions more readily available consciously, whereas the other functions are more unconsciously used. For example, if a person has a Thinking preference, he will naturally make decisions based on what is reasonable and logical. Under stress, however, when this detachment does not seem to work, he may suddenly become overly emotional, letting the Feeling part in him take over in an uncontrolled manner.

Carl Jung described the individuation principle[8] as the "ego," the conscious part of the personality, needing to meet the "shadow," its unconscious center, in order to become whole and let the "self" emerge. While a person cannot hope to render conscious everything that is unconscious, that person can at least become aware of his least preferred functions and make an effort to access and develop that potential.

The self is the completed form of the ego. It represents *unity* achieved when you have synthesized, in particular, differences between your various functions (conscious and unconscious). This concept of unity, at a *psychological level*, could be compared to unity achieved at a *cultural level* by leveraging cultural differences (see chapter 2).

Practically, awareness is the first step for developing ability: if a person knows that he tends to solve problems in a sensing fashion, he may practice approaching them intuitively. It will take effort, but nothing prevents him from tapping into both Sensing and Intuition. In this case, one's "individuation" progresses: "So much darkness is brought to light that, on one hand, the entire personality is lightened up, and on the other hand, the conscious part, inevitably, gains in scale and depth."[9]

Many other models and instruments exist to identify psychological preferences, for example, referring to Transactional Analysis, an "egogram" can be built: a percentage is attributed to each subego state, representing the relative amount of energy devoted to each. In other words, a person may realize that he often behaves as a Normative Parent but doesn't rely much on his Spontaneous Child. As a result, the Normative Parent "muscle" is well developed but the Spontaneous Child has atrophied.

The Fundamental Interpersonal Relations Orientation-Behavior (FIRO-B)[10] is particularly useful. This instrument explores three critical areas related to interpersonal relationships: Inclusion (social interactions), Control (taking the lead, making decisions, empowering), and Affection (personal relationships, openness).

What is new in this coaching assessment is that you will also help your coachee examine cultural orientations. Referring to Part II, you are now in a position to help him determine both his cultural orientations and his abilities. Invite your coachee to complete the "Cultural Orientations Framework Worksheet" in chapter 3 (pages 62–64).

The cultural perspective illuminates reality in an alternative way. As I have shown, behavior is often a cultural manifestation. For example, let us pretend that the leader you are coaching has received feedback that he is too direct. Realizing that his orientation is toward direct communication will help him recognize and apply feedback that emanates from a culturally indirect source. Your coachee may conclude in his assessment that he has a weakness—being able to communicate indirectly. The good news is that he now has a strategy to overcome that weakness: learning lessons and practices from indirect cultures.

When you work with cross-cultural teams or facilitate a merger between companies, adding the cultural dimension in the assessment may well turn out to be a critical success factor. You will be able to point out interesting patterns and fruitful connections for the team or group you are coaching. Having a clear picture yourself will certainly help your group to articulate effective target objectives and to identify ways to progress toward meeting those objectives.

Others' Expectations

The stakeholders are, in a general sense, clients. These are the people your coachee serves: direct reports, superiors and colleagues, external clients, partners, and shareholders.

As I indicated, the self-assessment should include their expectations both in terms of performance and competencies. If the stakeholders' viewpoints are missing, your coachee will need to put in place the mechanisms that allow him to collect information: surveys and conversations. It is a good idea in particular to invite your coachee to schedule a meeting with his boss and direct reports to gather their expectations and feedback.

Family and friends are often not part of the equation if your coaching is performed in the work environment. You need to be sure, though, that they are brought into the picture, in the spirit of honoring both the being and doing orientations. Encourage your coachee to invite his spouse to dinner and ask for reasons for current happiness and for what he could do to make the relationship even more fulfilling.

If you think about it, the person you are coaching probably deserves much of his success. Hard work, perseverance, and courage may be the reason he is where he is today. But to be honest, good fortune was probably a factor too. He may enjoy living in peace in a democratic country. Had he been born a few centuries or decades ago, he would have had to fight for that privilege. Many people in the world today are not in this privileged position. They must exert all of their energy and creativity to find food, escape terror, or fight dictatorship. At a more personal level, journeys are rarely a linear progression. Your coachee may have gone through difficult times, and perhaps, when he was in a rut, somebody lent a helping hand. That person believed in him, listened, or gave valued advice. In chapter 4, we discussed the need to supplement control with humility. Adopting the latter perspective could inspire your coachee to give something back to his immediate community and also to the world at large. People who need help the most may be far away.

Again, the goal is not to make everyone happy. Who can do that? But it is worth helping the person you are coaching to develop a clear picture of other people's expectations. Later on, he will identify ways to leverage different expectations: serving others while serving himself. Sometimes tradeoff choices will be required: favoring an important work project, giving family a greater place, or engaging in the community. Finally, invite your coachee to give himself permission to be healthily selfish, too. By taking great care of himself, he will be able to sustain the ability to give to others.

Chapter 12
Articulate Objectives with the Global Scorecard

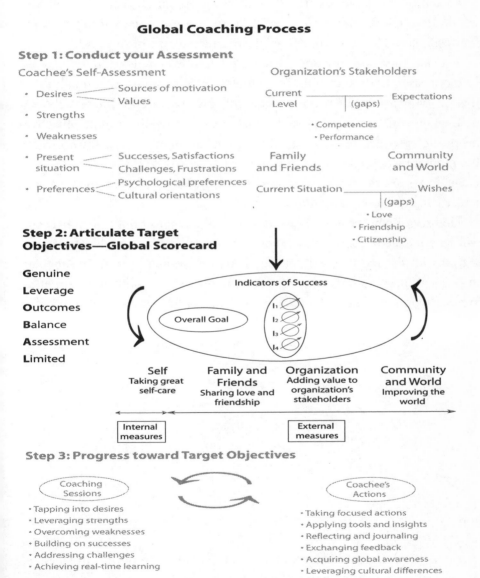

Global Coaching Process

Step 1: Conduct your Assessment

Coachee's Self-Assessment

* Desires ——— Sources of motivation
              Values
* Strengths
* Weaknesses
* Present ——— Successes, Satisfactions
  situation ——— Challenges, Frustrations
* Preferences ——— Psychological preferences
              Cultural orientations

Organization's Stakeholders

Current ——————— Expectations
Level   (gaps)

          • Competencies
          • Performance

Family   Community
and Friends   and World

Current Situation ——————— Wishes
                    (gaps)
          • Love
          • Friendship
          • Citizenship

**Step 2: Articulate Target
Objectives—Global Scorecard**

Genuine
Leverage
Outcomes
Balance
Assessment
Limited

Indicators of Success

Overall Goal

I₁
I₂
I₃
I₄

Self   Family and   Organization   Community
Taking great   Friends   Adding value to   and World
self-care   Sharing love and   organization's   Improving the
                      friendship   stakeholders   world

Internal   External
measures   measures

Step 3: Progress toward Target Objectives

Coaching
Sessions

• Tapping into desires
• Leveraging strengths
• Overcoming weaknesses
• Building on successes
• Addressing challenges
• Achieving real-time learning

Coachee's
Actions

• Taking focused actions
• Applying tools and insights
• Reflecting and journaling
• Exchanging feedback
• Acquiring global awareness
• Leveraging cultural differences

I start this chapter with advice I have given you before, but its importance in your own process of becoming a global coach cannot be overemphasized. So it is that I challenge you, the coach, to put yourself in the coachee's position as you work through this chapter. Hence, I address you as the coachee, the learner.

By now, you are ready to advance on your journey. The obvious question is "Where am I heading?" Indeed, "If you don't know where you are going, you'll probably end up somewhere else."[1]

Coaching, by definition, is goal and results oriented. So at the onset, you will have to ask yourself, "How will I know in a year (or whatever my time frame is) that I have succeeded? What will my measure of success be?"

For sure there are situations that are inherently complex and ambiguous. In those cases there is no point in prematurely determining a thorough list of specific objectives. The precision will only give you a false illusion about a destination you cannot yet possibly visualize. You need to let those objectives become clearer, let them emerge during the coaching process. You will seize the moment when closure can be reached on adequate measures of success. Coaching is an art. You have to use your intuition and your judgment on a journey that is rarely straightforward.

However, in most cases it is possible to establish early on the objectives you will set out to achieve. It will take effort and discipline. The tendency is to just get on with the journey, without clarifying the desired outcomes. Articulating target objectives helps provide focus, rigor, and discipline to the process. While discipline is important for focus and implies closure, flexibility and open-endedness are necessary for radical change and a journey in uncharted territory.[2] Your journey will consist of a progression toward these targets.

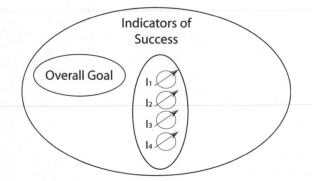

Metaphorically, you determine the overall destination of the airplane and devise a tailored instrument panel with select indicators that will help monitor progress and pilot the plane. It may even be useful to weight each indicator of success in terms of its relative importance for overall success. Nevertheless, the targets may change or evolve along the way.

In this chapter, I will challenge you to adopt a global perspective. A global perspective refers to the *what* and the *how* questions: What are the objectives that could truly indicate that you are achieving global success? How could you go about determining these objectives? First, to address the "what" question, I have developed a new framework, called the Global Scorecard, for devising appropriate measures of global success. Second, regarding the "how" question, I propose the "GLOBAL" acronym, which captures six goal-setting principles for global coaches. As you learn about the Global Scorecard, I invite you to jot down possible objectives you may consider for your own journey. Let yourself freely explore the various possibilities. This is a time for divergence. You don't need to make any commitment yet. Then, once you read about the GLOBAL acronym, I suggest you move to convergence, that is, you reach closure by articulating appropriate target objectives (see chapter 10 for a review of divergent and convergent thinking).

I also encourage you to use these tools as you lead and coach individuals, teams, and organizations.

The Global Scorecard

The Global Scorecard is a tool designed to facilitate the goal-setting process. It includes two types of objectives: the projected outcomes and the drivers of success. Profit, for example, can be viewed as the ultimate outcome, and employee satisfaction as an enabler. Alternatively, profit may be the driver and employee satisfaction the desired outcome. Means or end, any important objective should be part of your Global Scorecard. As Robert Kaplan and David Norton point out in *The Balanced Scorecard*, in France "Companies have developed and used for more than two decades the *Tableau de Bord*, a dashboard of key indicators of organizational success. The Tableau de Bord is designed to help employees "pilot" the organization by identifying key success factors."[3] The Global Scorecard goes beyond the scope of the traditional Tableau de Bord. It uses its visual dashboard representation but applies it to more categories of objectives to form a truly global picture.

The Global Scorecard

Devising appropriate measures of global success (drivers and outcomes)

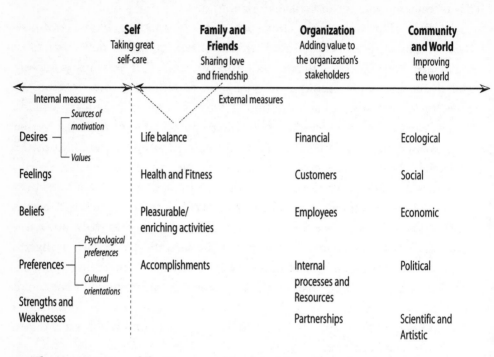

The perspective of the Scorecard is global in at least three ways: it serves a broad variety of stakeholders, it integrates external and internal realities, and it evokes the concepts of wholeness and unity.

1. Serving a broad variety of stakeholders

    First, the Global Scorecard encompasses four interconnected categories, which, together, allow you to adopt a global view. These categories represent different areas of responsibility, people you want to take care of, and various stakeholders you have to serve.

    - Self: Taking great self-care
    - Family and Friends: Sharing love and friendship
    - Organization: Adding value to your organization's stakeholders
    - Community and World: Improving the world

    Traditional coaching tends to favor certain categories. Personal coaching has typically emphasized the self, while executive coaching has concentrated on the organization. For sure, even traditional coaching has devoted some of its attention to the other areas, but certainly not in the systematic fashion described in this chapter. The synergy that can be achieved when you consider these four stakeholder categories globally is truly remarkable. After a short summary of the four categories, I will address each of these stakeholders in depth. I will summarize the case researchers have begun to make, which illustrates, for example, how improving the world (particularly through sustainable development or corporate citizenship) positively affects the organization's bottom line.

I do not intend to reinvent the wheel, however. Several institutions have developed useful sets of indicators. I will refer you to these sources, for example, the *Balanced Scorecard* and the *EFQM Model* (European Foundation for Quality Management), which represent collections of metrics primarily in the organization category, although the EFQM Model, unlike the Balanced Scorecard, has a "society results" category that clearly embraces improving-the-world targets. Two other examples I shall mention are the standards "SA8000" (Social Accountability) and "ISO 14000" (International Organization for Standardization); their norms relate to improving the world.

What has been missing is a comprehensive framework for conceptually and practically tying together previous and disparate scorecards and extending the overall scope. This is exactly what the Global Scorecard does. It allows you to set targets, which are truly indicative of both high performance and high fulfillment, in the service of the four sets of stakeholders: self, family and friends, organization, and community and world.

In my experience, the latter category is least known and considered in the goal setting of traditional coaching today, although this is changing rapidly. It represents a critical necessity and a wonderful opportunity, which is why I have chosen to devote more room to it than to the better-known categories.

2. Integrating the external and internal realities

    Second, the approach is global in that it integrates both
    external and internal realities. As the being/doing duality
    has revealed, your success is not solely measured by visible
    achievements. The gauge can also be internal, for example,
    reaching a state of happiness and serenity. Moreover,
    internal and external realities mutually reinforce each other.
    By being more serene, you can also be more productive.

3. Achieving wholeness and unity

Finally, the term *global* also evokes the concept of wholeness and unity (see chapter 2 for an explanation of the concept of unity). At the risk of sounding utopian once again, let me suggest that this ideal state represents the ultimate destination of the human journey, which may never be reached but which we can strive to approach. Externally, unity would characterize a mature society where differences are fully appreciated and leveraged. Internally, each human would make the most of his natural talents and cultural orientations. And furthermore, people would have discovered and developed alternative psychological functions and cultural orientations. Unity and peace would exist within people and be reflected outside.

Self: Taking Great Self-Care

Your life is precious and you deserve to make the most of it. Based on the assessment in chapter 11, you need to determine what success will look like for you. By extension, the Global Scorecard can also be used by groups and organizations. In this case, the "Self" category can be viewed as a set of measures attesting that the individuals making up the group or the organization are taking great care of themselves. Climate surveys and tailor-designed indexes could provide indicators of success. Aggregate profiles of instruments measuring psychological preferences (such as the MBTI) or cultural orientations (such as the COI) and aggregate 360-degree feedback profiles (see chapter 11) offer vehicles for team coaches and leaders to use the Global Scorecard with their teams and organizations.

Again, a goal is to look for synergy, for opportunities to serve other people. But it is important to articulate what is right for you as well. Remember, you don't need to share your Global Scorecard with anyone. Your coach (only if you want to) is an exception, and he will keep the information strictly confidential. In any case, the contract is only with you. You need to be true to your desires.

The subcategories in the Self section closely match those already explored in the assessment. The contents, however, need to be articulated in the form of specific targets. For example, in the *desires* subcategory, your assessment may reveal that one of your values is creativity. In the goal-setting step, one objective could be that your work involves more creativity. Your impression today is that there is 20 percent creativity and your objective is 60 percent by the end of the year. This is an internal and subjective measure. Yet, your own perception of whether your desires are being met is important. To render the measurement more accurate, ask yourself, "What does 20 percent represent and what would 60 percent look like?" This could trigger external objectives, formulated, for example, in terms of time devoted to certain creative projects.

Based on your assessment, you may set specific targets in the *preferences* subcategory. However, in general your objectives will relate to abilities, not to the preferences themselves. For example, if you are an Extravert, the goal is not to become an Introvert but to make productive use of your less-preferred introverted side. You could, for instance, engage in meditation, save time for some solitude, start a learning journal, and so on.

Cultural orientations can be treated here like psychological preferences, with a nuance. Since culture is a process and not a given (unlike psychological preferences), your objective could also be to shift your orientations altogether, for example choosing to view time as a plentiful rather than as a scarce resource. These changes will typically be in the form of new values and new beliefs, hence the *values* and *beliefs* subcategories.

Incidentally, you may notice overlaps between the subcategories. A value, for example, could be a desire and a preference. Furthermore, values and beliefs can sometimes be psychological rather than cultural manifestations. These considerations do not matter practically for goal setting. Indeed, the main point when you set your objectives is to keep sight of various interrelated aspects of the inner reality.

The *strengths and weaknesses* subcategory could be measured by 360-degree feedback: the measure here integrates the scores from your observers and your own scores. In fact, the targets should represent your projected self-perception once you have received feedback from other people. In other words, you are invited to consider their view, but in the Self category, you are ultimately in charge of evaluating the progress you have made. Because the Global Scorecard is confidential, there is no temptation to distort the figures and paint a rosier picture than the reality.

One of the most important aspects of the Global Scorecard is that it includes people's inner reality. The internal world has been traditionally neglected by business consultants who are habitually more at ease with finance, IT, marketing, and strategy than with psychology and spirituality. The inner reality is nevertheless essential for personal as well as business success.

For example, a senior business executive I coached expressed the belief that success is ephemeral but problems are lasting. This belief had constructively helped him to stretch himself, set new goals, and never indulge in complacent passivity. On the other hand, he realized that this belief led him to not enjoy or celebrate success. The coaching process gave him an opportunity to understand how this prevented him from feeling serene and happy and to experience stress and frustration instead. He saw how his belief also hindered his effectiveness. By failing to celebrate the unit's success, he did not seize opportunities to market its remarkable achievements vis-à-vis top management.

As a result, he did not attract the investments and projects his unit could have been entitled to, which would have also been beneficial for the entire organization. Interestingly, this marketing specialist would not have imagined relying on quality products and services alone, without sophisticated marketing, to persuade potential clients. Yet, until our coaching together, he had held the belief that his achievements should speak for themselves. Moreover, his belief had proven to be effective in the past, as he had earned recognition and had received several promotions without ever "selling" personal victories to management. Changing old beliefs that had helped him to an enviable senior position was not easy. But he decided to set new beliefs as objectives. These ended up constituting key drivers to his success, measured both in terms of feelings (feeling serene and happy rather than stressed-out and uneasy) and of business success. After a few months, the intellectual conjectures, "Success can last" and "It is all right and useful to celebrate accomplishments," had sunk in emotionally and turned into real convictions. Day after day, the new beliefs had a positive impact that further reinforced them, creating a virtuous circle.

Because of their crucial role in situations like these, "beliefs" and "feelings" are part of the Global Scorecard. The targets of these internal-world drivers and outcomes lie outside the domain covered by traditional scorecards such as the Balanced Scorecard.

The "external measures" in the Self category include life balance, health, pleasurable activities, and accomplishments.

Life balance no longer refers to your subjective impression but to observable criteria. These indicators will typically come in the form of time measures, for example how much time you plan to spend on specific activities that make you happy. You will need to be precise so that you can regularly check your progression toward the target. Bear in mind that the quality of time is a subjective measure and belongs to the internal subcategories (e.g., sources of motivation). For example, one executive confided to me that he really enjoyed the moments with his family; he did not have the quantity but certainly had the quality. The intensity replaced the abundance, and this was adequate to make every family member feel happy. His colleagues were not aware of his experience and, watching him put in long work hours, wrongly assumed he did not have proper "life balance."

Health and fitness is critical, too. The Romans used to say, "*Mens sana in corpore sano*" (Healthy mind, healthy body). Your well-being and your performance are dependent on your health and fitness. You may decide to conduct a health and fitness assessment and set specific targets accordingly. Doctors, nutritionists, and physical coaches or trainers can help you determine objectives: cholesterol level, blood pressure, body-fat percentage, resistance, endurance, and so on. If you smoke, your objective could be to stop smoking. As the Chinese suggest, you can be the richest man, but without health your wealth amounts to nothing. Hopefully, you won't turn the pursuit of health and fitness into an ascetic obsession (unless it is your desire to do so!). You can still enjoy food while adopting healthy eating habits. Occasional deviations from the "ideal" diet should please your taste buds without damaging your body. Exercise can be a lot of fun. Choose a sport you like and engage in it with family and friends.

Pleasurable and enriching activities are those that make you happy and stimulate you. You may have listed them in the "timeline" exercise and in your assessment; these are the ones you will want to pursue. For example, in the Baxter Renal UK team, members found out about colleagues who enjoyed practicing various martial arts, were unexpected fans of football teams, and liked car racing. Some fancied activities in service of others: coaching sports teams for underprivileged children, assisting the people of Turkey after a recent earthquake, or acting as a guide for blind skiers. The objectives in this subcategory are formulated in terms of time devoted rather than in achievements. Making room for these activities is in fact your purpose here.

Accomplishments, on the other hand, represent your projected achievements. For example, perhaps you really want to improve certain aspects of your leadership skills. The perceptions of others in a 360-degree feedback assessment could be the measure here. The target could also be, for example, having written the book you always wanted to write, having started the company you dreamed of, or having secured the job you were shooting for. Accomplishments may relate to hobbies: improving your golf handicap, winning an amateur football competition, or having your paintings displayed in an art gallery.

Taking great self-care does not exclude taking care of other people. In fact, you can often take great self-care *while* you share love and friendship. This brings us to the second category in the Global Scorecard, family and friends.

Family and Friends: Sharing Love and Friendship

Family and friends are usually the people who matter to us the most, but this is not necessarily reflected in our lifestyle. Work is often the priority. To the question, "What would you do if you only had one year to live?" I invariably hear managers dreaming about sailing around the world with their spouse and children. Yet, in their real life, the sad truth is that they do not spend nearly as much time as they would like with the people dearest to them.

In Western society, the family structure has been evolving: blended families, recomposed families, not to mention more single people. In the Family and Friends category, the structure and composition don't matter. What counts is that you set objectives that reflect your life priorities, and this usually includes the people important to you. If you realize you don't have special people to share love and friendship with (possibly as a consequence of submersing yourself in work), your objective may well be to create those intimate and social connections.

The subcategories here are identical to the ones in the external Self category. This does not mean that the actual objectives are the same. For example, you will have your own pleasurable/enriching activities as well as some with members of your family or friends. You can schedule regular restaurant dates with your spouse, golf games with your friends, and time to read an enjoyable book or take a walk alone.

The important point is that work and life have often been viewed as competing priorities: a gain in one area means a loss in the other. The best you could hope for was to make tradeoff choices, trying to achieve some balance. The *Harvard Business Review* article "Work and Life: The End of the Zero-Sum Game" offers research results that corroborate my own experience and make the case for an alternative approach: leveraging work and life priorities.[4]

In the traditional perspective, managers decide how their employees' work and personal lives should intersect and often view work-life programs as just so much social welfare. A new breed of managers, however, is trying a new tack, one in which managers and employees collaborate to achieve work and personal objectives to everyone's benefit.

These managers are guided by three principles. The first is to clearly inform their employees about business priorities and to encourage them to be just as clear about personal priorities. The second is to recognize and support their employees as whole people, not only acknowledging but also celebrating their roles outside the office. The third is to continually experiment with the way work gets done, looking for approaches that enhance the organization's performance and allow employees to pursue personal goals.

The managers who are acting on these principles have discovered that conflicts between work and personal priorities can actually be catalysts for identifying inefficiencies at the workplace. For example, one manager and his staff found a way to accommodate the increased workload at their 24-hour-a-day command center while granting the staff more concentrated time off.[5]

Ask yourself a few questions about leveraging your work and your personal time. Do you consider that a job necessarily needs to be performed between 9:00 A.M. and 5:00 P.M., or are you open to considering flexible and creative arrangements as long as the business objectives are achieved? What about doing some work from home using telecommunication tools such as e-mail, voice mail and teleconferencing? What about considering job sharing and part-time schedules? At the end of the day, what matters is not the time you have spent working but the value you have added to your organization. When you are also committed to your family and friends, you have to find new solutions to increase productivity. Of course, you need to develop an "OK–OK" mindset characterized by mutual trust to make nontraditional approaches work.

This being said, it helps when organizations and governments are committed to developing policies that make it possible to have it all, career and family life. Sylvia Ann Hewlett's research[6] shows that there is still a long way to go, particularly in the United States, to counteract job pressures (e.g., comments like "If she is not prepared to work the client's hours, she has no business being in the profession"). But Hewlett indicates how effective work-life policies can and do ultimately benefit employees and their organizations alike.

Organization: Adding Value to the Organization's Stakeholders

For leaders and executive coaches, organization is the prime category. Coaching efforts may contribute to other areas, but at the end of the day, the coaching investment can only be sustained if it serves the organization by adding value to its stakeholders.

The indicators in the organization category can be divided into five subcategories: financial, customers, employees, internal processes and resources, and partnerships. The organization's vision and mission provide the general direction. Its strategy stresses the sources of competitive advantage, or, in other words, the chosen path to success. The vision, mission, and strategy are not measured as such. What is measured is their effective implementation in service of various stakeholders: customers, employees, shareholders, and other partners.

Serving multiple stakeholders at once is ideal. For example, if you consistently provide superior service, worthy of a premium price in your customers' view, you will encourage customer loyalty and bring in positive cash flow. Both the customers and the shareholders will be pleased. You leverage your efforts and achieve several objectives at the same time.

Sometimes trade-off choices are inevitable: you obviously cannot pay each employee a fortune or hand out quality products to customers for free (they would really love it though!) and still make gigantic profits (shareholders deserve an incentive as well).

However, there are in my experience many missed opportunities for achieving synergy. The reason for not taking advantage of such opportunities is often a short-term financial focus. For example, by emphasizing cost cutting over value creation, organizations end up alienating customers and employees alike, fostering a vicious circle of frustration and precipitating failure. Let's take interactive Websites as an example. The rationale for proposing fully automated processes is to build cost-effective mechanisms to generate superior financial performance. But a company should only cut costs so much. Without minimum service, customers feel they don't count. If the company adds insincere rhetoric about customer service (or similarly about employees supposedly being "our main asset"), it makes matters worse by fostering resentment and alienation. Whenever they have a better alternative, these customers and employees will go elsewhere.

You need to set creative objectives, animated by the desire to serve all categories of stakeholders. This will promote a virtuous circle, where satisfied employees devote their best efforts to serving customers who enable the organization's financial success. This in turn will attract further investments for the organization's operation and development, increasing the capacity to serve customers and employees, and so on.

Finally, let me note that measurements can either be direct or indirect. For example, to determine employee satisfaction, you could consider measuring employee turnover. This variable is an indirect measure: high turnover may be the result of dissatisfaction, but it can also be a consequence of other factors. Proper direct measurements (in this case, using a climate survey[7]) are more accurate but not necessarily readily available.

Measurements may be objective or subjective. In the second set, you will find perception measures, which imply the use of surveys and indexes. Subjective measures are essential in the customers and employees subcategories. Their perceptions are indeed the reality you have to deal with.

In the next pages, you will find a definition and examples of generic objectives for each subcategory. I have tried to be concrete, yet avoid going into too much detail. For readers interested in learning more about the subject, I have given references and mentioned additional resources.

Financial: ensuring financial success. Examples of generic objectives include growth (revenues growth rates, sales growth rates in targeted markets), profitability (operating income, gross margin, return on investment, return on equity, return on assets, economic value added), cash flow, share price, dividends, meeting of budgets, and so forth.

Customers: addressing targeted customer needs with a win–win value proposition. Generic objectives might include market share, customer loyalty, customer satisfaction, customer profitability, customer acquisitions, product/service attributes, image, and reputation. Customer loyalty can be measured objectively ("duration of relationship, effective recommendations, frequency/value of orders, lifetime value, number of complaints and compliments, new and/or lost business, customer retention"[8]) and subjectively ("intention to repurchase, willingness to purchase other products and services from the organization, willingness to recommend the organization."[9])

Employees: attract, retain, develop, and harvest human talent in a win–win fashion. Examples of generic objectives include employee satisfaction, employee retention, employee productivity, competencies, and goal alignment. Employee satisfaction can be measured objectively but indirectly (retention, turnover, absenteeism, strikes) or directly but subjectively (climate survey, including such factors as "work itself, working conditions, stress-free, co-workers, diversity, supervision, top leadership, pay, benefits, job security, promotions, feedback, planning, ethics, quality, innovation, general contentment").[10]

Internal processes and Resources: building effective and efficient internal processes and securing appropriate resources (excluding human resources). Such objectives include innovation, quality (defect rates, percent returns), efficiency, cycle times, and others. Innovation or creativity can be measured, for example, by using the instrument/survey *Keys*, by Teresa Amabile and the Center for Creative Leadership. *Keys* is a direct but subjective instrument designed to assess the climate for creativity. The factors relate either to the employees subcategory or to internal processes and resources and focus on (1) "stimulants to creativity: freedom, challenging work, sufficient resources, supervisory encouragement of creativity, work group supports, organizational encouragement of creativity; and (2) obstacles to creativity: organizational impediments, workload pressure."[11]

Objective but indirect measures might include the number of patents produced yearly and the number of suggestions received by employees.

The EFQM lists the following key resources and generic objectives: "buildings, equipment and materials (defect rates, inventory turnover, utility consumption, utilization); technology (innovation rate, value of intellectual property, patents, royalties); information and knowledge (accessibility, integrity, relevance, timeliness, sharing and using of knowledge, value of intellectual capital)."[12]

Partnerships: forging mutually beneficial partnerships, providing similar or complementary products and services. In this case general objectives might include "supplier performance, supplier price, number and value added partnerships, number and value added of innovative products and services solutions generated by partners, number and value added of joint improvements with partners, recognition of partner's contribution."[13]

Partnerships can take several forms. Alliances, as compared with mergers and acquisitions, "provide a way to dip a toe in the water with minimum risk.... [They] fit the current fashion for outsourcing: a company that retreats to its core competencies needs plenty of partners to fill all the non-core roles such as [say] manufacture or distribution. And companies that want a global reach need local partners to enter foreign markets."[14]

To further explore this topic and help you devise relevant measurements in the organization category, I recommend the *Balanced Scorecard*, which provides indicators in four areas: "Financial, Customer, Internal Business Process, and Learning and Growth."[15] In the corporate world, the tool provides a systematic approach to keeping all the important organizational indicators in sight. It consists of key metrics to help managers consistently drive their business in the desired direction, implementing their business strategy.

According to Kaplan and Norton, "the scorecard outcomes and performance drivers should measure those factors that create competitive advantage and breakthroughs for an organization." This, of course, leaves Self, Family and Friends, and Community and World out of the picture, when no precise link can establish that these aspects are "vital for the success of the business unit's strategy."[16]

But from a global coaching perspective, the Balanced Scorecard or the classical Tableau de Bord can only be part of the picture. Our scope goes beyond helping to achieve business success by translating the business strategy into action or by piloting the organization to high performance. We want to invite coachees to consider how they can constructively improve their communities and the world in addition to realizing business success (see endnote[17] for more information on how the Global Scorecard can complement the commonly used Balanced Scorecard).

The EFQM Excellence Model is another useful resource. This model offers a "non-prescriptive framework based on nine criteria. Excellent results with respect to Performance, Customers, People and Society are achieved through Leadership driving Policy and Strategy, People, Partnerships and Resources, and Processes."[18]

The EFQM model recognizes multiple stakeholders as well as the organizational responsibility toward society.

Community and World: Improving the World

Have you ever reflected on the meaning of success and wondered how your actions serve your community and the world at large? Once you embark on this type of self-questioning, you may find yourself quite disheartened if you cannot see a larger purpose than business success as an end in itself. For example, one executive could no longer muster his usual high energy level. He had started to reflect on the legacy he was going to leave behind, and what he saw did not appeal to him. Suddenly, achieving record profit targets seemed futile. He came to realize that what was missing was a sense of genuine pride in doing something useful for humanity. And once he had gained this insight, he could no longer pretend, he could no more get excited solely by stretch targets and by the prospect of becoming "number one."

Following extensive research, Paul Ray and Sherry Ruth Anderson coined the term *Cultural Creatives*[19] to characterize fifty million Americans who are forming an emerging third subculture alongside the better known Moderns (the dominant culture, committed to material progress) and Traditionals (socially conservative and pious). In my experience the Cultural Creatives are becoming a force to be reckoned with and not only in the United States.

As it turns out, Cultural Creatives are very concerned about improving the world.

> Sixty-five percent say "having our work make a contribution to society" is very or extremely important. Fifty-four percent say "wanting to be involved in creating a better society" is very or extremely important....They are the people most concerned about the condition of our global ecology and the well-being of the people of the planet....Eighty-one percent of the Cultural Creatives say that they are very or extremely concerned about "problems of the global environment: global warming, destruction of rain forests, destruction of species, loss of the ozone layer." Seventy-eight percent say, "Americans need to consume a much smaller proportion of the world's resources." Seventy-three percent see "living in harmony with the Earth" as very or extremely important. And 68 percent say, "We need to develop a whole new way of life for ecological sustainability.[20]

Ray and Anderson give the example of Cultural Creatives who gave away their intellectual property on the ecological hypercar (i.e., car of the future with today's aerospace technologies, using, for example, carbon fiber materials to cut weight in half and save on fuel). They were more interested in saving the planet than in "making a bundle."

The core group of Cultural Creatives, about twenty-four million people in the United States, are also very concerned about social justice. They are interested in social action and social transformation. Interestingly, their desire for personal growth coincides with their service to others and with social activism, confirming the intuitive premises of global coaching and the Global Scorecard. In fact, Cultural Creatives have developed a habit of leveraging dualities: for them, "reality includes heart and mind, personal and public, individual and community."

In 2001, *le Guide éthique du consommateur* (*The Ethical Guide for the Consumer*) was published in France for the first time, building on the U.S. version *Shopping for a Better World*, which was born a decade earlier and sold over one million copies.

> The public is starting to open their eyes and to demand
> greater transparency in the face of new risks such as the
> BSE, the "mad cow" disease; genetically modified foods;
> chicken ridden with dioxin, beef with hormones; ecological
> catastrophes such as oil slick[s], which hit entire regions;
> and finally the risks to employment security that affect large
> parts of the population. Today we are entitled to know what
> is on our plates, what enterprises are doing to the planet, and
> how they treat their employees.[21]

The guide is written for consumers, employees, and investors. It is a tool that allows the simplest consumption act to become a vote. Traditionally, people often adopted "schizophrenic" behaviors, verbally condemning unethical corporate behaviors but forgetting those considerations at buying time, just going for the best deal. This is changing, and *le Guide éthique du consommateur* is an attempt to help consumers make educated choices. "Ethics oversight associations" are being created to determine specific criteria and to evaluate corporate ethical performance. The meaning of ethics goes beyond mere compliance with the law. It includes serious ecological and social concerns and a real commitment to making the world a better place. To date these ethics oversight associations exist in many countries throughout the world, including the United States, Canada, the United Kingdom, Germany, France, Benelux, Japan, India, Italy, and Sweden.

In 1987, *sustainable development* was defined for the first time by a panel headed by Sweden's Gro Harlem Brundland as "growth that meets our needs without compromising the ability of future generations to meet theirs." In 1992, representatives from 150 countries met to discuss their common concern for the environment at the Rio Earth Summit. In 1995, a world meeting in Copenhagen affirmed that "economic development, social development, and protecting the environment constitute interdependent elements that reinforce each other in the sustainable development process, context of our efforts to ensure a better life for all."

Many nongovernmental organizations (NGOs) also bring a constructive contribution and should be acknowledged here. Promoting ecological and social enhancements is the very mission of several international organizations such as Greenpeace, World Wildlife Fund, Médecins Sans Frontières, and Amnesty International, to cite but a few.

"Improving the world" may have previously appeared as an idealistic and somewhat naïve concern. Recent events are making it very clear that it should become a necessary pursuit. Related objectives should be incorporated in everyone's scorecard.

Interrelated objectives in the Community and World category have been grouped in five subcategories: ecological, social, economic, political, and scientific and artistic. You will find in this section examples of indicators and resources to help you explore this topic further. I would ask you to imagine more indicators moving from merely (but importantly) eliminating nuisances and abuses to proactively creating a better world.

Ecological (or Environmental): protecting natural ecosystems, preserving the earth, reducing pollutions (water, air, land, and noise), biodiversity. One resource for achieving ecological objectives is the Sustainable Reporting Guidelines,[22] which provide examples of specific indicators as well as numerous references and a reporting mechanism for organizations that are eager to engage in sustainable development. Also of value is ISO 14031, part of the ISO 14000 series,[23] which presents a standard framework for environmental management. ISO 14031 contains a number of generic environmental performance indicators designed for internal management reporting and control purposes as well as guidance on the process for indicator selection.

In 1997, Baxter Renal Division[24] became the first company division in the world to gain global ISO 14001 certification. Baxter has defined five environmental goals to be achieved before the end of the year 2005:

- Decrease hazardous air emissions by 80 percent
- Decrease hazardous waste by 35 percent
- Decrease other waste by 35 percent
- Increase energy efficiency by 10 percent
- Reduce packaging material by 20 percent

Social: enforcing human rights, improving social conditions and well-being across the globe, providing adequate food and housing to all people, combating diseases and improving health, promoting education, developing the practice of sports and leisure. In addition to the Sustainable Reporting Guidelines just cited, SA8000 is a useful reference.[25] SA8000 specifies standards for social accountability. The criteria cover nine areas: child labor, forced labor, health and safety, freedom of association and the right to collective bargaining, discrimination, disciplinary practices, compensation, and management systems (to conform to this standard and other applicable laws, continuous improvement, etc.).

Taking a broader view, outside the world of organizations, certain objectives are essential. They relate to human rights and dignity, embedded in the minimum standards of freedom, food, housing, and education. There is still a long way to go before these fundamental targets become a reality worldwide. Yet beyond promoting human rights and dignity, I also want to suggest increasing well-being. This can be achieved through achieving various objectives, for example, by making sports and leisure available for everyone.

Economic: creating economic value, funding projects through financial investments and donations, improving material standards of living for all people worldwide. A useful reference in the economic domain is, again, the Sustainable Reporting Guidelines, but more research is necessary to accurately portray the economic performance of an organization.

The Guidelines also suggest integrated indicators:

1. Systemic indicators that "link performance at the micro-level (e.g., organizational) with economic, environmental, or social conditions at the macro-level (e.g., regional, national, or global)," for example, "workplace accident or discrimination cases at the organizational level expressed in relation to regional or sectoral totals."

2. Cross-cutting indicators that "bridge information across two or [all] three elements of sustainability—economic, environmental, or social—of an organization's performance." In some instances, integrated indicators combine systemic and cross-cutting approaches. For example, expressing an organization's air emissions in relation to regional totals as well as estimates of human health effects of such emissions combines the systemic (micro/macro) with the cross-cutting (environmental/social) dimensions of integrated indicators.

Coaches cannot, of course, be experts in all these areas. A more reasonable goal is to know where resources can be found and to be able to recommend those resources during the goal-setting process. Your coachee will very often delegate the task of suggesting specific indicators of success to expert

colleagues or consultants. Nevertheless, the leader is still responsible for setting the general direction and for going beyond the traditional scorecards.
What matters is that in the end the selection of indicators represents (1) the
appropriate measure of success and (2) the destination you as coach will help
your coachees reach.

Political: developing democracies,[26] *building world peace, enabling ecological, social, and economic progress.* Many of your coachees work in organizations, but all of you are citizens who can actively contribute to achieving these
goals by promoting constructive governments, institutions, associations, and
nongovernmental organizations. Certainly, engaging in political activities is
one means of improving society. Resources in this domain are well known
and readily available.

*Scientific and Artistic: tapping into human creativity and intelligence to
promote scientific progress and its constructive applications, and also favoring culture, aesthetics, and beauty.* Scientific progress comes with its ethical dangers and dilemmas: nuclear technology and genetic engineering, to
name but two, represent double-edged swords. Still, without entering those
important debates here, I simply want to mention the promotion of arts and
science as possible goals. These activities are the expression of human creativity and potential and are worth considering for coaches whose purpose is to
help unleash human capabilities. Sciences and the arts do not always add
value directly. Fundamental research, for example, is exciting and risky; you
don't know what you will discover or how long it will take. Yet it is typically
necessary to generate the next breakthrough and to improve the world. It is
important, therefore, to remember these endeavors, and to keep them in sight
on your radar screen when setting your priorities.

The Case for Sustainable Development/Corporate Citizenship

The Bright Side

In 1997, a group of companies, which included Unilever, gathered and
formed a consortium, the theme of which was "Sustainable Strategies and
Shareholder Value." A key question emerged during the meeting: "Is there a
link between sustainable strategies and shareholder value?"

In 1998, the Consortium affirmed,

> Though the purpose of this Consortium has never been to
> provide scientific proof that such [a] link exists, we found
> much anecdotal evidence that supports this theory…

It is especially through improvements in *reputation*,
increases in *innovative* capacity, savings through *efficiency*
gains, and improved market advantage through better
awareness of stakeholders' and customers' perceptions and
needs that increased shareholder value can be realized....

The Consortium members share the view that
environmental issues will increase in importance in the
future and that it is better to anticipate and be prepared
than to eventually be *forced* into providing more sustainable
products and processes and services.[27]

The Dow Jones Indexes, together with the SAM (Sustainable Asset Management) Sustainability group, launched the following initiative in 1999:

Corporate Sustainability is a business approach, which
creates long-term shareholder value by embracing
opportunities and managing risks deriving from economic,
environmental, and social developments.

Dow Jones Sustainability Group Index (DJSGI) is
the world's first global sustainability index, tracking
the performance of the leading sustainability-driven
companies....

The DJSGI consists of more than 200 companies that
represent the top 10 percent of the leading sustainability
companies in 64 industry groups in the 36 countries covered
by the Dow Jones Global Indexes (DJGI). (Note: Baxter
and Unilever are selected industry group leaders, part of the
DJSGI.)

At the end of August 2000, the market capitalization of
the Dow Jones Sustainability Group World Index exceeded
5 trillion U.S. dollars...."[28]

John Prestbo, chief editor of the Dow Jones Indexes, noted that the supe-

Dow Jones Indexes
(Sustainability-driven Companies versus the Others)

Performance Indicators	Sustainability-driven Companies (DJSGI World Index)	Others (DJGI World Index)
ROE	14.89%/14.73%	8.43%/9.87%
ROI	11.09%/8.86%	7.37%/6.97%
ROA	5.81%/5.49%	3.63%/4.77%

Average 1st semest 2000/ 1995–1999 (DJSGI—report September 2001)

rior performance of companies integrating corporate sustainability in their business strategies is evidenced by some key financial parameters. I have represented his data in the following table:

"Should Companies Care?" writes Geoffrey Colvin in *Fortune*. He answers, "Sure, if caring brings a profit. And businesses are discovering that it pays to be concerned about society."

Colvin goes on to say,

> Companies today are doing more of what the activists want than they ever have done before, and it's not because they're being socially responsible. It's because they're listening to the markets. If it seems surprising that as the world has become more virulently capitalist, it has also become more concerned about the environment, child labor, and human rights…
>
> The fact is that today consumers care about those things more than ever. A substantial number now base buying decisions on who made their Nike shoes or where Exxon Mobil got its gasoline or what McDonald's does with its paper waste. The trend is hardly universal—plenty of people still just want the lowest price—but it's utterly clear…
>
> At least as important as consumers' caring, employees care. One trend in business is that employees, especially the best young employees, want a sense of purpose in their work. They want to know that what they do at work is good and right in some large sense. Since most companies are in a desperate war for talent, they'd better be able to make that case.
>
> Consumers care and employees care. That means equity markets care. And that means CEOs care.[29]

In his research report "Doing Good and Doing Well: Making the Business Case for Corporate Citizenship," Simon Zadek argues that the business case can be broken down into four broad, interrelated categories:

1. *Defending the Reputation (pain alleviation)*. This is mostly about avoiding potential financial losses. Monsanto (genetically modified organisms), Nike (child labor), and Shell (Brent Spar oil platform and Nigeria) were subject to media attacks on their reputation. Even if companies are not necessarily significantly affected in the short term, reputation still plays out over the long term. As it turns out, for the companies mentioned, the blows to their honor acted as wake-up calls. They went beyond taking remedial action to become proactive "corporate citizens."[30]

2. *Traditional Business Case (cost benefit).* Zadek comments,

"This generally involves specific activities where there are relatively tangible financial gains to be made. Such activities affect actual and potential employees through, for example, building greater diversity, quality of workplace, and links to home life. It also can involve targeted actions to gain specific contracts (e.g., affirmative action contracts), planning permission (e.g., for retail units), or resource management and exploitation rights (e.g., water utilities, energy, and mining operations)."

3. *Strategic Business Case.* Zadek argues,

"At this level, corporate citizenship becomes an integral element of the company's broader strategic approach to long-term business performance. There may be a fundamental shift in product and service delivery, for example, away from non-renewable resources towards renewable ones, or away from product sales to service rentals. Another example would involve investment in a wider global role for the business; for example, in public policy or the promotion of human rights and other elements of an emerging global framework for business. Such strategic dimensions of corporate citizenship cannot be easily subjected to standard financial cost–benefit analysis. They are part of a broad pattern of investments by the business that build on each other and together create potential financial gains."

4. *New Economy Business Case.* Zadek's fourth case, admittedly a subset of the third, relates to

"the capacity of the business to learn, innovate, and effectively manage risk in an increasingly dynamic and complex business environment." This means, for example, appreciating the emergence of a "Cultural Creatives" subculture and a growing concern by the population for preserving the planet and promoting social justice. The business case needs to integrate ecological and social parameters because, as should be obvious by now, these factors are moving up on the stakeholders' agendas.[31]

The Global Scorecard offers a global perspective, which encompasses all these elements. It provides in essence a framework for leaders, teams, and organizations to translate a truly global strategy into concrete objectives.

The Dark Side: Obstacles and Threats

Despite the inherent societal advantages of sustainable development and notwithstanding a business case that makes it possible to leverage business and ethical concerns, the truth is that preserving the world, let alone improving it, is often not regarded as a priority.

Let me indicate elements that unfortunately still prevent leaders and organizations from committing to sustainable development. Then I shall evoke some of the realities that make sustainable development absolutely necessary.

Greed, conflicts of interest, and lack of ethics constitute obstacles, apparent in the following example. The television report "Les grandes enquêtes: En toute légalité"[32] described the perverse system of maritime transport. Some ship owners do not perform vital repairs, they abandon crews without pay, and they register their ships in countries where safety standards are lax (legally so, unfortunately). "Classification societies" are the companies that inspect ships and deliver a certificate when they consider a ship is fit to travel. Even if many of these companies perform their duties with integrity and place safety above any other consideration, conflicts of interest still represent a danger. If a classification society is too strict, it risks losing clients, the unscrupulous ones, to more accommodating competitors.

About one-fifth of the fifty thousand ships in the world are not up to safety standards, causing repeated ecological and human catastrophes. Many organizations still use these "trash-boats," saving money and displaying false records attesting all is in accordance with regulations. The TV report followed the history and movements of the rusty ship *Reno*, duly registered, sadly, and owned by the same devious man whose boat, the *Cordigliera*, sank in 1996 with twenty-nine men on board.

Under these circumstances, the better-known oil slicks relayed by the media (e.g., the *Erika*, the *Jessica*) should not come as a surprise.

Cynicism and a lack of conscience can have dramatic consequences. But what appears to constitute evil behavior may well be the shadow side of the relentless pursuit of profit and the competitive struggle to survive and prosper, both of which characterize liberal capitalism and, at its worst, exclusive short-term orientation.

Jürgen Dunsch writes in the *International Herald Tribune*, "Shareholder value has also seen its name dragged in the mud. It has been used too often simply for short-term stock-market gains or to justify the elimination of jobs. Managers now dance to the tune of stock analysts instead of developing long-term entrepreneurial concepts."[33]

Negligence in terms of global responsibility and accountability is another obstacle to sustainable development. Isabelle Callens conducted a survey with 481 industrial enterprises in Belgium: 60 percent were passive or reactive (doing nothing or merely reacting to environmental legislation), and only 8 percent could be considered proactive (initiating actions to preserve the environment in all areas: research and development, production, marketing, suppliers, etc.).[34]

Furthermore, in the cultural sense, the feeling that things will not change may create a sense of powerlessness. The best intentions for improving the world are then repressed. Ray and Anderson indicate that in 1999, the Moderns represented 48 percent of the American population, or 93 million out of a total of about 193 million adults: "The simplest way to understand today's Moderns is to see that they are the people who accept the commercialized urban–industrial world as the obvious right way to live. They're not looking for alternatives. They're adapting to the contemporary world by assuming, rather than reasoning about, what's important, especially those values linked to economic and public life."[35]

The world news media relays the sad reality of threats that make sustainable development and an improved world even more necessary. Atrocious wars,[36] human rights abuses, and criminality still plague humanity. The gap between the rich and the poor (individuals and nations) is also a serious issue. The debt of the Third World engenders vicious circles that rich nations must help to break even if finding appropriate ways to contribute requires careful thinking.

Here is what *The Economist* had to say about the widening gulf between the rich and the poor:

> There are more rich people than ever before, including some
> 7 million millionaires, and over 400 billionaires.... As for the
> poor, the gap between them and the rich is rising, even in
> the industrialized countries, where for much of the twentieth
> century the gap had narrowed. In America, between 1979
> and 1997 the average income of the richest fifth of the

population jumped from nine times the income of the poorest fifth to around 15 times. In 1999, British income inequality reached its widest level in 40 years…. Focusing resources and policy on poverty would be worthwhile simply on humanitarian grounds. But also, the disadvantages of growing up in extreme poverty pose a challenge to a belief in equality of opportunity. And helping the underclass rejoin society is in the interests of all. The main task here is for governments to provide a proper welfare safety net; provide and protect public education in the poorest areas; provide remedial training and schooling; provide adequate incentives to help the poor get back into (or just get into) work through which they can support themselves. Yet today's many rich individuals can also play a role.[37]

While some of us are fortunate to envision living a happy and meaningful life (possibly using coaching to make that happen), others are merely striving to survive from day to day, meal to meal. Lessening poverty and hunger is not solely a question of morality or compassion. It is in everyone's best interest. Victims cannot understand or accept that people are simply indifferent to their suffering. This rancor can easily be transformed into hatred, which will inevitably backfire.

On the ecological front, the degradation of beautiful ecosystems and the necessity to preserve the Amazonian equatorial forest, the Polar Regions, and other magnificent sanctuaries is well known. Closer to many of us, though, poorly planned urbanization; destruction of green areas; unbearable noise, traffic, and air pollution decrease quality of life for all, not to mention the increased suffering among the least privileged who can't afford a comfortable home to which they can escape.

But as the International Energy Agency suggests regarding energy policies, "Liberalising power markets can make it harder to subsidise renewable energy sources, and reducing emissions from transport might involve unpopular moves such as raising fuel taxes or ending perks like company cars."[38] To surmount this type of difficulty, it seems that our mentalities need to evolve from, say, a purely capitalistic or a solely materialistic culture, to embracing multiple perspectives instead.

Leveraging Economic, Social, and Ecological Cultures

An Important Pursuit

The dominant materialistic, capitalistic culture, incarnated by the Moderns, requires a counterbalancing perspective. The point is not to condemn liberal capitalism, which has and still does foster considerable economic progress. Global coaches propose calmly considering the merits of various other views, inviting teams to leverage the traditional right (liberal capitalism),[39] the left (socialism), and ecologists (green) in order to build thriving democracies. These political views can be tied to the cultural orientations discussed in Part II, notably doing (profit), being (people), and harmony (planet). The ideals are different, respectively: economic prosperity, social justice and well-being, preserving the earth and living in harmony with nature. These preferences are not mutually exclusive and, as I argue, should be leveraged as much as possible. For corporations committed to sustainable development, the last two political preferences complement the indomitable profit to form a "triple bottom line."

The business case for sustainable development shows that reconciling and leveraging these diverse views is possible. But in order to make the triple bottom line plausible, one must be aware of one's own political cultural orientation and be ready to review it. Again, this is not about giving up your preference. It is about enriching it with other perspectives: leveraging perspectives.

The application of this three-part approach obviously goes beyond the corporate world. The goal is to help reconcile "Davos" and "Porto Alegre." The annual symposium in Davos is the rendez-vous of the world business elite. Select politicians and journalists also take part. Davos has become the symbol of a capitalistic form of globalization. The Porto Alegre symposium, which takes place during the same period in Brazil, was initiated as a reaction against the prevailing approach to globalization. A key message among the protesters is that social and environmental concerns should become essential drivers, and globalization should serve humanity as a whole. Reconciling Davos and Porto Alegre, then, means creating economic value, fostering ecological progress, enforcing human rights and dignity, and improving standards of living of all people worldwide, thus *promoting a better world*.

As a coach, you have an opportunity and, I believe, a responsibility to enhance the potential and help reduce the obstacles by suggesting the incorporation of this societal perspective of improving the world into the coachee's goal-setting. As a manager or executive, the leader you coach might aim to influence his corporation, as much as he can, to commit to sustainable development; to the fostering of a holistic economic, social, and ecological approach to business; and to proactively creating a better world. There is still a long way to go, but many constructive initiatives already exist and, as the Chinese say, every journey starts with a single step.

Examples of Two Responsible Companies

Baxter for a Greener World. On August 4, 1997, Baxter leaders adopted and signed a company environmental, health, and safety policy stipulating that Baxter will be a global leader in environmental, health, and safety (EHS) management. This is consistent with Baxter's business interests, ethics, and shared values. Specifically, Baxter commits to the following:

Sustainable Development: We will strive to conserve resources and minimize or eliminate adverse EHS effects and risks that may be associated with our products, services, and operations.

Employees: We will provide a safe and healthy workplace, striving to prevent injuries and illnesses, promoting healthy lifestyles, and encouraging respect for the environment. We will ensure that our employees have the awareness, skills, and knowledge to carry out this policy.

Compliance: We will meet all applicable EHS laws and Baxter EHS requirements, including our own EHS management standards.

Business Integration: We will integrate EHS considerations into our business activities.

Customers: We will work with our customers to help them address their EHS needs.

Suppliers and Contractors: We will work with our suppliers and contractors to enhance EHS performance.

Community and Government: We will participate in community and government EHS initiatives.

Baxter commits to continuous improvement in environmental, health, and safety performance. We will set goals, measure progress and communicate results.

Compliance with this policy is the responsibility of every employee.[40]

The Thetford manufacturing plant in Norfolk, United Kingdom, exemplifies leveraging environmental and business performance.

In the 1990–1999 period, on a per unit of production basis, the following reductions occurred: electricity by 58 percent, gas by 54 percent, water by 65 percent, landfill waste (1994–1999) by 36 percent, hazardous waste by 56 percent. At the same time production was increased by 30 percent. Our success is built on the commitment of our employees, who strive to maintain and improve a safe and healthy workplace, whilst producing quality products and minimizing our impact on the environment.

Among many other facts, Baxter was also able to report the following achievements:

- During 1997 Baxter recycled 16,000 tons of plastic packaging. This represents 2,300 trucks full of oil!
- Baxter's achievements also had a positive impact on global warming: 50,000 tons of CO_2 not added to the atmosphere.
- During 1997 Baxter recycled 5,800 tons of paper and cardboard, which saved just over 80,000 trees! Through photosynthesis, 80,000 trees, over their lifetime, will remove approximately 70,000 tons of CO_2 from the atmosphere.[41]

IBM: What Does It Mean to Lead? This is IBM's response in its year 2000 Annual Report:

In our business, there's technical leadership, thought leadership, financial leadership, marketplace leadership—all the things documented in this report. But any company that aspires to make a lasting contribution to the world must lead in ways that spread far beyond the confines of the marketplace, and winning, and profit. It is leadership by serving, leadership by caring, leadership in the community. It's the kind of leadership we think about when we think about the world our work will leave for our children. At IBM, it's how we apply our financial strength, resources and minds...to change things, to make our planet a better place.[42]

Here are some examples:

- Of special urgency with the rise of the Internet are protections of the individual's right to privacy. In 2000, IBM appointed its first chief privacy officer—a senior executive charged with guiding all the company's policies and practices in this area, and with working across the public and private sectors to advance protections of consumer and citizen privacy.
- IBM's largest ongoing corporate commitment remains its $45 million grant program, Reinventing Education, which has the potential to touch one in five children in U.S. public schools as well as children in seven other countries, including Singapore, site of IBM's latest grant.
- IBM is perennially among the world's most generous corporations. In 2000, it contributed more than $126 million to programs around the world that help people in need. Individual employees added another $49 million through matching grants and donations to nonprofit organizations and educational institutions. And of incalculable value was the more than 4 million hours of their time and expertise IBMers volunteered to a broad range of local causes.
- IBM's participation in voluntary initiatives to address global climate change and its latest offering to facilitate the reuse and recycling of PCs are just two examples of environmental efforts that contributed to the significant recognition the company received in 2000 for environmental excellence.[43]

The GLOBAL Goal-Setting Principles

The Global Scorecard is, as you now know, designed to help you and coachees you work with determine your/their objectives. However, it is easy to be overwhelmed: there is so much to do but only limited time and resources. How does one select appropriate objectives?

To help you answer this question, the GLOBAL acronym represents six important principles you and those you coach should take into consideration. I have already alluded to some.

Genuine	Choosing objectives you would pursue out of a mere sense
L	of obligation is not a recipe for success. Remember Spinoza's
O	notion that desire is the very essence of man. The goals you set
B	have to resonate with your desires so that you will **genuine**ly and
A	passionately want to achieve them.
L	

G
Leverage
O
B
A
L

To have maximum impact, you will want to "kill more than one bird with one stone." (I prefer the French version, *"faire d'une pierre deux coups,"* which leaves the birds alone.) In other words, you will look for opportunities to serve several stakeholders and achieve multiple objectives at once. For example, you might engage in a work project that benefits your customers, contributes positively to society, preserves ecology, and gives you satisfaction. To **leverage**, you have to consider various cultural perspectives and make the most of them through synthesis (e.g., leveraging economic, social, and ecological cultures).

G
L
Outcomes
B
A
L

You will literally project yourself into the future, trying as best you can to depict what success will look like. These **outcomes** should provide an accurate picture of where you set out to go. The objectives need to be truly indicative of both high performance and high fulfillment. Forming that image is an important step in realizing the goal. Athletes develop a mental image (visual but also auditory and kinesthetic) of their next race before actually performing it. You will devise indicators, which will represent the outcomes of your success. These metrics will also grant the ability to monitor progress.

G
L
O
Balance
A
L

It would be fantastic if we could always leverage various objectives. But in reality, you will also have to make trade-off choices. Achieving **balance** is your next best tactic when leveraging appears inaccessible. When confronted with two alternatives (target A and target B), balancing (or making a trade-off decision) means you choose (1) to adopt either A or B or (2) to compromise (i.e., adopt a part of A and a part of B). Balancing is *a zero-sum game*: more of something implies less of something else. It is a dynamic of the *or*, always a *balancing act*, associated with *scarcity* (you cannot have it all). Leveraging, by contrast, is a *positive-sum game*: more of something does not imply less of something else. In fact achieving more of A could help you achieve more of B, and vice versa, forming a virtuous circle, resulting in *synergy*. It is a dynamic of the *and*, of *abundance* (you can have it all).

This said, balancing is still often viewed both as sufficiently challenging and desirable (e.g. achieving *life balance*). If you cannot do it all at once, you may decide to favor certain organizational objectives or decide that your family will be your priority. In any event, the targets you will choose have to reflect the balance you strive for. Balance refers to the four external categories cited as well as external/internal realities (balancing external and internal criteria of success).

G
L
O
B
Assessment
L

The goal-setting process is based on a thorough **assessment** (see chapter 11). Moreover, once you have determined your indicators of success, you will assess the present value of these indicators. This will give you a point of reference. For example, your market share may be 80 percent today and the objective is to reach 90 percent in a year. Or the client satisfaction index is 60 today and has to increase by 10 percent in six months. Very often to determine the measure of success you will have to gauge the present value of the variable. This may involve significant work when a survey is necessary for the assessment.

G
L
O
B
A
Limited

You cannot do it all. Setting priorities and concentrating your efforts accordingly is a key success factor. Articulating a **limited** set of objectives will allow you to focus on and shoot for what really matters. Hopefully, you will be able to leverage various objectives, realizing solid gains while only going for a few well-chosen targets. Your main targets could well be limited to 3 to 5.

Chapter 13
Progress toward Target Objectives

Global Coaching Process

Step 1: Conduct your Assessment

Coachee's Self-Assessment

- Desires —— Sources of motivation
            —— Values
- Strengths
- Weaknesses
- Present —— Successes, Satisfactions
  situation —— Challenges, Frustrations
- Preferences —— Psychological preferences
              —— Cultural orientations

Organization's Stakeholders

Current .... Expectations
Level | (gaps)

· Competencies
· Performance

Family   Community
and Friends   and World

Current Situation _____ Wishes
                   | (gaps)

· Love
· Friendship
· Citizenship

Step 2: Articulate Target Objectives—Global Scorecard

Genuine
Leverage
Outcomes
Balance
Assessment
Limited

Indicators of Success

Overall Goal

I₁
I₂
I₃
I₄

Self
Taking great
self-care

Family and
Friends
Sharing love and
friendship

Organization
Adding value to
organization's
stakeholders

Community
and World
Improving the
world

Internal
measures

External
measures

Step 3: Progress toward Target Objectives

Coaching
Sessions

- Tapping into desires
- Leveraging strengths
- Overcoming weaknesses
- Building on successes
- Addressing challenges
- Achieving real-time learning

Coachee's
Actions

- Taking focused actions
- Applying tools and insights
- Reflecting and journaling
- Exchanging feedback
- Acquiring global awareness
- Leveraging cultural differences

Once the destination is determined, the task is to cast off into the winds and tides, adjust the sails, and put your skills and resources to work. You will circumvent some obstacles and take on others, and you will most definitely learn valuable lessons along the way.

To help others progress toward their objectives, I again invite you to first coach yourself to success by striving to achieve the objectives on the "Global Scorecard." Unfortunately, when you coach yourself, even though only you have to show up to coaching sessions, you may find you are more prone to skip sessions, letting the rigor slip. Don't give in to the temptation. If you don't hire a coach, I would recommend partnering with select friends or colleagues you trust. They will support you and help you maintain a systematic and disciplined approach.

It takes a great deal of self-awareness to be able to step back, appreciate what is going on at multiple levels, assess your progress, explore new options, decide on next actions, and muster the courage to move forward. If you have not had prior self- or team-development experience, it becomes virtually a mission impossible to leverage your full potential on your own.

Peter Leyland from Baxter Renal was one of those courageous leaders who kept his promise to team members that they would engage in a long-term coaching journey. The team retreats were never isolated feel-good events but were part of a systematic process. Insights gained were to be immediately put into practice. Excitement generated in a comfortable, secluded environment would have to stand the harsh test of business reality. Team members confided later on that the continuity of the coaching process was a key success factor. Also, Peter Leyland continued acting as a coach with his team, making my job as external coach much easier.

The coaching journey can be and often is exciting. It helps to be curious and eager to learn. But even then, the process is likely to be challenging at times. The journey requires blasting out of one's comfort zone and being willing to go backward in order to move forward, to stretch and resist the temptation to revert to old habits. This is the rite of passage to reach higher levels of performance and fulfillment.

Martin Luther King claimed he was not afraid of the constant threats on his life. Not long before he was assassinated, he declared, "The day you are afraid of dying, you stop living." Most of us, fortunately, don't have to risk our lives to pursue our journeys. Yet, we are still afraid. By playing it safe, however, we take the greater risk of ultimately losing ourselves, letting our desires remain unattainable dreams, and leaving our potential underutilized. The self-questioning, cognitive and emotional work, and disciplined practice of new competencies may be discouraging. In these moments of doubt, remind your coachees (and yourself) of their desires, their best engines for action. Cherish the journey, for it is your coachees' lives and yours as well that unfold!

Roles of the Coach

Communicator. In chapter 1, I described the coach's communication role. It is redundant to even mention this role since coaching sessions take the form of dialogues. Apart from mastering communication techniques, the coach's awareness and sense of caring enable him to actively listen, ask powerful questions, and make judicious suggestions. Moreover, as explained in chapter 9, global coaches are sensitive to various cultural communication patterns. They are able to use the differences advantageously, relying on direct and indirect communication, high-context and low-context communication, and so on.

Process Designer. A less visible coaching role is that of process designer. Coaches really add value when they devise tailored processes that significantly increase the chances of achieving individual and collective targets.

Knowing that my clients typically view time as a scarce resource, I tell them that my goal is to make sure we use their limited time in the most productive fashion. Coaches know how to create a learning experience conducive to progress, how to build an environment where talents can shine and synergies occur. Before a session, the coach will reflect on the gaps between the current situation and the desired future. He will use his experience and imagination to determine the nature and flow of experiences required to bridge the gaps. The coaching activities, as a sequence and as a whole, are carefully weighted in relation to the target objectives. No two coaching sessions will be the same, which is in sharp contrast with standard teaching programs, where the agenda is predetermined.

·The coach will anticipate reactions and be prepared to face various scenarios. In a team situation, he may also discuss some possibilities with select members. For example, I remember coaching a team whose president had a tendency to dominate. Prior to the team meeting, we discussed how this tendency would affect the team and we talked about the importance of modelling the change we wanted to promote. As a result, the president acknowledged upfront to others on the team his habit of taking control. He expressed his desire to adopt instead a style that was more empowering. He also said that if he fell back into his old ways, he would welcome feedback any time this happened. As it turned out, in the middle of a sensitive conversation during the retreat, the president could not help once again pressing his point. When he received feedback from a team member, because he was mentally prepared for constructive criticism, he had the lucidity to thank the team member. This showed he was serious about improving. His leadership encouraged other people to exchange feedback and to take responsibility for their own behaviors.

Despite the important design work that takes place before coaching sessions, the agenda produced is still framed as tentative. As the individual or group process actually unfolds, the coach is ready to take a different course and adapt to his coachees' progress. Coaches need to be constantly attuned to what is going on and will invariably need to improvise: confronting the individual or the team, reframing the purpose, proposing a different activity, etc. Designing on the spot makes coaching both difficult and exciting.

Human Generalist. Coaches must be what Frederic Hudson calls human generalists.[1] They may not have a degree in the humanities, for example in psychology or sociology, but they need to know about behavioral psychology, human growth and adult learning, leadership development, group dynamics, organizational change, and so forth. I have argued throughout this book that coaches also need to master intercultural knowledge and skills. During sessions, coaches draw from this knowledge and experience to select perspectives, tools, and techniques. They select what is likely to provide optimum possibilities for leveraging and help coachees discover new ways to address their challenges.

Business Management Generalist. Certain coaches must also be business management generalists. This is undoubtedly the case for business leaders. While this requirement may not be necessary for all professional coaches, it does apply in particular to executive coaches. Just as some coaches come into the field with advanced degrees in psychology and a background in psychotherapy, some will bring a business management degree and significant leadership experience. Professional coaches working in an organizational context must be familiar with strategy, finance, marketing, economics, and business management in general. This knowledge allows the coach to appreciate the client's perspective and to be a credible partner in the business aspects of the dialogue. It is sign of respect, too. Coaches expect their clients to learn about human dynamics; likewise, the coach must demonstrate his interest in their universe, which is business. He needs to be able to question assumptions and offer alternative perspectives to a business strategy or a marketing plan, discuss specific business objectives and progress toward those targets, and contribute something of value to the business conversation. Nonetheless, professional coaches' expertise, unlike that of business consultants, still lies primarily in human processes.

Transferer of Knowledge. In my view coaches are also responsible for transferring knowledge. Coaches don't simply help resolve coachees' issues. They actually share their knowledge so that coachees can become better coaches. For example, the coach will briefly explain his frame of reference. Beyond listening, questioning, and suggesting, the coach presents the underlying models, giving the coachee the opportunity to acquire skills for dealing autonomously with future challenges. This approach usually implies sessions that last for more than one hour.[2]

Effective Learning

Coaching benefits are twofold. On one hand, coachees can articulate and reach their objectives more effectively. Coaching sessions are focused on reaching those objectives. On the other hand, coachees enrich their "toolbox" and learn. The value is short-term and long-term.

Learning through coaching is effective for a number of reasons.

- The information received during coaching sessions is *relevant*. We are all swamped with information, but coaches strive to impart knowledge that can actually help coachees on their journey. The incentive to learn is greater when what is learned is pertinent. For example, one executive was complaining about his poor work–family life balance. I gave him a copy of "Work and Life: The End of the Zero-Sum Game,"[3] and we discussed balance. Another executive needed to understand and use politics to obtain the organizational support necessary to succeed. I handed him the article "Constructive Politics: Essential to Leadership."[4] Relevant information really speaks to the coachee because it can immediately be put to use. It resonates with his current challenges and taps into his desires: wanting more balance in the first example or more power in the second.

- Learning occurs *just in time*. Not only is the information relevant in terms of its content, but it is also delivered to address coachees' issues here and now. This makes it even more pertinent, allowing learning to take place when the curiosity and eagerness to do so are at a peak. One doesn't need to be an expert in adult learning to figure out that, under these circumstances, learning is facilitated.

- The knowledge acquired is *immediately put into practice*. For example, the Myers-Briggs Type Indicator is most interesting for the coachee when he can see how the model plays out in the way he addresses his challenges and how the awareness helps determine more effective options. Learning can really occur—and stick—because the chance to practice what has been learned is immediate. The reality test obliges the coachee to study and question the theories. Understanding is enhanced.

- A *variety of techniques* is used to honor alternative modes of learning while also stretching coachees outside their comfort zones. The diversity of methods also helps to prevent monotony and maintain interest. I have mentioned a number of techniques throughout the book: dialogues, role plays, experiential activities, artistic exercises and creativity methods, feedback from instruments (e.g., 360-degree leadership assessment, psychological preferences), and so on.

- *Learning occurs at different levels*. It follows a single, double, and triple-loop pattern. Richard Kilburg has shown how the concepts from Chris Argyris and Robert Hargrove play a key role in executive coaching.[5] "In single-loop learning or incremental improvement, we use the feedback from the consequences to change the specific actions we used to implement the strategies." For example, a motorist may choose a different route next time if he has been stuck in traffic.

"In double-loop learning, or reframing, we use the feedback to alter the constructed framework that we use to understand ourselves and the strategies we select to address the situation." For example, the motorist may decide to commute at a different time to avoid the traffic. Rather than going to the office at 8 A.M., he could leave after the rush hour is over. He could do some work at home before leaving for the office or stay at the office later to make up for the delayed departure time.

"In triple-loop learning, or transformation, the feedback might lead to a change in the context, in how our individual identities are constructed, or in the culture of the organization." For example, the motorist can decide to give up his car altogether, favoring alternative modes of transportation: the train, where he could spend commuting time reading, or the bicycle, which would allow him to get physical exercise. He could also promote new work patterns, leveraging modern telecommunication and working from home.

As I have shown, coaches invite reflection that takes the form of a dance between external reality and the internal representation of that reality, each mutually influencing the other. Coaches can serve their coachees when they help them juggle the three loops, but transformation is not easy to grasp. This book has already shown how we can be prisoners of a certain worldview. The clash of cultures, on the other hand, challenges our certainties and opens up new transformational possibilities. Coaching across cultures, which emphasizes viewing reality from multiple cultural perspectives, provides a perfect opportunity for giving substance to Hargrove's third loop.

Structure of Coaching Sessions

The structure I use in my coaching sessions tends to comprise three parts: reviewing challenges and progress, addressing challenges and providing tools, and setting up next steps. These parts may progress in a seamless flow or be clearly delineated.[6]

Please keep in mind that by now, ground rules for the creation of a safe and constructive environment have been established, as have mutual trust, respect, and complicity. This allowed us to conduct the assessment and to articulate objectives. The purpose of the sessions is now to progress toward these objectives and to learn something in the process. Of course, the conversation can always lead to making a new assessment and setting new objectives. In a fast-moving environment, I know I can expect sudden changes (e.g., an opportunity for a promotion, a new acquisition, etc.) that will make flexibility necessary.

Reviewing Challenges and Progress

After initial greetings and smalltalk (as appropriate culturally), after serving beverages and ensuring everybody is comfortably seated, the coaching conversation can begin.

In one-on-one coaching, the first question typically is "How are you?" It is not meant as a simple ritual where "Fine, thank you" is the expected answer.

Let's assume that the previous coaching session ended with some coachee resolutions: a developmental assignment, achieving milestones on projects, or taking specific actions. Predictably, you will ask, "How did it go?" If the coachee is juggling multiple projects, you will ask, "What would you like to discuss?" You then convey the importance of setting priorities here and now and your commitment to work on whatever matters most to the coachee. You must also keep sight of the overall objectives (say the one-year objectives) and challenge the coachee, if necessary, to keep them in mind and include them in the conversation. You are attuned to verbal and nonverbal responses, so that if an issue seems to worry the coachee but is not verbally expressed, you can raise it and properly deal with it.

One coachee was suffering from poor communication with his teenage son. We spent some time on that issue. This turned out to be a learning opportunity for the executive, who appreciated how he could avoid entering into negative psychological games. With a sense of relief, the executive was then prepared to discuss progress on various work projects.

When you review progress, you first celebrate success. In the simplest form, the celebration comes as an acknowledgment. It is easy to forget where we have come from and to take for granted the path already covered. But before rushing for the next hurdle, the small victories need to be applauded. Reviewing success also reinforces learning about what works well: "Yes, I was more effective when I maintained an OK–OK mindset," "Yes, launching a sustainable development initiative increased employees' pride and motivation," "Yes, I was surprised I was able to manage a particularist approach when before I was stuck on the universalist side."

Addressing Challenges and Providing Tools

Then you discuss what is still a problem. The NLP model in Appendix 2 suggests valuable questions related to challenges: "What prevents you from achieving …?" or "What would happen if you succeeded?" You help your coachee determine the nature of the obstacles and reflect on ways to overcome them, so that the projected image acts as an attractor.[7]

A systematic approach typically allows the coachee to discover new options. Your talent as coach is necessary here to enable coachees to tap into their potential and resume progress toward their objectives. Even though each situation is unique, the challenges likely to arise during the sessions most often fall into universal categories, which make up the various chapters of Part II: problem solving, time management, boundary setting, organizational arrangements, communication, and so on.

As I said earlier, I tend to devote additional time to present relevant tools and models to help the client I am coaching to address current challenges and to provide learning opportunities that will be applicable in the future as well as the present. The coachees' "toolboxes" are gradually filled and they become better coaches themselves.

The dialogue gradually shifts from present (addressing pending challenges) to future (addressing new challenges): "What do you need to do next to progress on your journey?" and "What are the main challenges you face?"

Coaching sessions can actually be viewed as a laboratory. In this safe environment, coachees can rehearse at ease, make mistakes, and consider alternative courses of actions.

Phone conversations, when the coachee has an important presentation to deliver or a key meeting to attend and wants to receive feedback from or bounce ideas off you, complement regularly scheduled sessions.

Setting Next Steps and Developmental Assignments

Coaching is action oriented; therefore, you will help the coachee identify actions that are likely to boost him toward achieving his objectives. The dialogue now moves into the future.

A key to real progress lies in the commitment and dedication of the coachee to applying the learnings from your sessions back at work in real situations, and to capturing insights in a learning journal that can be discussed in the following sessions. Specific assignments will help structure that process. The fact that the objectives are intrinsically motivating for the coachee, rather than pushed on him, is essential to sustain his daily long-term developmental efforts and lasting progress.

One executive, for example, established his list of important projects, which were tied to his selection of objectives, which itself was based on a sound assessment. He described each project with bullet points in the following categories: objective, problems, milestones, key stakeholders, actions, and successes so far.

One assignment was to prepare a first set of documents on all his major projects. Most were work related, but a few had to do with his family and community life. Prior to each session, he regularly updated the documents. He brought some projects to completion and started new ones. The written documents gave us a chance to focus coaching dialogues on specific challenges without losing sight of the big picture. We then used our combined creativity to find solutions to these challenges.

When interpersonal communication is an issue, I often invite the coachee to record actual challenging conversations in the learning journal, prior to our next session. I insist on his noting both successes and failures. If we have already discussed models like Transactional Analysis, the Myers-Briggs Indicator, or the "Cultural Orientations Framework," I may propose that my client reflect on how these played out and on what he could have done differently to ensure a more productive outcome. That way the theory can really be mastered and put to use to increase effectiveness in real situations. Moreover, I am helping the client to become his own coach.

In the case of a team retreat, the collectively agreed-upon next steps and completion dates are captured in writing and shared with the entire team. The team leader then ensures actions are taken on time. He acts as a coach, and his role becomes critical to the success of the team, especially since the next retreat with the external coach may not take place until a year later.

Ongoing Feedback

To protect confidentiality, you will refrain from sharing the personal content of your sessions. An exception could be with select colleague coaches, but always with the approval of the coachee.

If you, as coach, are also a leader who takes on other roles, boundaries are more difficult to establish. They need to be clarified upfront. Trust will be based on integrity. For example, you will need to think beforehand about how you plan to handle conflicts of interests such as the following:

- Your direct report reveals personal problems that may negatively affect the team project. Your dilemma is that he would have hidden those issues from you if you were not the coach he trusted.
- You appreciate that it would be in the coachee's best interest to pursue a business opportunity outside of the organization, but you really need him on your team.

If you commit to being a coach, I believe that you should put the interest of your coachees first and be ready to live with the consequences. In most cases, you will be able to creatively leverage the different needs and priorities, and this will result in genuine and wholehearted commitment from your employee. But sometimes your agenda will have to come second.

Confidentiality prevents you from sharing with third parties your evaluation of the coachee's progress. However, such an evaluation is not necessary. The coachee's results will speak for themselves. Moreover, as a professional coach you can always ask your coachee to solicit feedback directly from his stakeholders. If you are in contact with your coachee's manager, you may suggest that he regularly engage in feedback sessions with your coachee. The manager can show his support by noticing when progress is made and by helping to remove obstacles along the way.

Just as you encourage your coachee to solicit feedback, you will regularly ask for his feedback as well. At the end of each session, the exchange can be brief: "How did the session go for you?" More questions will follow, the content of which depends on the response you get. The enquiry can also be more elaborate and systematic, especially if you feel that something was not quite right, or if you want to know what worked well.

I recommend that you maintain a record of your coaching conversations. For example, you may summarize the topics and content of the dialogue and review how many of the various elements of a productive coaching session you actually covered:

- Tapping into desires (sources of motivation and values)
- Leveraging strengths
- Overcoming weaknesses
- Building on successes
- Addressing challenges (including through leveraging cultural differences)
- Real-time learning (including enriching the coachee's toolbox in pursuit of target objectives)

Midterm reviews may be appropriate and final feedback is indispensable. You can find examples of these questionnaires in Appendix 3, "Soliciting Written Feedback on Your Coaching."

Building tracking mechanisms as you go along allows learning to occur at the individual, team, and organizational levels. But when you collect data, you have to guarantee that confidentially is protected and strict boundaries are preserved. Aggregate results will also allow you to compute statistics as well as perform qualitative analyses.

Achieving Global Success

When you have progressed and at last reached your objectives, it is easy to forget where you have come from. You may already be projecting yourself into the next coaching assignment. Your coachee may be contemplating his next challenge or feeling overwhelmed by what still lies ahead.

Instead, I invite you to pause and take time to celebrate. Appreciating the road already traveled should give your coachee increased confidence about his ability to set out on a new journey, overcoming more obstacles and unleashing more human potential. What remains to be done will suddenly appear more accessible and less intimidating.

Since most of your time with coachees is spent on the journey, you both may start treasuring the journey itself more than the destination. This journey, aimed at the future, yet built on the past and anchored in the present, may ultimately be the global success I have been referring to.

Global success is, I believe, this full-hearted commitment to consider life globally, by creating richer lives for ourselves and for those other lives we touch and hopefully affect in positive ways.

Global success will not be achieved if we ignore cultural differences or if our ambition is merely to tolerate diversity. This book has invited you to leverage diversity, that is, to proactively reconcile and synthesize differences. In Part II, I proposed specific cultural differences to be considered as well as particular ways to leverage them. In Part III, I invited you to translate those insights into actions and tangible results. You have discovered a systematic process to assess your situation, set important and meaningful objectives, and reach those objectives (as well as help your coachees reach theirs).

It is my wish that the journeys of leaders and coaches described in this book will stimulate you to discover many more ways to take advantage of diversity for global success.

Final Words—Bringing Disciplines, Cultures, and People Together

Like so many of us, I watched with horror as the events of 11 September 2001 unfolded in the United States. The tragedy changed many lives abruptly and forever. Continued terrorist attacks and warfare in many parts of the world remind me constantly of the dark side of humanity and its destructive potential. Yet as coaches, knowing this reality, we must keep striving to help unleash what is most noble in people, building on the remarkable constructive side of human potential.

Recent events continue to provide more evidence that we live in an interconnected world, for better and for worse. This book has invited you to take a cross-cultural and global view. Contributing to improving the world overall is not just a matter of responsibility and ethics, it is an absolute necessity. Through our actions, we can serve the world at large and promote the conditions of human peace and unity.

It is said in the Talmud, "The man who saves one man saves the entire world." It is also written, "Every man shall say, 'It is for me that the world was created'." And again, "Every man shall say, 'The world rests on me'."

My heart is filled with appreciation for all the heroes risking and sacrificing their lives to save humanity: the courageous firefighters and rescue workers who paid a steep price in New York on 11 September; the remarkable soldiers who saved Europe during World War II; the European Resistance who refused to give in to Nazi barbarism; Commandant Massoud, who hated war but fought for freedom and tolerance in Afghanistan; the enlightened Mahatma Gandhi and Nelson Mandela, for whom nonviolence was the best weapon; and the anonymous workers providing humanitarian aid to distressed populations, away from media attention, in the most dangerous and isolated places on earth. Our role as global coaches seems so much safer and more comfortable in comparison. Yet we too can play a part. As leaders in international corporations, as executive coaches for those organizations, and as people, we can have a considerable impact.

We have an opportunity to help foster the conditions of a better world. Before changing others, however, we must make sure we become better human beings ourselves. Let us really listen to others, seeking to understand their perspectives. Let us deal with cross-cultural differences with an attitude of openness, curiosity, and eagerness to learn. Let us strive to leverage diversity as a source of richness, not as a threat. Let us achieve business success but without being so obsessed by financial performance that we forget to care for society. Let us enjoy life to the fullest but without turning our backs on those who suffer.

If you will allow my affective cultural orientation (remember chapter 9) to speak up, I will use the following metaphor. In the human brain, synapses are the joints between neurons, which are our nerve cells. Synapses allow the regrouping and succession of neurons into a gigantic number of possible combinations or circuits. It is those circuits that make possible the complex functioning and incredible performance of our nervous system. Synapses, flexible and organic bridges, constitute superb cross-fertilizers.

The brain's accomplishments, which we often take for granted, are multiple and really incredible: vision, audition, taste, physical coordination, cognitive and emotional intelligence, memory, and so forth. What is remarkable is that the true potential is only realized because the synapses allow all the neuronal parts to function in synergy.

I suggest human potential can be unleashed when coaches act as synapses,[1] drawing influx from various disciplines and cultures. Coaches do not need to be the best experts in sciences, engineering, finance, arts, technology, or history. Coaches do not have to be scholars, specialists in civilizations. How could they master it all? But effective coaches have engaged in a life-long learning journey. Their contribution is in bringing these different disciplines and cultures together, in tapping into the multifaceted wisdom. They leverage the various perspectives and adopt a global view. They help establish the synthesis necessary to address multidimensional issues. Coaches can help form ad hoc circuits of human knowledge that illuminate particular challenges in fresh ways.

Coaches also act as synapses when they help bring various people into contact, enhancing the quality of communication, fostering the circulation of positive energy, and ultimately enabling human synergy. These bridges allow individual potential to multiply exponentially, unleashing the collective capabilities of teams, communities, and society at large.

Over fifty years ago, Martin Buber addressed a Jewish audience. I feel that his call is for all of us, the organizations in which we work, and the planet we all share:

> The purpose is not an everlasting struggle to the death between sects or classes or nations. Our purpose is the great up-building of peace....
>
> We...are charged to perfect our own portion of the universe....
>
> Only an entire nation, which comprehends people of all kinds, can demonstrate a life of unity and peace, of righteousness and justice....
>
> Only nations, each of which is a true nation living in the light of righteousness and justice, are capable of entering into upright relations with one another.[2]

For you and all those you can touch, make the most of your journey.

Appendices

Appendix 1
Transactional Analysis

Transactional Analysis (TA), a theory created by Dr. Eric Berne, has been around since the 1960s, going in and out of fashion. In some instances, the message of TA has been caricatured, often giving a false impression of simplism. In other instances, the ideas have been woven into "new" models. The TA theory elegantly captures fundamental elements of interpersonal communication and self-awareness. Explaining TA is beyond the scope of this book, but you will find some key notions in this appendix. You will also find some of the TA tools I share with coachees to help them improve their communication.

Eric Berne uses the word *stroke* to refer to the fundamental unit of social interaction. A stroke may be not only a sentence we address to someone but also any nonverbal signal to that person (for example, a smile or a frown).

An exchange of strokes constitutes a *transaction*, which is the unit of social intercourse; hence, the overall title transactional analysis, or the analysis of transactions. If I say, "How are you?" you could reply in various ways. You could provide a ritual response: "I am fine, thank you!" You could, alternatively, start to complain about your problems, express joy, or simply return the question. The point is that we always have various options when we initiate a stroke or react to one.

It is important to note that "any social intercourse has a biological advantage over no intercourse at all."[1] The implication is that destructive communication is preferable to no communication. In other words, when constructive communication is absent, destructive communication tends to occur instead. Likewise, you cannot eliminate destructive communications. You can only replace them with more constructive forms. Your child will cry to get your attention. The worst thing you could do would be to systematically ignore him. If you blame him for crying (negative stroke), at least you have acknowledged his existence. But, hopefully, you can meet his biological hunger for strokes in a more positive way by playing and having fun with him.

Beyond developing an OK–OK mindset (see chapter 1), Eric Berne indicates various specific ways to engage in constructive communications (i.e., deploy positive energy). He also shows how we frequently and most often unconsciously promote destructive communications (i.e., unleash negative energy), which he refers to as *playing games*.

I shall briefly present some of the concepts and show how to put them to use in coaching situations.

Dramatic Triangle

Steve Karpman's *dramatic triangle* illustrates the three roles people can adopt when they "play games."

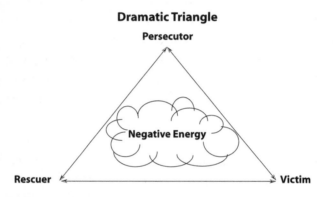

When we "play games," we reinforce a negative image we have of ourselves and/or of others.

For example, a sales manager (coachee), could struggle with a salesperson (employee) playing "Yes, but...."

A possible dialogue between them might go:

Salesperson:	I cannot reach those sales targets.
Sales manager:	I know a great seminar on the subject of selling. Why don't you take it?
Salesperson:	Yes, but this is theory. I need practical solutions.
Sales manager:	Why don't you go speak to Claude? He has worked with these clients for many years. He could give practical advice.
Salesperson:	Yes, but Claude is always busy. Plus things have changed since he was involved with my clients.

The sales manager gives unsolicited advice repeatedly, playing "Rescuer," while the salesperson takes the "Victim" part, expressing his helplessness. At some point, the sales manager might switch to the "Persecutor" role, angrily demanding that the salesperson figure it out himself but "meet those targets," possibly threatening to fire him if objectives are not met.

In any event, negative energy has been exchanged, with no constructive solutions.

In this situation, the sales manager could refrain from giving advice that will be discarded. The dialogue could become:

> Salesperson: I cannot reach those sales targets.
>
> Sales manager: What's preventing you from reaching them?
>
> Salesperson: I don't know. I work as hard as always. Our clients don't seem to be as excited about what we have to offer.
>
> Sales manager: What could we do to make them more excited?
>
> Salesperson: I'm not sure.
>
> Sales manager: How could you find out?
>
> Salesperson: I suppose I could call Mr. X and Ms. Y and have a conversation with them.

Through questioning, the sales manager is helping his employee find solutions while also building his responsibility for resolving the problem. This is surely not rocket science. Yet even intelligent people with the best of intentions "play games." Eric Berne reports a series of games people frequently play such as "Let's You and Him Fight," "Now I've Got You, You Son of a Bitch," and so on. Only a detailed analysis of actual interactions of coachees reveals where their communication went astray, and may pinpoint certain patterns. This process is comparable to studying strokes in a chess game, celebrating the good ones and finding ways to avoid similar bad moves in the future. A coach helps the coachee to first become aware of how he communicates, especially in delicate situations. Then they explore alternative options together to bring about effective and constructive communication.

Centers of Resources (Ego States)

Transactional Analysis also suggests different "ego states" that we all possess and exhibit in communication. The three main states are called "Parent," "Adult," and "Child."

When Eric Berne says, "This is your Parent," he means "You are now in the same state of mind as one of your parents (or a parental substitute) used to be, and you are responding as he would, with the same posture, gestures, vocabulary, feelings, etc."

The purpose in coaching is not to analyze how the real parents actually behaved, or how the coachees reacted when they were children, but to help them become aware of the Parent, Adult, and Child they carry within them and of the ways in which they use what constitute three centers of resources, represented in the figures that follow.

The notion of *autonomy* that coaches strive to develop is in fact elegantly defined in the TA theory. Autonomy is achieved when you are positively able to use all your ego states and subego states. (This is equivalent to saying that you have a habit of adopting the OK–OK mindset.) *Symbiosis* or *dependency*, in contrast, happens when you resort to playing psychological games; this necessarily implies a mindset other than OK–OK. For example, an autonomous person will know how to be firm, without being aggressive. Autonomous people take ownership for their own actions and feelings rather than blaming others. They look for solutions. Autonomy is in fact inseparable from constructive communication and is a key ingredient of leadership.

Our Three Centers of Resources
(ego states)

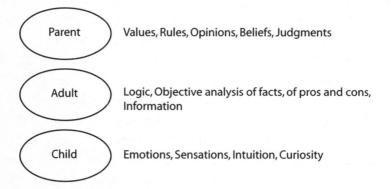

Parent — Values, Rules, Opinions, Beliefs, Judgments

Adult — Logic, Objective analysis of facts, of pros and cons, Information

Child — Emotions, Sensations, Intuition, Curiosity

Contamination occurs when the Parent or the Child is confused with the Adult. For example, saying "You cannot trust anybody" indicates the Adult is contaminated by the Parent (the statement is an opinion rather than factual evidence) and perhaps also by the Child (the person may be afraid of trusting).

Contamination

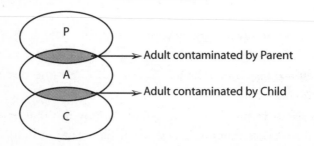

P

A → Adult contaminated by Parent

→ Adult contaminated by Child

C

Subego States with Their
Effective (+) and Ineffective Uses (-)

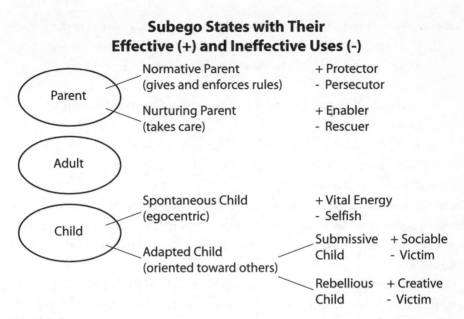

Parent

- Normative Parent (gives and enforces rules) — + Protector / - Persecutor
- Nurturing Parent (takes care) — + Enabler / - Rescuer

Adult

Child

- Spontaneous Child (egocentric) — + Vital Energy / - Selfish
- Adapted Child (oriented toward others):
  - Submissive Child — + Sociable / - Victim
  - Rebellious Child — + Creative / - Victim

Transactions

Transactions can be represented by arrows in a transactional diagram. Consider the following example involving Fred, Zone Vice President, and his direct report, Bob, Area Manager. I coached Bob, using TA to address his communication challenge.

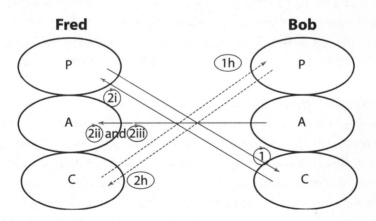

1. Fred (Normative Parent)→Bob (Submissive Child)[2]
   Fred: "*We have to stop these non-added value activities.*"
   We first need to decode this indirect message. It means
   "You have to stop wasting your time with endless discussions
   because we need closure on this issue—deciding on a
   suitable candidate to be the senior sales person in Holland."

Our conversation also reveals a hidden (h) stroke. Fred is concerned:

1h. Fred (Submissive Child)→Bob (Nurturing Parent)

Fred: "*I am afraid for the Benelux. We need quick decisions to improve sales figures.*"

In reality, Bob reacted emotionally, responding to the verbal stroke with:

2i. Bob (Rebellious Child)→Fred (Normative Parent)

Bob: "*I am only sticking to the original plan. We have discussed this already.*"

(Note: It turns out Bob is also sending an indirect message (2h): "You stupid moron, stop bugging me. I have already told you that we cannot rush this important decision and that we need to ensure buy-in from all stakeholders.")

As we review this exchange, it becomes clear to Bob that he took Fred's bait, that is, Fred's unconscious invitation to enter the dramatic triangle to "play a game." Fred is the Persecutor and Bob unconsciously chose to play the Victim (rebellious version). The risk of escalation is real. Fred could become a more aggressive Persecutor, and Bob a more sarcastic Victim. The relationship is damaged and trust diminishes, especially when this game becomes a habit or a pattern. Ultimately, the professional relationship can be terminated. I once had a manager who confused straight talk with "playing games." He alienated his superiors and eventually got fired.

I had invited Bob to actually keep track of what happened in a learning journal. Calmly looking at his conversation with Fred from a distance during our coaching session, Bob discovered healthier options that he could have chosen or could choose in the future under similar circumstances.

Bob could have chosen to react to the hidden stroke about sales in Benelux countries with his Nurturing Parent, reassuring Fred by saying, "Don't worry,..." But Bob was not sure whether Fred was sending a hidden signal. Moreover, a stimulus directed to Fred's Submissive Child could have been perceived in this instance as ironic, triggering an attack by Fred's Persecutor. Bob preferred considering a response from his Adult by asking the following question:

2ii. Bob (Adult)→Fred (Adult)

Bob: "*This is what I have done so far. We are progressing according to plan and I am confident that the decision will be made within the next week. Do you have any concerns?*"

Alternatively:

    2iii.   Bob (Adult)→Fred (Adult)

        Bob: *"I share your desire for productivity by concentrating*
        on added-value activities. This is the reason why I have
        eliminated the following activities. So I would appreciate
        knowing which other non-added activities, in your opinion,
        should still be discarded."

With these words, Bob first emphasizes what Fred and Bob have in common. Communication is inherently about finding common ground, a basis for unity. In this case Bob reaffirms the fact that he agrees with his boss' desire to concentrate on added-value activities. He also names the value they share, productivity. Bob ends up asking for feedback, demonstrating an open mind, while saving his boss' face.

Knowing their history, I knew that if Bob simply responded by asking, "Which non-added value activities are you referring to?" Fred could have interpreted the message as ironic and too direct.[3] In both cases, Fred may perceive that the stroke is coming from the Persecutor rather than from the Adult and may continue the exchange in the dramatic triangle.

The coach in this situation provides the models to decipher the dynamics causing the coachee to find the communication situation challenging. Then the coach, through questioning as much as possible (to let the coachee discover solutions himself), enables the coachee to explore his concrete options to build more constructive communication. A tennis coach would help a player in a similar fashion to expand his repertoire of shots (hitting the tennis "ball-stroke" replaces sending a "communication-stroke"), to be able to respond most effectively in a variety of situations.

You can use a similar process to help the coachee prepare for any interpersonal communication. This can be, for example, managing an important negotiation, conducting a performance appraisal, delivering a difficult message, resolving a conflict, responding to criticism, coaching for development, and so on.

You can go into theoretical refinements when needed, but there is no point in bombarding the coachee with theories not readily put into practice. On the other hand, the art of coaching implies selectively presenting tools and using them to address real challenges. While the coachee resolves his issues, he also expands his toolkit by enhancing his ability to autonomously deal with similar situations in the future.

Appendix 2
Neuro-Linguistic Programming

John Grinder and Richard Bandler set out to study the subjective experience of the human being. The study had to be, at the same time, "global, formalized and verifiable through the observation and its results."[1]

The experience of reality and communication is represented in the figure below:

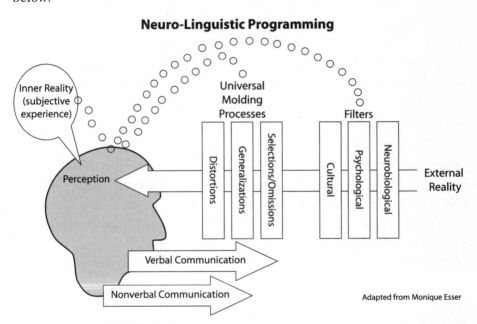

Neuro-Linguistic Programming

Adapted from Monique Esser

Filtering the External Reality

Grinder and Bandler's major contribution for the practicing coach is their description of the conversion process that takes place from the external reality to the inner representation we derive from that reality, and vice versa.

Understanding these processes is the first step toward consciously altering them and possibly overcoming obstacles to our effectiveness and success. In the same way optical lenses can alter shapes and colors in photography, mental filters can create a unique subjective experience different from objective reality.

Neurobiological filters are beyond our scope. We all know, for example, that we cannot "see" external reality in its entirety. It is humbling to remember that we can only see light and hear sound within a certain range of frequencies.

Psychological filters constitute an important category. The Myers-Briggs Type Indicator (see chapter 11) provides a concrete example of these kinds of filters and suggests different biases we all have in the form of preferences.

Cultural filters are another important category, although less well known by coaches in my experience. This book primarily focuses on cultural filters, describing them and suggesting concrete implications for coaching (see the "Cultural Orientations Framework" and its use in Part II).

Universal Molding Processes (meta-model)

Grinder and Bandler have additionally described three universal molding processes, which can be both useful and limiting.

Selection/Omission is the process through which we selectively place our attention on certain dimensions of our experience while excluding others. Useful, for example, when we set priorities, selection becomes limiting when we only listen to certain people or to certain topics and fail to tap into other sources of potentially great ideas.

Generalization is the process through which a specific experience comes to represent the entire category of which it is a member. Generalizations are essential to learning. We study a number of similar cases and naturally build general laws, which facilitate the resolution of new cases. It becomes limiting when we fail to appreciate the specificity of a situation and we give in to stereotyping and clichés.[2]

Distortion is the process that allows us to represent the connections between parts of external reality. Establishing connections is crucial in any creative enterprise, such as combining ingredients to prepare a gourmet meal or elaborating theories to explain a phenomenon. But distortions can also be limiting when we start believing our combination of ingredients is the *only* true possibility or when we grant an absolute status to our theories, thereby preventing further discoveries.

The meta-model[3] (see pages 269–71) describes common selections, generalizations, and distortions that pepper our communications. IBM, for example, has adopted this model to guard against the limitations we create for ourselves and for others when we fall prey to those phenomena and confuse events or facts with our interpretations of them.[4] The meta-model suggests specific remedies in the form of questions to remove the confusion, reestablish a subjective reality more in conformity with the external reality, and improve communication. *Meta* refers to the position from a distance (which allows for the elimination of what prevents us from knowing the external reality as it is) in order to overcome the effects of selection, generalization, and distortion. In coaching, the meta-model is often extremely useful in helping the coachee gain clarity about his own experience and as a tool in helping him improve his communication.

You can use the meta-model in combination with Transactional Analysis. The meta-model in fact provides useful "Adult–Adult" questions for addressing the issues of omissions, generalizations, and distortions in our interpersonal communications.

Meta-Model

Omissions

1. **Simple omissions**

   Examples—coachee's statements: "I am angry."
                                   "I am confused."

   Questions—coach's responses: "With whom/what?"
                                   "About whom/what?"

2. **Index of reference missing**

   Examples—coachee's statements: "It does not matter."
                                   "One does not know."

   Questions—coach's responses: "What does not (matter)?"
                                   "Who/what/what type/more
                                   precisely/more specifically?"

3. **Nonspecific verbs**

   Examples—coachee's statements: "Peter hurt me."
                                   "Anne won."

   Questions—coach's responses: "How, specifically?"
                                   "In which manner?

4. **Nominalizations**[5]

   Examples—coachee's statements: "Motivation is important."
                                   "I regret my decision."

   Questions—coach's responses: "Alright, and how do you motivate
                                   yourself/others?"
                                   "How, specifically, did you decide?"

Generalizations

1. Universal quantifiers

Examples—coachee's statements:	Always, never, all, nobody, every time (and so forth).
	"Nobody pays attention to my suggestions."
Questions—coach's responses:[6]	"Nobody?" (emphasizing and exaggerating)/ "Really nobody?"
	"Isn't there one person who pays attention?"

2. Modal operators (internal rules)

Examples—coachee's statements:	Necessity: I have to, I should, one must (and so on).
	Possibility: I should not, it is impossible (and such).
	"I cannot give up."
Questions—coach's responses:[7]	"What prevents you from giving up?"
	"What would happen if you did?"

Distortions

1. Cause-Effect links

Examples—coachee's statements:	"She makes me angry."
	"He does not greet me. He hates me."
Questions—coach's responses:	"How, specifically, does she make you angry?"
	"How does the fact that he does not greet you prove/imply that he hates you?"

2. Mind reading

Examples—coachee's statements:	"I know this annoys you."
	"He thinks I am lying."
Questions—coach's responses:	"How do you know that?"
	"On what do you base this hypothesis?"

3. **Vanished author**

Example—coachee's statement:	"Scots are avaricious."
Question—coach's response:	"Who says that?"

Appendix 3
Soliciting Written Feedback on Your Coaching

Just as you encourage your coachees to solicit feedback, you should regularly ask for your coachees' feedback.[1] Apart from on-going feedback, I recommend asking for written feedback so you can review your coaching in a systematic fashion. You may need to customize your questionnaire, but you could use the following examples as templates.

Midterm Feedback

The following questionnaire was used with an organization my company worked with, where we coached seven executives. The feedback process took place after a six-month period of coaching. As explained beforehand to participants, a report with comments provided verbatim and anonymously was shared with the group. Responses to the questions on objectives were not included to protect confidentiality. References to the company have been removed here.

Respond to the following using the scale provided.

5 = Strongly Agree; 4 = Agree; 3 = Neutral; 2 = Disagree; 1 = Strongly Disagree

- How valuable has the coaching been so far?
  5   4   3   2   1

- How enjoyable has the coaching been so far?
  5   4   3   2   1

- Do you find that the coaching is a good investment for you personally?
  5   4   3   2   1

- Do you find that the coaching is a good investment for the organization?
  5   4   3   2   1

Respond to the following in narrative form.

- What are your comments overall about the coaching process and sessions?
- What has the coaching helped you achieve?
- What have you learned as a result of the coaching?
- What do you find most valuable and what do you like best about the coaching?
- What do you find least valuable and what do you dislike about the coaching?
- How could the coaching be more effective?
- What specific feedback can you give your coach?

Objectives (responses strictly confidential)

- Please prepare a list with the key objectives you are aiming to achieve (based on the <specific organizational goal-setting process> and on your initial discussions with your coach).
- For each objective, how will you know and measure, at the end of <year>, that you have achieved it? How important is the objective to you personally?
- What progress have you made so far?
- What possible obstacles remain?
- How do you plan to remove those obstacles and leverage your assets to achieve your objectives by the end of <year>?

Final feedback

I have used the following questionnaire (slightly modified to protect confidentiality) to solicit feedback at the end of a one-year coaching intervention with a senior executive. My client, a renowned international organization, later decided to use a slightly adapted version of this questionnaire to conduct its own survey.

- What have you learned this year as a result of the executive coaching program?
- How has the program been valuable to you? Please indicate specific benefits.
- How has the program been valuable to <organization's name>? Please indicate specific benefits.
- What objectives have you achieved this year? (Please refer to your "Global Scorecard.") How has the coaching process helped?

- To what extent have you reached the goals you set? How has the coaching process helped?
- What are the challenges you still face or have begun to face?
- What is your overall feedback regarding the coaching process?
- What is your feedback to your executive coach?
- How capable are you of coaching others ?

Glossary

coach A person coaching. In this book, a coach can refer to a leader as coach (a leader whenever he adopts a coaching style), a professional coach (internal/external coach, executive coach, corporate coach, team coach, personal coach), or to anyone eager to deploy human potential through coaching. *See* Introduction.

coachee A person being coached (*see also* client).

coaching The art of facilitating the unleashing of people's potential to reach meaningful, important objectives. *See* chapter 1.

coaching across cultures An enlargement of traditional, monocultural coaching that strives to unleash more human potential in order to foster global success by making the most of alternative worldviews and by embracing cultural differences as a source of enrichment. *See* Introduction, chapter 2. (equivalent: *global coaching*)

client A person/team being coached, or an organization having contracted coaching services. As a person being coached (*coachee*), the client can be external (when coached by a professional outside his organization) or internal (when coached by a leader or a colleague from the same organization).

culture The set of unique characteristics that distinguish a group's members from another group. *See* chapter 2.

cultural orientation An inclination for responding in a certain culturally driven way to a universal challenge. In this book, the universal challenges considered are grouped into seven *categories*: sense of power and responsibility, time management approaches, definitions of identity and purpose, organizational arrangements, notions of territory and boundaries, communication patterns, and modes of thinking. Each category encompasses one or more *cultural dimensions* (seventeen in total). Each dimension comprises two or three *cultural orientations* (thirty-six in total). *See* Part II.

Cultural Orientations Framework A coaching tool comprising cultural categories, dimensions, and orientations, designed to assess cultural orientations and establish a cultural profile. *See* chapter 3.

global "Relating to or embracing the whole of something, or of a group of things."[1] In this book, "something"/"group of things" can refer to the planet earth, to its diverse cultures, or to various areas of success.

GLOBAL Acronym representing six important principles for determining appropriate targets of global success. *See* chapter 12.

global coaching (*see* coaching across cultures).

Global Coaching Process Coaching process that considers success globally and integrates a cross-cultural perspective. *See* Part III.

Global Scorecard A tool designed to help an individual (or by extension a group/organization) set target objectives in four key interconnected areas: self, family and friends, organization, and community and world. *See* chapter 12.

global success A state characterized by high performance and high fulfillment, having achieved the personal/collective targets of the "Global Scorecard." *See* chapter 12. Global success also lies in the journey. *See* chapter 13.

identity The fundamental characteristics that make a person or a society unique, which constitute his/its dynamic synthesis of his/its multiple cultures (typically, a person belongs to several groups, and a society is made up of several groups). *See* chapter 2.

The way we define our personal identity is culturally biased, emphasizing who we are (being) and/or what we do (doing), and referring to the self (individualist) and/or to the group (collectivist). *See* chapter 6.

interculturalist A professional involved in intercultural work, typically a culture-generalist who masters broad cross-cultural knowledge and who understands common global cross-cultural challenges. Can also be expert in particular cultures, for example specific nations or civilizations. *See* Preface; Introduction.

leader A person who gets results through people. Among several leadership roles, coaching is an important one. *See* Introduction; chapter 1.

leverage Achieve more output with a given input, by using a lever. In this book, the input is human potential in general, and cultural differences in particular. The lever is coaching across cultures (*see* coaching across cultures). The output is performance and fulfillment, aiming at global success (*see* global success). *See also* chapter 2 and Part II (on how to leverage various cultural orientations). Referring to different alternatives, say A and B (an alternative being, for example, an objective or a cultural orientation), leveraging differences means achieving synergy by realizing/adopting A and B (making the most of A and B). *See* chapter 3; chapter 12.

politics An activity that builds and maintains your *power*, taking into account, especially, social interdependencies (other people aiming to build and maintain their power, with goals competing, compatible, or in synergy with yours). *See* chapter 7.

power The ability to achieve your meaningful, important goals. *See* chapter 7.

preference "A greater liking for one alternative over another or others."[2] In this book, the alternatives considered are either psychological (psychological preferences) or cultural (cultural orientations) (*see also* cultural orientation). *See* chapter 3; chapter 11.

unity A form of completion, wholeness, or globality. The synthesis of differences rather than a bland version (uniformity) in which disparities have been eliminated. *See* chapters 2, 11, and 12.

Notes and References

Preface

[1] *Interculturalism* is the discipline of the *interculturalists*, a term that refers to professionals involved in cross-cultural work. Their background is typically in human studies areas such as cultural anthropology, international relations, psychology, and intercultural communication. Interculturalists are researchers, academics, consultants, trainers, educators, politicians, peace workers, or mediators. They are culture generalists who master broad cross-cultural knowledge and who understand common global cross-cultural challenges. Some can also be experts in particular cultures, for example specific nations or civilizations.

[2] I first presented "coaching across cultures" at the second Linkage International Coaching and Mentoring Conference in London in 1999.

[3] Chris Bangle, "The Ultimate Creativity Machine—How BMW Turns Art into Profit," *Harvard Business Review*, January 2001.

Introduction

[1] In this book, the term *coach* encompasses the following roles: *leader as coach* (a leader whenever he/she adopts a coaching style) and *professional coach* (internal/external coach, executive coach, corporate coach, team coach, personal coach). See chapter 1 for more information on these roles. Note that an *external coach* provides coaching services to a client organization whereas an *internal coach* is typically a human resources professional acting as coach vis-a-vis staff members.

[2] Clearly, your nationality is only one part of your cultural identity. You may be British, but you also have a certain religion (or no religion), profession, organization you work for, team you work with, gender, social class, and such. This book takes the approach of looking at culture in a general sense, rather than concentrating on cultural comparisons between nations. Culture will also be viewed as a dynamic process.

Chapter 1

[1] "Global Executive and Organizational Development," IBM, June 2001.

[2] Although the definition highlights the differences between coaching and related disciplines (therapy, consulting, teaching), the boundaries are not sharply drawn; overlap can exist. But as I indicate in my note 6, it is important to work within the confines of one's competencies and mandate. It is also valuable to learn about and appreciate potential contributions from related disciplines. Richard Kilburg (*Executive Coaching*, American Psychological Association, 2000) offers

an interesting argument, showing how the distinction between coaching, consulting, and therapy can be blurred.

3   Except for personal coaching, where the individual coachee is the only stakeholder. Even then, the coachee will typically articulate certain objectives in the service of others. Beyond a possible genuine desire to serve others, this situation simply arises by virtue of the interdependencies characteristic of social life: prosaically, "I need to serve others if I expect others to serve me, and help me achieve my objectives."

4   See figure "Map of Team Members' Desires," page 114.

5   *Intelligence*, defined by *The New Oxford Dictionary of English* as "the ability to acquire and apply knowledge and skills," exists in multiple forms, as Howard Gardner has argued (see *Frame of Mind: The Theory of Multiple Intelligences*, Basic Books, 1983). In chapter 10, I elaborate on the concept of intuition and its importance for powerful thinking. But beyond thinking (evidencing the intelligence of the head), it is worth mentioning the intelligence of the heart (i.e., emotional intelligence), of the body (i.e., bodily intelligence), and of the spirit (i.e., spiritual intelligence). All forms of intelligence have a role to play in coaching, which strives to unleash people's potential, without placing limitations on the nature of that potential.

6   When a person experiences difficulties moving forward and keeps stumbling over the same obstacles, therapy may be necessary. In some cases, the use of medications may even be indicated to relieve some of the suffering, even before psychotherapy can take place (or at least together with psychotherapy). In any event, ethically, it is necessary to consider the best interest of one's client, to work within the boundaries of one's competency and mandate, while developing an ability and openness to recommend different help as appropriate.

7   Richard Kilburg, *Executive Coaching*, American Psychological Association, 2000.

8   Frederic Hudson, *The Handbook of Coaching*, Jossey-Bass, 1999.

9   The "Global Coaching Process," which will be described in detail in Part III, is an extension of the coaching process briefly described here. By integrating the cultural dimension, the scope of the assessment and the range of possible target objectives are increased, as well as the means to reach these objectives. The three-step structure however is identical.

10 For more information, please refer to Appendix 2 — Neuro-Linguistic Programming.

11 The ICF was founded in 1992. Its mission is to build, support, and preserve the integrity of the coaching profession. ICF is the most important international coaching association today (2001). Its membership has been doubling annually: 1,000 members in 1999, 2,000 in 2000 and 4,000 in 2001. The ICF has defined ethical standards of conduct and core coaching competencies (e.g., active listening and powerful questioning). It has also developed a serious and much needed credentialing program for professional coaches and coach training agencies. See www.coachfederation.org

12 Thomas Leonard is the founder of Coach U, a virtual university, and is the author of *The Portable Coach*, Scribner, 1998.

13 These include the following coaches and authors, whose books can serve as useful references:

   • Cheryl Richardson's central premise is that you deserve to take "extreme self-care." (*Take Time for Your Life—A Personal Coach's 7-Step Program for Creating the Life You Want*, Broadway, 1998; *The Life Makeovers*, Bantam, 2001)

   • Laura Berman Fortgang invites you to *Take Yourself to the Top* (Warner Books, 1998) and to live your best life (*Living Your Best Life*, Tarcher/Putnam, 2001).

   • Talane Miedaner shows how to *Coach Yourself to Success—101 Tips from a Personal Coach for Reaching Your Goals at Work and in Life* (Contemporary Books, 2000).

14 See, for example, Alyssa Freas, "Strategic Executive Coaching's Bottom-Line," www.linkageinc.com, 2001.

15 Sometimes, defining the *vision, strategy*, and *culture* is an outcome of the coaching process.

16 "Summary Findings from the International Executive Coaching Summit: A Collaborative Effort to Distinguish the Profession," compiled by Dr. Lee Smith and Dr. Jeannine Sandstrom, 1999.

17 Philippe Rosinski, "Coaching Executive Teams," workshop at the 3d Linkage European Coaching and Mentoring Conference (London, 2000)—see Conference Proceedings, July 2000.

18 "The Team Intervention Process: How It Worked for Baxter Renal," 1st Linkage European Coaching and Mentoring Conference (Amsterdam, 1998); see Conference Proceedings, October 1998.

19 *Training Magazine*, June 2001.

20 *Harvard Business Review*, March/April 2000.

21 These six styles are as follows: Coercive (demands immediate compliance), Authoritative (mobilizes people toward a vision), Affiliative (creates harmony and builds emotional bonds), Democratic (forges consensus through participation), Pacesetting (sets high standards for performance), and Coaching (develops people for the future). According to Goleman, the more traditional styles, coercive and pacesetting, have their use in crisis situations and get quick results from a highly motivated and competent team, but they have a negative impact on the corporate climate. The other four styles, on the other hand, have a positive impact on the organization's working environment, which in turn impacts business performance. Goleman claims that climate accounts for nearly one third of results and his research shows that leaders who used styles that positively affected the climate had decidedly better financial results than those who did not.

22 David Campbell, for example, considers seven "crucial, constant, continuing" leadership tasks. They are vision, management, empowerment, politics, feedback, entrepreneurship, and personal style.

    Campbell then proposes five important leadership characteristics, which are subdivided into twenty-one more specific scales, which are necessary to perform the leadership tasks:
    • Leadership: the act of being out in front, making new and creative things happen
    • Energy: a recognition of the physical demands required of leaders
    • Affability: an acknowledgment that leaders need to foster teamwork and cooperation and make people feel valued
    • Dependability: being credible, reliable and able to allocate organizational resources and manage details
    • Resilience: the ability to show optimism, mental durability, and emotional balance.
    See David Campbell, *Manual for the Campbell Leadership Index*, National Computer Systems, 1991; Dianne Nilsen and David Campbell, *Development Planning Guide for the Campbell Leadership Index*, NCS, 1991.

23 Notes for executive coaches, "Leadership for Growth Competencies," Unilever, 2000.

24 Unilever Home and Personal Care Europe. I led the design during my days as the Director of Custom Programmes at the Center for Creative Leadership, tapping into CCL's expertise in leadership development training and research.

25 From "Strengthening Leadership at IBM—An Assessment Handbook for Executives," IBM, 1997.

26 Ibid.

27 Dean O'Hare's address at the Chubb Leadership Development Seminar, USA, July 31, 2000.

[28] Let me acknowledge Chubb's human resources and learning and development executives Christopher Hamilton, Jenifer Rinehart, Helen Faulkner and Deby Bradley, with whom I have worked and who took a proactive role in this.

Chapter 2

[1] Sandra Vandermerwe, "How Increasing Value to Customers Improves Business Results," *Sloan Management Review*, Fall 2000.

[2] The real name has been modified to protect anonymity. For confidentiality, I have also altered some of the details.

[3] The booklet *Swedishness* (Bengt Anderson, SandbergTrygg, 2000) offers insights on the Swedish culture. It has helped me in deciphering behaviors I had observed in Sweden or that Mark was describing. The generalizations here about Swedes are merely common trends, not always verified. They should not therefore be interpreted as stereotypes (see Appendix 2—NLP on "generalizations").

[4] *La Société Interculturelle*, Editions du Seuil, 2001.

[5] Edgar Schein, *Organizational Culture and Leadership*, 2d ed., Jossey-Bass, 1992.

[6] Fons Trompenaars, *Riding the Waves of Culture*, Irwin, 1993.

[7] Edgar Schein introduced the concept of levels of culture referring to artifacts, espoused values, and basic underlying assumptions. The model I present here, however, is not Schein's model. The onion ring relates to my definition of culture, which refers to visible and immersed characteristics.

[8] A similar analysis could be performed with leaders as coaches.

[9] Master Certified Coach Application Form, International Coach Federation, 1998.

[10] What is truly important (i.e., the real values considered here) may be obviously different from "official" (abstract) values. The implications of that distinction are similar to those briefly discussed for abstract versus real norms.

[11] See chapter 6, endnote 2, for the distinction made by Kluckhohn and Strodtbeck between Being-in-Becoming (growing) and Being (being).

[12] I also use the term *belief*, which is close enough to *assumption*, in that both terms refer to something one accepts as true (see *The New Oxford Dictionary of English*, Oxford University Press, 1998) and sometimes confuses with truth. Beliefs or assumptions can be unconscious to the point that one is not even aware of holding them (e.g., at a conscious level, you may take for granted that time is money, being unaware that you are unconsciously making that assumption or holding that belief). However, beliefs and assumptions can be brought to consciousness (notably through coaching or training). At the conscious level, the nuance is that a belief is a "firmly held opinion or conviction" (*The New Oxford Dictionary of English*), whereas an assumption is merely considered a temporary premise for the purpose of argument.

[13] Milton Bennett, "Towards Ethnorelativism: A Developmental Model of Intercultural Sensitivity," in *Education for the Intercultural Experience*, edited by R. Michael Paige, Intercultural Press, 1993.

[14] *Denial* is the term used by Bennett for stage 1.

[15] Max Pagès, a French social psychologist evoked such an experience, when he attended a seminar in the United States in the 1950s. "It became very clear to me that it was I, Max, but not my culture which was accepted. I was treated as just another American who had this exotic peculiarity of being a Frenchman, which was something like, say, a particular style of shirt. In general no curiosity existed about the intellectual world I was living in, the kinds of books I had written or read, the differences between what is being done in

France or Europe and in the United States." (Max Pagès, 1971, quoted by Geert Hofstede in *Culture's Consequences*, 2d ed., Sage, 2001).

16 Website: www.sietar.org

17 Website: www.interculturalpress.com

18 "Beyond Cultural Identity: Reflections upon Cultural and Multicultural Man," in *Culture Learning: Concepts, Application and Research*, edited by Richard W. Brislin, University Press of Hawaii, 1977.

19 *The New Oxford Dictionary of English*, Oxford University Press, 1998.

20 Likewise, in finance, you can leverage your equity by using debt. Borrowing money can allow you to achieve more earnings per share. If you can make productive use of more money, then debt will help you to do more with your limited capital. The lever effect will boost your earnings. But with debt, your risk increases: losses (negative earnings) will inflate too. If you win, you win big. If you lose, you lose big as well.

21 See "Dialectical versus Binary Thinking" page 57 for the type of thinking required to be able to leverage differences.

22 This process can be viewed as an extension of Carl Jung's individuation principle to the realm of culture.

23 Source: "Global research project study of 115 merger operations by A. T. Kearney in 1998–1999," in "Fusions: La guerre des cultures," *Enjeux Les Echos*, January 2001.

24 See "Fusions: Les 20 principales opérations annoncées en 2000," in "Bilan du Monde" Edition 2001, *Le Monde*.

25 My observations that follow are consistent with those made by other authors. See among others, Richard Lewis, *When Cultures Collide*, 2d ed., Nicholas Brealey, 1999 and Joerg Schmitz, *Cultural Orientations Guide*, Princeton Training Press, 2000. Several orientations have been leveraged in this situation, notably control–harmony (see chapter 4), individualistic–collectivistic (chapter 6), hierarchy–equality (chapter 7), and direct-indirect communication (chapter 9).

26 See also chapter 8 for information on giving feedback while preserving harmony.

27 See Michael Tang, *A Victor's Reflections and other Tales of China's Timeless Wisdom for Leaders*, Prentice-Hall, 2000.

Chapter 3

1 See Terence Brake, Danielle Walker, and Tim Walker, *Doing Business Internationally*, McGraw-Hill, 1995.

2 See Meena Wilson, Michael Hoppe, and Leonard Sayles, *Managing Across Cultures—A Learning Framework*, Center for Creative Leadership, 1996.

3 Edward C. Stewart and Milton J. Bennett, *American Cultural Patterns: A Cross-Cultural Perspective*, rev. ed., Intercultural Press, 1991.

4 Geert Hofstede, *Culture's Consequences*, 2d ed., Sage, 2001.

5 Hippocrates was a Greek physician and is regarded as the father of medicine.

6 See Pierre Cauvin and Geneviève Cailloux, *Les Types de Personnalité*, ESF éditeur, 1994.

7 Carl Jung, *Psychological Types*, Princeton University Press, 1971 (revision of the original English translation, 1923).

8 See Isabel Briggs Myers, *Introduction to Type*, 6th ed., Consulting Psychologists Press, 1998.

9 Jung recognized the crucial role of parental influence in someone's development, but nevertheless noticed that natural predispositions, which are biological, were the determinant factor for establishing one's personality, at least under normal circumstances (see *Psycho-*

logical Types). Even if personality can and does change, it probably does not change very much.

[10] Alfred Korzybski (1879–1950) was an engineer by training but devoted most of his life to studying the functioning of the human spirit. He analyzed in particular the interdependencies between language and our representation of reality. His point was that language is not merely a creative and structuring process. It is also illusory and limiting. Korzybski's idea was to raise our awareness about the structure of our particular language and to learn to refer to actual reality with more accuracy and precision. Monique Esser (*La P.N.L. en perspective*, Editions Labor, 1993) has shown how his work is one of the epistemological roots of Neuro-Linguistic Programming (see Appendix 2).

[11] ICF Conference, Vancouver, 2000.

[12] Stewart and Bennett, *American Cultural Patterns*. The authors observe a further link between the two realities: "Objective culture can be treated as an externalization of subjective culture which usually becomes reified; that is, those institutions which are properly seen as extensions of human activity attain an independent status as external entities. They seem to exist 'out there,' and their ongoing human origins are forgotten."

[13] Michel Fustier, *Pratique de la dialectique*, ESF, 1986.

[14] James Collins and Jerry Porras, *Built to Last*, HarperBusiness, 1994.

[15] To keep it simple, for the two dimensions with three possible orientations (i.e., control–harmony–humility and past–present–future), "harmony" and "present" could be viewed as the zero point, in the middle of the continuum.

[16] For the value of "diversity," the scale was given the following meaning, based on the seven-stage model for dealing with cultural diversity presented in chapter 2: positive numbers referred to "ethnorelative stages" (+5 meaning, for example, "consistently leveraging diversity") while negative numbers were associated with "ethnocentric stages."

Chapter 4

[1] Florence Kluckhohn and Frederick Strodtbeck, *Variations in Value Orientations*, Row, Peterson, 1961.

[2] Terence Brake, Danielle Walker, and Tim Walker, *Doing Business Internationally*, McGraw-Hill, 1995.

[3] Craig Storti, *Figuring Foreigners Out: A Practical Guide*, Intercultural Press, 1999.

[4] Kluckhohn and Strodtbeck, *Variations in Value Orientations*.

[5] Eun Kim, *The Yin and Yang of American Culture: A Paradox*, Intercultural Press, 2001.

[6] John Heider, *The Tao of Leadership*, Bantam, 1985.

[7] Kluckhohn and Strodtbeck, *Variations in Value Orientations*.

[8] Storti, *Figuring Foreigners Out*.

[9] Idries Shah, *The Way of the Sufi*, Penguin-Arkana, 1968.

[10] "What Makes Us Strong?" in *One Voice*, IBM, 2001.

[11] "We're All of These Things," in *One Voice*, IBM, 2001.

[12] Stephanie Mehta, "What Lucent Can Learn From IBM," *Fortune*, 25 June 2001.

[13] "From Mindshare to Marketshare," in *One Voice*, IBM, 2001.

[14] *One Voice*, IBM, 2001.

[15] See, for example, Christophe Bouchet, "Cyclisme: dopage à l'italienne," *Le Nouvel Observateur*, 12–18 juillet 2001.

[16] See Catherine Berthillier and Anne de Loisy, "Les naufragés du dopage," in *Envoyé spécial*, Antenne 2 (French public television), 5 July 2001.

[17] Certain sections of this paragraph paraphrased from Donald Smith, "Costa Rica Deals with Environmental Pressures," *NationalGeographic.com*, December 2000.

[18] Jim Loehr and Tony Schwartz make the point that "executives face unprecedented demands in the workplace" and are in fact "corporate athletes" who need to be trained accordingly ("The Making of a Corporate Athlete," *Harvard Business Review*, January 2001).

[19] Shah, *The Way of the Sufi*.

[20] Michael Porter, "Strategy and the Internet," *Harvard Business Review*, March 2001.

Chapter 5

[1] Daniel Boorstin, *The Discoverers*, Random House, 1983.

[2] Edward C. Stewart and Milton J. Bennett (*American Cultural Patterns*, Intercultural Press, 1991) explain,

> Contemporary American values of time can be traced back to colonial days in Virginia where an early change in attitude toward time and labor occurred. The discovery of the profitability of tobacco in colonial Jamestown impelled agents of the Virginia Company to manipulate land and labor to maximize production. By the 1620s, the concept of time thrift had begun to replace the original work discipline that placed no emphasis on hourly output and required only four hours of daily labor (Richard Brown, *Modernization: The Transformation of American Life, 1600–1865*, 1976). The time thrift idea received a strong boost early on from Benjamin Franklin in his admonition, "Remember that time is money." Support from technology arrived in the form of mass-produced timepieces. By 1840 cheap clocks were everywhere and soon became a necessity in American households.

> Wilson, Hoppe and Sayles use the terminology "scarce–plentiful" in reference to time. The question is this: "Is the orientation to the use of time urgent or relaxed?" (*Managing Across Cultures: A Learning Framework*, Center for Creative Leadership, 1996).

[3] "Génération vitesse," *Le Nouvel Observateur—hors-série*, Mars/Avril 2001.

[4] François Aelion, *Manager en Toutes Lettres*, Les Editions d'Organisation, 1995.

[5] Nancy Adler, *International Dimensions of Organizational Behavior*, South-Western College Publishing, 1991.

[6] "Assis sans rien faire," in "Génération vitesse," *Le Nouvel Observateur—hors-série*, Mars/Avril 2001.

[7] "Avons-nous encore le temps?" in "Génération vitesse," *Le Nouvel Observateur—hors-série*, Mars/Avril 2001.

[8] Edward T. Hall, *Beyond Culture*, Anchor/Doubleday, 1976.

[9] Ibid.

[10] Fons Trompenaars, *Riding The Waves of Culture*, Economist Books, 1993.

[11] Hall, *Beyond Culture*.

[12] Edward T. Hall, *The Dance of Life: The Other Dimension of Time*, Anchor/Doubleday, 1983.

[13] Fermat's Last Theorem, as it is known, stated that $x^n + y^n = z^n$ has no whole-number solutions for a number greater than 2. The simplicity of the enunciation only matched the difficulty of rediscovering Fermat's lost proof. See Simon Singh, *Fermat's Last Theorem*, Fourth Estate, 1997.

[14] See Rainer Zerbst, *Antonio Gaudi*, Taschen, 1990.

[15] My discussion on "universalism–particularism" (see chapter 7) also sheds light on ways to resolve this type of issue.

[16] *The New Oxford Dictionary of English*, Oxford University Press, 1998.

[17] Michelle Conlin, "Sabbaticals—Give a Geek a Break," *Business Week*, 10 July 2000.

[18] Jean-Yves Tadié and Marc Tadié, *Le Sens de la mémoire*, Gallimard, 1999.

[19] "La Mémoire"—Jean Cambier—collection 2001, Editions le Cavalier Bleu.

[20] See "Cultivez vos neurones," in "Les nouvelles clefs de la mémoire," *Le Nouvel Observateur*, 17–23 Mai 2001.

[21] Quotes from Fons Trompenaars, *Riding The Waves of Culture*.

[22] John Hennessy, "Building an Education That Won't Wear Out," *Stanford*, January/February 2001.

[23] One could argue that Socrates' goal was ultimately to cleverly have people reach his own conclusions. If this is true, Socrates' agenda would differ from coaching, and his maieutics Socratics would not equate to coaching but could still be viewed as a powerful coaching technique.

Chapter 6

[1] Claude Lévi-Strauss, *Tristes Tropiques*, Plon, 1955.

[2] Florence L. Kluckhohn and Frederick Strodtbeck (*Variations in Value Orientations*, Row, Peterson, 1961) refer to three modes of human activity: Being, Being-in-Becoming and Doing.

"In the Being orientation the preference is for the kind of activity that is a spontaneous expression of what is conceived to be 'given' in the human personality. As compared to either the Being-in-Becoming or the Doing orientation, it is a non-developmental conception of activity. It might even be phrased as a spontaneous expression in activity of impulses and desires....

The Being-in-Becoming orientation shares with the Being one a great concern with what the human being is rather than what he can accomplish, but here the similarity ends. The idea of development, so little stressed in the Being orientation, is paramount in the Being-in-Becoming one.... The Being-in-Becoming orientation emphasizes that kind of activity that has as its goal the development of all aspects of the self as an integrated whole.

The Doing orientation is so characteristically the dominant one in American society that there is little need for an extensive discussion of it. Its most distinctive feature is a demand for the kind of activity that results in accomplishments that are measurable by standards conceived to be external to the acting individual...What does the individual do? What can he or will he accomplish? These are almost always the primary questions in the American scale of appraisal of persons."

Brake, Walker, and Walker (*Doing Business Internationally*, McGraw-Hill, 1995), while referring to Kluckhohn and Strodtbeck, simply use the pair Being/Doing to describe the preferred mode of activity. In this book, I also use the pair Being/Doing, with the understanding that Being is the equivalent of both Being and Being-in-Becoming. In other words, Being could mean a preference for living (spontaneously) and/or for growing (developing one's self). As Kluckhohn and Strodtbeck pointed out, the difference with doing lies in the "concern with what the human being is rather than what he can accomplish."

[3] Paraphrased from *Finding the Middle Ground: Insights and Applications of the Value Orientations Method*, edited by Kurt Russo, Intercultural Press, 2000.

[4] See Paul Hersey and Ken Blanchard, *Management of Organizational Behavior: Utilizing Human Resources*, 6th ed., Prentice-Hall, 1993.

[5] One difference with my definition of *being* is that in the situational leadership model, relationship behaviors are instrumental. They take place in the context of a particular job. You say, "Job well done!" and not necessarily "I appreciate you as a person, regardless of your job performance." Referring to Transactional Analysis terminology, you provide

"conditional reinforcements" rather than "unconditional reinforcements." Both types are necessary.

6   Timothy Gallwey, *The Inner Game of Tennis*, Random House, 1974, 1997; *The Inner Game of Golf*, 1998 rev. ed., and *The Inner Game of Work*, 2001.

7   This example also illustrates leveraging individualistic and collectivistic orientations.

8   See chapter 7 and also Philippe Rosinski, "Constructive Politics: Essential to Leadership," *Leadership in Action* 18, no. 3 (1998).

9   See also chapter 4 about control and Appendix 1, "Transactional Analysis" about the Victim role.

10 See the last research update on "Benchmarks" by the Center for Creative Leadership in 2000.

11 Brian Hall, *Values Shift*, Twin Lights, 1995.

12 Cheryl Richardson, *Take Time for Your Life*, Broadway Books, 1998.

13 John Whitmore, *Coaching for Performance*, 2d ed., Nicholas Brealey Publishing, 1996.

14 This is a classic dimension. Talcott Parsons (*The Social System*, Macmillan, 1951) writes about the private versus collective interest dilemma, distinguishing the Self Orientation from the Collectivity Orientation. Kluckhohn and Strodtbeck refer to three subdivisions: the Lineal and the Collateral (two types of collectivism) and the Individualistic. Geert Hofstede contrasts Individualism and Collectivism (*Culture's Consequences: International Differences in Work Related Values*, Sage, 1980). Fons Trompenaars uses Parsons' relational orientations as a starting point and, in a clear and practical fashion, differentiates Individualism and Collectivism while suggesting ways to reconcile the differences (see chapter 5, "The Group and the Individual," in *Riding the Waves of Culture*, Irwin, 1993).

15 Craig Storti, *Figuring Foreigners Out*, Intercultural Press, 1999.

16 Ibid.

17 James Collins and Jerry Porras, *Built to Last*, HarperBusiness, 1994.

18 "Japan's Decline Makes One Thing Rise: Individualism, *The Wall Street Journal* Europe, 29–30 December 2000.

19 I generalize the concept of individualism and apply it to a nation (or a region) as opposed to Europe, which is the collective entity, the group of nations.

20 Bengt Anderson, *Swedishness*, SandbergTrygg, 2000.

21 See chapter 2, "Synthesizing Western and Asian Cultures in Chubb Insurance." I noticed important differences among Asians, as expected. For example, Singaporeans live in a remarkably multicultural society, where several cultures and religions peacefully coexist. Their official language is English, and they are influenced by the West to a significant degree. This makes it easier for them to converse in English and to speak up, compared, say, to their colleagues from Japan or Korea.

22 Groupthink is a "phenomenon in which the norm for consensus overrides the realistic appraisal of alternative courses of action" (Stephen Robbins, *Organizational Behavior*, Prentice-Hall, 1989). Individuals who hold a position that is different from the dominant majority are under pressure to suppress, withhold, or modify their true feelings and beliefs.

23 Confronted with a crisis situation, the team leader may have to make a quick and unilateral decision. This certainly is not coaching, but, then, we do not claim that coaching is a panacea.

24 I have used this activity with several executive teams, including the management of Chubb Human Resources Europe and Baxter Renal UK. I presented it at the "Coaching Executive Teams" workshop I conducted at the Linkage Coaching and Mentoring Conference (London, July 2000). The coaching application is mine, but I have borrowed the collage idea from "Leading Creatively," a seminar from the Center for Creative Leadership.

[25] See Appendix 1 — Transactional Analysis.

Chapter 7

[1] Sun Tzu, *The Art of War*, translated by Samuel Griffith, Oxford University Press, 1963.
[2] Following the definition from the *Petit Larousse Illustré 1996*.
[3] Henry Mintzberg, *Mintzberg on Management — Inside Our Strange World of Organizations*, The Free Press, 1989.
[4] See Geert Hofstede, *Culture's Consequences*, 2d ed., Sage, 2001.
[5] Gareth Morgan, *Images of Organization*, 2d ed., Sage, 1997.
[6] Chistopher Bartlett and Sumantra Ghoshal, "Managing Across Borders: New Organizational Responses," *Sloan Management Review*, Fall 1987; and *Managing Across Borders: The Transnational Solution*, Harvard Business School Press, 1989. Nancy Adler, *International Dimensions of Organizational Behavior*, 3d ed., South-Western College Publishing, 1997. Stephen Rhinesmith, *A Manager's Guide to Globalization*, McGraw-Hill, 1996.
[7] See Thomas Cummings and Christopher Worley, *Organizational Development and Change*, 6th ed., South-Western College Publishing, 1997.
[8] Power Distance is one of Geert Hofstede's dimensions (*Cultures and Organizations*, McGraw-Hill, 1991). Hofstede compares high-power distance countries (hierarchy) in Latin Europe (France and Spain), Latin America, Asia, and Africa with low-power distance nations like Great Britain and its former dominions and non-Latin Western European countries.
    Terence Brake, Danielle Walker, and Tim Walker use the terms *Hierarchy/Equality* (*Doing Business Internationally*, McGraw-Hill, 1995). Meena Wilson, Michael Hoppe, and Leonard Sayles prefer the terms *Unequal/Equal* (*Managing Across Cultures — A Learning Framework*, Center for Creative Leadership, 1996).
[9] Quotes in this paragraph and the previous one are from Craig Storti, *Figuring Foreigners Out: A Practical Guide*, Intercultural Press, 1999.
[10] *Confucius — Entretiens du Maître avec ses disciples*, translated from Chinese by S. Couvreur, Editions Mille et Une Nuits, 1997.
[11] See chapter 11 for more information on 360-degree feedback surveys and chapter 8 on exchanging feedback.
[12] While organizational politics is often seen as an evil, leaders can engage in a constructive form of politics. See "Constructive Politics" later in this chapter.
[13] Conversation with Jackie Chang, 26 June 2001.
[14] Israel and Austria had the lowest power distance index in Hofstede's research (in *Cultures and Organizations*).
[15] This also reveals a direct communication orientation (see chapter 9).
[16] *Fortune*, 25 June 2001. According to *Fortune*, Sanford Weill of Citigroup made $150,688,160 in 2000; Jack Welch of General Electric, $125,340,263.
[17] Philippe Rosinski, "Constructive Politics: Essential to Leadership," *Leadership in Action* 18, no. 3 (1998).
[18] As explained in chapter 1, this is not true for mentoring, which is sometimes confused with coaching and which does not necessitate equality. Mentors are usually older and more senior than mentees. They share their experience and wisdom. Mentors also explain to newer professionals how to play the game and open doors. Some mentors have good coaching skills but others can be very poor coaches. The latter may have great advice to pass on but little self-awareness and capacity to empathize with the person's situation. Conversations can remain relatively superficial.
[19] Leaders vary in their relative orientation toward service, depending not only on the

strength of their commitment to others and the number of others they are trying to help but also on their capacity to listen, empathize, trust, respect, share, and care.

[20] Philippe Rosinski, "Constructive Politics."

[21] Although Talcott Parsons introduced the concept of universalism/particularism, Fons Trompenaars deserves the credit for providing a clear explanation for today's business professional. His sole emphasis, however, remained in contrasting national cultures. The dimension in fact can be used to describe cultural groups of any kind. Talcott Parsons, *The Social System*, Macmillan, 1951; Fons Trompenaars, *Riding the Waves of Culture*, Irwin, 1993.

[22] Trompenaars, *Riding the Waves of Culture*.

[23] Storti, *Figuring Foreigners Out*.

[24] Trompenaars, *Riding the Waves of Culture*.

[25] Ibid.

[26] The communication dimension "high context/low context" (see chapter 9) is also at play in this example.

[27] Trompenaars, *Riding the Waves of Culture*.

[28] Charles Hampden-Turner and Fons Trompenaars, *The Seven Cultures of Capitalism*, Doubleday, 1993.

[29] See "Unilever Annual Review 2000 — Meeting Everyday Needs of People Everywhere."

[30] Hofstede (*Cultures and Organizations*) used "uncertainty avoidance" as one of his four dimensions to describe cultural differences. Wilson, Hoppe, and Sayles adopted the terminology "stable/dynamic" (*Managing Across Cultures*). Brake, Walker, and Walker (*Doing Business Internationally*) chose the terms "order/flexibility." Stability is meant to represent a high degree of uncertainty avoidance and change, a low one.

[31] The quotes in the previous two paragraphs are adapted from Gert Jan Hofstede, Paul Pedersen, and Geert Hofstede, *Exploring Culture: Exercises, Stories, and Synthetic Cultures*, Intercultural Press, 2002.

[32] Jim Loehr and Tony Schwartz, "The Making of a Corporate Athlete," *Harvard Business Review*, January 2001.

[33] James Collins and Jerry Porras, *Built to Last*, HarperBusiness, 1994.

[34] "Chubb and Its People," ed. 3/96.

[35] See Michael J. Kirton, ed., *Adaptors and Innovators*, Taylor and Francis, 1989.

[36] See the discussion on "Constructive Politics."

[37] Henry Mintzberg, *Mintzberg on Management*.

[38] Brake, Walker, and Walker (*Doing Business Internationally*) use a similar dimension, "competitive/cooperative," to describe a cultural reality overlooked by most cross-cultural consultants, including Hofstede and Trompenaars. However, their definition is significantly different from mine. They define *competitive* as follows: "achievement, assertiveness, and material success are reinforced," and they define *cooperative* as "stress...placed on the quality of life, interdependence, and relationships." This definition, in my opinion, does not clearly demarcate the pair "competitive/cooperative" from the "doing/being" dimension. I have attempted to stay closer to the essence of the concepts in the definitions I propose. For example, quality of life may be a consequence of collaboration but is not its essence. By the same token, quality of life is not incompatible with competition. Some people have a great time competing!

[39] See "Comment Jacques Rogge a conquis le trône," *Le Soir*, 20 July 2001.

[40] "Renault's Alliance with Nissan — Halfway Down a Long Road," *The Economist*, 18 August 2001.

[41] To protect confidentiality, I am not divulging specific information about the company, the industry, or the territory itself.

42 The dimension "protective/sharing" is also at play here (see chapter 8).

43 See Transactional Analysis vocabulary in chapter 1 and Appendix 1.

44 Senior managers use "elevator speech" to refer to the capacity to convey your message in thirty seconds or so, which is the approximate duration of an impromptu meeting in the company's elevator.

45 "There is power from knowing and having access to key people in the environment outside the organization, people who are seen as being able to help the organization in some significant way—for instance, a potential large customer or an influential public figure. In addition, having a relationship with the knowledge people who are generating new ideas adds power." (Philippe Rosinski, "Constructive Politics").

Chapter 8

1   William Shakespeare, *Antony and Cleopatra*.

2   Edward T. Hall, *The Silent Language*, 1959; *The Hidden Dimension*, 1966; *Beyond Culture*, 1976 (Anchor/Doubleday).

3   Talcott Parsons, *The Social System*, Macmillan, 1951.

4   Especially when the culture also has a "scarce" time orientation.

5   Michel Polac, *Journal*, Presses Universitaires de France, 2000.

6   I want to acknowledge the Center for Creative Leadership (CCL); feedback has been a core component of CCL leadership development programs since the 1970s.

7   Referring to Transactional Analysis, we can say that judging and giving advice come from the Normative Parent state, while giving feedback comes from the Adult and the Child. The Normative Parent, even if intended in a positive fashion, may be perceived in its negative form, the Persecutor, and trigger a "psychological game." Even when perceived positively, the Normative Parent typically addresses the Submissive Child. Feedback is destined instead to the Adult, who then needs to feed the information to all his ego states and decide on possible changes, bearing the responsibility for installing those changes rather than changing because someone else has asked him to.

8   This is an adaptation of the Center for Creative Leadership's S-B-I model (Situation–Behavior–Impact).

9   Referring to Transactional Analysis, this equates to playing the Rescuer role, assuming your interlocutor is a Victim. Unintentionally, you invite the other to enter the "dramatic triangle" and play a "psychological game" with you.

10 The real first name has been modified to protect anonymity.

11 Exceptions include situations where you are victims of physical aggression, torture, abuse, and so forth. Please refer to chapter 4: we most often have more choices than we admit to or are able to imagine, but we still need to "humbly" accept the fact that we are not always in control.

12 TA has coined key "constraining messages," which appear to constitute wise injunctions but have perverse effects. "Be perfect" and "Be nice" are examples. Antidotes come in the form of "permissions," as is explained later.

13 See, for example Claire Aubé, "L'e-mail sans ses maux," *Enjeux Les Echos*, June 2001. See also chapter 9 about communication patterns.

14 Coaches need to master competency in assertiveness. Assertiveness training may have gone out of fashion these days, but the content is still very relevant. Being assertive means operating from an "OK–OK" position: being firm and calm rather than aggressive (OK–not OK), submissive (not OK–OK), or defeatist (not OK–not OK). To become more assertive and nourish mutual respect, you can proactively establish a list of qualities you possess (I'm OK) and a list of qualities you appreciate in the person you are dealing

with (He's OK). OK–OK is also an effective habit for constructively dealing with cultural differences. To this end, you are currently reading about merits and positive lessons from multiple cultural orientations.

15 This obviously does not excuse the manager who was responsible for his own behavior and had options other than playing a Persecutor role.

16 Of course, the Victim attitude does not in any way justify or excuse the abuse.

17 I have already evoked exceptional circumstances where leaving may not be an option. The concentration camp is an extreme example, where victims are a reality, even for those who do not fancy the Victim psychological role.

18 Cheryl Richardson, "Protect Yourself," in *Life Makeover for the Year 2001* (electronic newsletter), January 2001.

19 Quoted in "Protect Yourself," in *Life Makeover for the Year 2001* (electronic newsletter), January 2001.

Chapter 9

1 Cheryl Richardson, presentation at the "Linkage International Coaching and Mentoring Conference," London, September 1999.

2 This is also true in any culture but to a greater extent in high-context cultures.

3 Edward T. Hall and Mildred Reed Hall, *Understanding Cultural Differences: Germans, French and Americans*, Intercultural Press, 1990.

4 "La gestuologie et le langage du corps," in François Aelion, *Manager en Toutes Lettres*, Les Editions d'Organisation, 1995.

5 François Sulger, *Les Gestes Vérité*, Editions Sand, 1986.

6 *See* "How to Spot a Liar," *Time* magazine, 13 March 2000.

7 Valerie Sessa, Michael Hansen, Sonya Prestridge, and Michael Kossler, *Geographically Dispersed Teams: An Annotated Bibliography*, Center for Creative Leadership, 1999.

8 Some research is more surprising perhaps. "GDT members can pass along social context cues through communication technology. As time passes, GDT members may process socio-emotional information with greater effectiveness." For example, "smileys" constitute a code that did not exist before e-mail. Smileys represent your facial expression and convey your emotions. For example, :-) means "smile" (and will be automatically converted into ⇨ by some software programs), :) means "happy," <3 means "tenderness," >:-< means "crazy," and so on.

9 This also suggests a monochronic time orientation (chapter 5).

10 Hall contrasts the United States (low context) with Japan (high context) and France (in the middle). See Edward T. Hall, *Beyond Culture*, Anchor Books, 1976.

11 The universalist/particularist dimension (chapter 7) also has implications for contracting and policy making.

12 Richard Mead, *Cross-Cultural Management Communication*, Wiley & Sons, 1990.

13 Talcott Parsons (*The Social System*, Macmillan, 1951) contrasted emotionally charged and emotionally neutral cultures.

14 Kate Cannon offers the following definition: "Emotional intelligence is about using the power of emotion as a source of information, motivation, and connection" (in Geetu Orme, *Emotionally Intelligent Living*, Crown House, 2001).

15 See the coaching tool section in this chapter for a discussion on the relationship between coaching and influencing/persuading.

16 Quoted by François Aelion, "Convaincre ou Persuader?" (in *Manager en Toutes Lettres*, Les Editions d'Organisation, 1995).

17 Carl Jung, *Psychological Types*, Princeton University Press, 1971 (revision of the original English translation, 1923).

[18] This reveals other cultural dimensions as well, like universalism and inductive thinking in particular.

[19] See chapter 11 about desires and their important role in the "assessment" phase of the coaching process.

[20] David Whyte, *The Heart Aroused*, Currency Doubleday, 1994.

[21] Explanation paraphrased from John C. Condon and Fathi Yousef, *An Introduction to Intercultural Communication*, Macmillan, 1975.

[22] Sentence adapted from Terence Brake, Danielle Walker, and Tim Walker, *Doing Business Internationally*, McGraw-Hill, 1995.

[23] Explanation paraphrased from Condon and Yousef, *An Introduction to Intercultural Communication*.

[24] Explanation paraphrased from Joerg Schmitz, *Cultural Orientations Guide*, Princeton Training Press, 2000.

[25] Condon and Yousef, *An Introduction to Intercultural Communication*.

[26] Ibid.

[27] Brake, Walker, and Walker, *Doing Business Internationally*.

[28] Formality can be viewed as a form of distance characteristic of a protective culture (see chapter 8). Likewise, informality could be understood as a manifestation of a sharing culture.

So what is the rationale for proposing a formal/informal dimension as well as a protective/sharing one? The first pair is about *familiarity* while the second concerns *intimacy*. They often come together but you can also have one without the other. Intimacy without familiarity occurs, for example, when one confesses to a priest but also when one self-discloses and exchanges feedback with colleagues. Familiarity without intimacy occurs anytime one behaves informally without revealing much personal information.

Some of your friends or even your spouse may know less about you in some areas than your psychotherapist, your coach, a colleague, or even a stranger you conversed with on the plane. Coaches face the risk of confusing the two notions. Behaving informally will not necessarily make people feel closer to you. A Japanese or a French person could be turned off by U.S. informality, especially when no intimate relationship has been established.

[29] *Petit Traité des Grandes Vertus*, Presses Universitaires de France, 1995.

[30] I started to use videotaped role plays in the early 1990s. They worked well with diverse participants, in the private and public sector: executives, supervisors, engineers, policemen, and so forth.

[31] See Appendix 1 (Transactional Analysis) for examples of interpersonal communication and of how coaching (using TA in this case) can help identify more productive options.

[32] For a more detailed explanation of the GROW model, see John Whitmore, *Coaching For Performance*, 2d ed., Nicholas Brealey Publishing, 1996.

Chapter 10

[1] Quotes from Edward C. Stewart and Milton J. Bennett, *American Cultural Patterns: A Cross-Cultural Perspective*, Intercultural Press, 1991.

[2] Francis Bacon's book *Novum Organum* (meaning "new instrument," in particular, an "instrument of reasoning"; see for example edition translated and edited by Peter Urbach and John Gibson, Open Court, 1994) alludes to Aristotle's famous *Organum*.

[3] Gary Althen, *American Ways: A Guide for Foreigners in the United States*, 2d ed., Intercultural Press, 2002.

[4] *Petit Robert* dictionary 1973.

5   André Comte-Sponville, *Le bonheur, désespérément*, Editions Pleins Feux, 2000. The quotes are translated and adapted from this book.
6   Cheryl Richardson, "Are We Having Fun Yet?" in *Life Makeover for the Year 2000*, e-mail, 3 April 2000.
7   See also chapter 2 (abstract vs. real values)
8   Michael Maccoby, "Narcissistic Leaders: The Incredible Pros, the Inevitable Cons," *Harvard Business Review*, January/February 2000.
9   Peter Senge, *The Fifth Discipline*, Currency Doubleday, 1990.
10 Robert Kaplan and David Norton, *The Balanced Scorecard*, HBR Press, 1996.
11 Senge, *The Fifth Discipline*.
12 Referring to MBTI, his preference was very clearly for Intuition rather than Sensing.
13 Quotes from Sandra Vandermerwe, "How Increasing Value to Customers Improves Business Results," *Sloan Management Review*, Fall 2000.
14 Peter Hindle from Procter & Gamble, presentation at the CEPAC—Cercle de Développement Durable, 23 April 2002.
15 Quoted in Comte-Sponville, *Dictionnaire philosophique*, Presses Universitaires de France, 2001.
16 References on creativity (among others): Philippe Rosinski, *L'Ingénieur créateur*, Seminar University Louvain-la-Neuve, 1997; Philippe Rosinski, *Le Management Créatif*, Michel Chalude and Associates, 1993; Michel Fustier, *Pratique de la créativité*, ESF, 1991; Bernard Demory, *Créativité ? Créativité… Créativité!*, Les Presses du Management, 1990; Hubert Jaoui, *Créativité Pratique*, Epi, 1979.
17 See Tony Buzan, *Use Your Head*, BBC Books, 1974.
18 *Petit Robert* dictionary 1973.
19 See chapter 3 (postcards) and chapter 6 (collages).
20 See William Gordon, *Synectics, The Development of Human Capacity*, Harper, 1961.
21 Philippe Rosinski, *La méthode analogique*, Michel Chalude and Associates, 1993.
22 Alastair Rae, *Quantum Physics: Illusion or Reality?* Cambridge University Press, 1994; see also "Science at the End of the Century"; Michael Crichton makes a good argument in the introduction to his fiction novel *Timeline*, Century, 1999.

Part III

1   Joseph Campbell, *The Hero with a Thousand Faces*, Princeton University Press, 1949/1968.
2   Carol Pearson, *Awakening the Heroes within*, HarperCollins, 1991.
3   See "Chubb and Its People," Chubb, 1996.

Chapter 11

1   Michael Hammer and James Champy, *Reengineering the Corporation*, HarperBusiness, 1993.
2   James Champy , *Reengineering Management*, HarperBusiness, 1995.
3   Baruch Spinoza, *L'Ethique*, 1677 (French translation Edition Gallimard, 1954).
4   My article, "Leading for Joy" (European Forum for Management Development, Forum 1998/3), conveyed the notion that leading for joy is a path to perfecting people and the world. I later discovered that Spinoza had already written over three hundred years ago that "Joy is man's transition from a lesser to a greater perfection." Leaders and coaches can facilitate this noble human journey.

5 Both "Benchmarks" and the "Campbell Leadership Index" are examples of well-researched leadership development instruments. Benchmarks is a 360-degree leadership survey by the Center for Creative Leadership. The 2000 revised version comprises two sections: section 1 (leadership skills and perspectives), 16 scales, and section 2 (problems that can stall a career), 5 scales. The Campbell Leadership Index is a 360-degree leadership survey by David Campbell, distributed by NCS. It is made up of 5 orientations and 21 scales.

6 See, for instance, David Campbell, *Manual for the Campbell Leadership Index*, National Computer Systems, 1991.

7 From Sandra Hirsh and Jean Kummerow, *Introduction to Type in Organisations*, Oxford Psychologists Press, 1998.

8 See Carl Jung, *Types psychologiques*, Georg, 1950; *La guérison psychologique*, Georg, 1953 (French translations).

9 Carl Jung, *Ma vie*, Gallimard, 1967.

10 See *Introduction to the FIRO-B*, Consulting Psychologists Press, 2000.

Chapter 12

1 This is the title of David Campbell's book, Tabor Publishing, 1974.

2 Additionally, this polarity is both a matter of personality preference (contrast MBTI Judging with Perceiving preferences) and of cultural orientation (compare stability with change orientations).

3 Robert Kaplan and David Norton, *The Balanced Scorecard*, HBR Press, 1996.

4 This, incidentally, also constitutes a wonderful example of leveraging doing and being cultures, resulting in more of both. Note that life priorities often involve family and friends but can in some cases refer only to the self.

5 Steward Friedman, Perry Christensen, and Jessica DeGroot, "Work and Life: The End of the Zero-Sum Game," *Harvard Business Review*, November–December 1998.

6 "Executive Women and the Myth of Having It All," *Harvard Business Review*, April 2002.

7 Climate surveys measure employees' perceptions of their work environment and particularly the factors that affect job satisfaction and productivity. See example below in the *employees* subcategory.

8 *The EFQM Excellence Model*, European Foundation for Quality Management, 1999.

9 Ibid.

10 David Campbell, *Campbell Organizational Survey*, National Computer Systems, 1988–1995.

11 Teresa Amabile, *Keys*, Center for Creative Leadership, 1987–1998.

12 *The EFQM Excellence Model*.

13 Ibid.

14 "Just Good Friends," *The Economist*, 18–24 August 2001.

15 Kaplan and Norton, *The Balanced Scorecard*.

16 Ibid.

17 During the last decade Kaplan and Norton set out to systematize the use of metrics in management, traditionally taught in separate business classes (strategy, finance, marketing, organizational development, etc.), introducing the Balanced Scorecard. Its authors insisted on the fact that the Balanced Scorecard is more than a collection of critical indicators or key success factors, which they recognized had existed in France for two decades. "The multiple measures on a properly constructed Balanced Scorecard should consist of a linked series of objectives and measures that are both consistent and

mutually reinforcing." The linkages incorporate both cause-and-effect relationships and mixtures of outcome measures and performance drivers. These measures together should "tell the story of the business unit's strategy." Objectives that are neither drivers nor outcomes of the business unit's strategy should not appear on the Balanced Scorecard. Examples incorporate the interests of other stakeholders, employees, and society overall, when these are not directly aligned with the business strategy.

The Balanced Scorecard's innovation, which resides in the cause-and-effect linkages of indicators, is both advantageous and limiting. It is advantageous if your sole purpose, when working in the corporate world, is to help achieve competitive advantage. The methodology obliges you to eliminate non-added value activities and to systematically translate strategy into action. It is also limiting, in my view, because it invites you to consider solely business imperatives. Other important concerns are only taken into account when a link can be established with the financial indicators. For Kaplan and Norton, these appear to be the ultimate measures of organizational success.

The Balance Scorecard is nevertheless a good resource for coaches and coachees alike. It stimulates the formulation of relevant measurement in the organization category. But from a global coaching perspective, as I have indicated, the Balanced Scorecard or the Tableau de Bord can only be part of the picture. Our scope goes beyond helping to achieve business success by translating the business strategy into action or by piloting the organization to high performance. We want to invite coachees to consider how they can make a constructive difference in the world, whenever we sense their desire to help improve the world, in addition to realizing business success. Many people find this meaningful indeed. In some cases, for instance in the medical sector, business success is naturally aligned with improving the world. Haemo- and peri-dialysis devices can save patients with a renal condition and improve their lives. However, tradeoffs frequently exist. It may be cost-effective and a sound financial objective to manufacture shoes in places where social regulation is loose. But this strategy, which may provide a distinct short-term competitive advantage, could mean the exploitation of young children. In the Global Scorecard we include social indicators and other "improving the world" criteria that even out the Balanced Scorecard measures. The liberal capitalist logic is itself placed within a broader framework that includes personal, social, and ecological aspirations. As I indicated earlier, coaches, by definition, help people to articulate and to achieve meaningful and important objectives.

[18] *The EFQM Excellence Model.*

[19] Paul Ray and Sherry Ruth Anderson, *The Cultural Creatives*, Harmony Books, 2000.

[20] Ibid.

[21] Observatoire de l'éthique, *le Guide éthique du consommateur*, Albin Michel, 2001.

[22] See Global Reporting Initiative, www.globalreporting.org

[23] See the International Organization for Standardization, www.iso.ch, and the ISO Technical Committee 207 on Environmental Management (the committee responsible for developing the ISO 14000 series of standards and guidance documents) www.tc207.org

[24] *A Greener World*, Baxter, June 2000.

[25] The Council on Economic Priorities Accreditation Agency (CEPAA) developed SA8000 (1997) as a voluntary standard, www.cepaa.org

[26] Democracy assumes values of freedom and equality. Not every culture aspires to equality, which I have indeed contrasted with hierarchy in chapter 7. Democracies may not fit all societal conditions best. Winston Churchill had these words: "No one pretends that democracy is perfect or all-wise. Indeed, it has been said that democracy is the worst form of Government except all those other forms that have been tried from time to time." (Speech to House of Commons, 11 November 1947).

[27] Leif Johansson, "Foreword by the Chairman" in "Consortium Report," The Performance Group—Norway, 1998.

[28] "Dow Jones Sustainability Group Index," 6 September 2001. See www.sustainability-index.com

[29] Geoffrey Colvin, "Should Companies Care?" *Fortune*, 11 June 2001.

[30] Simon Zadek reports,

> Nike's approach to labor practices in its global supply chains is at a quite different stage of development than companies that have not faced the same force of public pressure. Indeed, at a recent high-level meeting of the UN-sponsored Global Compact, the company's CEO, Phil Knight, called for global mandatory social auditing standards to ensure that all companies in the future, including its less visible competitors, comply with basic social and environmental standards.
>
> Shell International declared, "We believe that our commitment to contribute to sustainable development holds the key to our long-term business success" ("The Shell Report 1999: People, Planet and Profits—An Act of Commitment"). Shell's wake-up call came through the public humiliation over the Brent Spar oil platform and the worldwide outrage over their alleged complicity in human rights abuses in Nigeria.... In subsequent years, Shell has reoriented many of its policies, from the initiation of a major diversity strategy within its ranks to accelerated investment in cleaner energy sources.
>
> To learn in more detail how Shell became a "professional of the ethically correct," see the article "Un peu d'éthique dans un monde de brut" by Laurence Bajot and Coralie Schaub, *Enjeux Les Echos*, September 2001.

[31] Simon Zadek, *Doing Good and Doing Well: Making the Business Case for Corporate Citizenship*, The Conference Board, 2000.

[32] Frédéric Brunnquell, "Les grandes enquêtes: En toute légalité" in *Thalassa*, France 3 (French television), 11 May 2001.

[33] Jürgen Dunsch, "Despite Shareholder-Value Hype, Capital Gains Is Not Basic Human Rights," *International Herald Tribune*, 21 October 2000.

[34] Christophe Lo Giudice, "Le principal incitant reste la contrainte," iMediair, 9 May 2001.

[35] Ray and Anderson, *The Cultural Creatives*.

[36] Some of these wars don't even make the news. Caught in the cycle of poverty and powerlessness, people die for no reason in meaningless wars. The rest of the world seems ignorant or indifferent to their suffering. Bernard-Henri Lévy has visited these "damned people" in Angola, Burundi, Sri Lanka, Sudan and Colombia. His recent book, *Réflexions sur la Guerre, le Mal et la fin de l'Histoire* (Grasset, 2001), helps to build our awareness so we can strive to change this situation.

[37] "Does Inequality Matter?" *The Economist*, 16 June 2001.

[38] Quoted in "Energetic Visionaries," *The Economist*, 1 September 2001.

[39] It must be noted that liberal capitalism itself comes in different blends. See Charles Hampden–Turner and Fons Trompenaars, *The Seven Cultures of Capitalism*, Doubleday, 1993. See also François Ewald, "Libéral mais pas asocial," *Enjeux les Echos*, September 2001.

[40] A *Greener World*, Baxter, June 2000.

[41] Ibid.

[42] "What Does It Mean to Lead?" in Annual Report 2000, IBM.

[43] Ibid.

Chapter 13

1 Frederic Hudson, *The Handbook of Coaching*, Jossey-Bass, 1999.
2 Admittedly, as I have indicated previously, other coaching practices exist, influenced in particular by one's cultural orientations.
3 See Steward Friedman, Perry Christensen, and Jessica DeGroot, "Work and Life: The End of the Zero-Sum Game," *Harvard Business Review*, November–December 1998.
4 See Philippe Rosinski, "Constructive Politics: Essential to Leadership," *Leadership in Action* 18, no. 3 (1998).
5 The following quotes are from Richard Kilburg, *Executive Coaching*, American Psychological Association, 2000.
6 The structure described here can also be used with teams. See chapter 1 for specific considerations on team coaching and more in chapter 6 (the individualistic/collectivistic dimension and "Collages to Reveal Your Common Purpose").
7 An attractor, by definition, exerts a force that is directed toward it. The concept has been used in chaos theory, popularized by James Gleick (*Chaos: Making a New Science*, Viking Press, 1997).

Final Words

1 Interestingly, the Greek etymology of *synapse* clearly conveys the notion of bringing together: *sun* (with) and *aptein* (to join).
2 Martin Buber, *On Judaism*, Schocken Books, 1967. This was part of an address Buber delivered in London in 1947.

Appendix 1

1 Eric Berne, *Games People Play*, Penguin Books, 1964. Eric Berne writes, "This has been experimentally demonstrated in the case of rats through some remarkable experiments by S. Levine in which not only physical, mental, and emotional development but also the biochemistry of the brain and even resistance to leukemia were favorably affected by handling. The significant feature of these experiments was that gentle handling and painful electric shocks were equally effective in promoting health of the animals."
2 Fred (Nurturing Parent)→Bob (Submissive Child). We mean here the Nurturing Parent subego state of Fred addresses the Submissive Child subego state of Bob. This "stroke" is represented by arrow 1 on the figure.
3 There is also a connection to culture here (see the direct–indirect dimension in chapter 9).

Appendix 2

1 Monique Esser, *La P.N.L. en perspective*, Editions Labor, 1993.
2 Hofstede defines the term *stereotype* as "a fixed notion about persons in a certain category, with no distinctions made among individuals" (e.g., "Dutch are tactless, honest..."). He notes that "What is unfounded...is the application of stereotype information about a group to any individual member of that group. The valid part of a stereotype is a statistical statement about a group, not a predic-

tion of the properties of particular individuals. Stereotypes are at best half-truths." Hofstede further explains, "Information about a population can be considered scientifically valid only when it meets the following criteria:
- It is descriptive and not evaluative (judgmental).
- It is verifiable from more than one independent source.
- It applies, if not to all members of the population, at least to a statistical majority.
- It discriminates; that is, it indicates those characteristics for which this population differs from others.

(Geert Hofstede, *Culture's Consequences*, 2d ed., Sage, 2001.)

[3]   Following John Grinder and Richard Bandler, several authors provide detailed descriptions of the meta-model; for example, *Agir en Leader avec la Programmation Neuro-Linguistique* by Pierre Longin, Dunod, 1993.

[4]   See "Global Executive and Organizational Development," IBM, June 2001.

[5]   I indicated that coaching is action oriented. Coaches need to beware of nominalizations (i.e., verbs converted into nouns) and be ready to subtly convert nouns (static) into verbs (dynamic) in their questioning. For example, if the coachee says, "I regret my decision," the coach could ask, "How specifically did you decide?" thereby inviting the coachee to explore his decision-making process. This exploration may reveal ineffective strategies, which the coachee can become aware of, enabling him to avoid repeating an ineffective strategy in the future. It could be that the coachee tends to rush into decisions, automatically giving in to his Judging preference (see Myers-Briggs Type Indicator, chapter 11). Or the coachee may have a tendency to please others at the expense of honoring his own needs, and so forth.

[6]   Another possibility is to propose a counter-example: "I remember your story of John who took on board your suggestion." You can simply follow your counter-example with silence.

[7]   Two options that are usually effective in this situation for identifying and removing obstacles are (1) analyzing causes and (2) imagining consequences.

Appendix 3

[1]   See "Ongoing Feedback" in chapter 13.

Glossary

[1]   *The New Oxford Dictionary of English*, Oxford University Press, 1998.
[2]   Ibid.

Bibliography

Adler, Nancy. 1991. *International Dimensions of Organizational Behavior.* South-Western College Publishing.

Aelion, François. 1995. *Manager en Toutes Lettres.* Les Editions d'Organisation.

Althen, Gary. 2002. *American Ways: A Guide for Foreigners in the United States.* 2d ed. Intercultural Press.

Anderson, Bengt. 2000. *Swedishness.* SandbergTrygg.

Bartlett, Chistopher, and Sumantra Ghoshal. 1989. *Managing Across Borders.* Harvard Business School Press.

Bennett, Milton. 1993. "Towards Ethnorelativism: A Developmental Model of Intercultural Sensitivity." In *Education for the Intercultural Experience,* edited by R. Michael Paige. Yarmouth, ME: Intercultural Press.

Berman Fortgang, Laura. 2001. *Living Your Best Life.* Tarcher/Putnam.

———. 1998. *Take Yourself to the Top.* Warner Books.

Berne, Eric. 1964. *Games People Play.* Penguin Books.

Brake, Terence, Danielle Walker, and Tim Walker. 1995. *Doing Business Internationally.* McGraw-Hill.

Briggs-Myers, Isabel. 1998. *Introduction to Type.* 6th. ed. Consulting Psychologists Press.

Campbell, Joseph. 1949, 1968. *The Hero with a Thousand Faces.* Princeton University Press.

Collins, James, and Jerry Porras. 1994. *Built to Last.* HarperBusiness. 1994.

Comte-Sponville, André. 2001. *Dictionnaire philosophique,* PUF.

———. 2000. *Le bonheur, désespérément.* Editions Pleins Feux.

———. 1995. *Petit Traité des Grandes Vertus.* Presses Universitaires de France.

Condon, John C., and Fathi Yousef. 1975. *An Introduction to Intercultural Communication.* Macmillan.

Cummings, Thomas, and Christopher Worley. 1997. *Organizational Development & Change.* 6th ed. South-Western College Publishing.

EFQM Excellence Model, The. 1999. European Foundation for Quality Management.

Esser, Monique. 1993. *La P.N.L. en perspective*. Editions Labor.

Friedman, Steward, Perry Christensen, and Jessica DeGroot. 1998. "Work and Life: The End of the Zero-Sum Game." *Harvard Business Review*, November/December.

Fustier, Michel. 1991. *Pratique de la créativité*. ESF.

———. 1986. *Pratique de la dialectique*. ESF.

Gallwey, Timothy. 2001. *The Inner Game of Work*. Random House.

———. 1974, 1997. *The Inner Game of Tennis*. Random House.

Gardner, Howard. 1983. *Frame of Mind: The Theory of Multiple Intelligences*. Basic Books.

Goleman, Daniel. 2000. "Leadership that Gets Results." *Harvard Business Review*, March/April.

Hall, Edward T. 1983. *The Dance of Life: The Other Dimension of Time*. Anchor/Doubleday.

———. 1976. *Beyond Culture*. Anchor/Doubleday.

Hall, Edward T., and Mildred Reed Hall. 1990. *Understanding Cultural Differences: Germans, French and Americans*. Intercultural Press.

Hammer, Michael, and James Champy. 1993. *Reengineering the Corporation*. HarperBusiness.

Hampden-Turner, Charles, and Fons Trompenaars. 1993. *The Seven Cultures of Capitalism*. Doubleday.

Heider, John. 1985. *The Tao of Leadership*. Bantam.

Hofstede, Geert. 2001. *Culture's Consequences*. 2d ed. Sage.

Hofstede, Gert Jan, Paul Pedersen, and Geert Hofstede. 2002. *Exploring Culture: Exercises, Stories, and Synthetic Cultures*. Intercultural Press.

Hudson, Frederic. 1999. *The Handbook of Coaching*. Jossey-Bass.

Jung, Carl. 1971 *Psychological Types*. Princeton University Press (revision of the original English translation, 1923).

Kaplan, Robert, and David Norton. 1996. *The Balanced Scorecard*. HBS Press.

Kilburg, Richard. 2000. *Executive Coaching*. American Psychological Association.

Kim, Eun. 2001. *The Yin and Yang of American Culture: A Paradox*. Intercultural Press.

Kluckhohn, Florence, and Frederick Strodtbeck. 1961. *Variations in Value Orientations*. Row, Peterson.

Leonard, Thomas. 1998. *The Portable Coach*. Scribner.

Lévy, Bernard-Henri. 2001. *Réflexions sur la Guerre, le Mal et la fin de l'Histoire*. Grasset.

Lewis, Richard D. 1999. *When Cultures Collide*. 2d ed. Nicholas Brealey.

Loehr, Jim, and Tony Schwartz. 2001. "The Making of a Corporate Athlete." *Harvard Business Review*. January.

Mead, Richard. 1998. *International Management*. 2d ed. Blackwell.

Miedaner, Talane. 2000. *Coach Yourself to Success*. Contemporary Books.

Mintzberg, Henry. 1989. *Mintzberg On Management—Inside Our Strange World of Organizations*. The Free Press.

Morgan, Gareth. 1997. *Images of Organization*. 2d ed. Sage.

Observatoire de l'éthique. 2001. *le Guide éthique du consommateur*. Albin Michel.

Orme, Geetu. 2001. *Emotionally Intelligent Living*. Crown House.

Parsons, Talcott. 1951. *The Social System*. Macmillan.

Pearson, Carol. 1991. *Awakening the Heroes Within*. HarperCollins.

Ray, Paul, and Sherry Ruth Anderson. 2000. *The Cultural Creatives*. Harmony Books.

Rhinesmith, Stephen. 1996. *A Manager's Guide to Globalization*. McGraw-Hill.

Richardson, Cheryl. 2001. *The Life Makeovers*. Bantam.

———. 1998. *Take Time for Your Life*. Broadway.

Rosinski, Philippe. 1998. "Constructive Politics: Essential to Leadership." *Leadership in Action* 18, no. 3.

———. 1998. "Leading for Joy: Lessons on Leadership from the Judaic Tradition." European Forum for Management Development, Forum no. 3.

Senge, Peter. 1990. *The Fifth Discipline*. Currency Doubleday.

Sessa, Valerie, Michael Hansen, Sonya Prestridge, and Michael Kossler. 1999. *Geographically Dispersed Teams—An Annotated Bibliography*. Center for Creative Leadership.

Schein, Edgar. 1992. *Organizational Culture and Leadership*. 2d ed. Jossey-Bass.

Schmitz, Joerg. 2000. *Cultural Orientations Guide*. Princeton Training Press.

Shah, Idries. 1968. *The Way of the Sufi*. Penguin–Arkana.

Spinoza, Baruch. 1677. *Ethics*. (edition in English by Penguin, 1996).

Stewart, Edward, and Milton Bennett. 1991. *American Cultural Patterns*. Intercultural Press.

Storti, Craig. 1999. *Figuring Foreigners Out*. Intercultural Press.

Sulger, François. 1986. *Les Gestes Vérité*. Editions Sand.

Tang, Michael. 2000. *A Victor's Reflections and other Tales of China's Timeless Wisdom for Leaders*. Prentice Hall.

Trompenaars, Fons. 1997. *Riding the Waves of Culture*. 2d ed. Nicholas Brealey.

Tzu, Sun. 1963. *The Art of War*. Translated by Samuel Griffith. Oxford University Press.

Verbunt, Gilles. 2001. *La Société Interculturelle*. Editions du Seuil.

Whitmore, John. 1996. *Coaching for Performance*, 2d ed. Nicholas Brealey.

Wilson, Meena, Michael Hoppe, and Leonard Sayles. 1996. *Managing Across Cultures*. Center for Creative Leadership.

Whyte, David. 1994. *The Heart Aroused*. Currency Doubleday.

Zadek, Simon. 2000. *Doing Good and Doing Well: Making the Business Case for Corporate Citizenship*. The Conference Board.

About the Author

Philippe Rosinski is an expert in executive coaching, team coaching, and global leadership development, sought by leading international corporations. His clients include Unilever, Chubb Insurance, Baxter Healthcare, and IBM.

His pioneering work in bringing the crucial intercultural dimension into the practice of coaching has won him worldwide acclaim. He is the first European to have been designated Master Certified Coach by the International Coach Federation.

Rosinski is currently principal of *Rosinski & Company*, a global consulting firm that helps leaders, teams, and organizations unleash their human potential to achieve high performance and high fulfillment. Previously, he was the Director of Custom Programs at the Center for Creative Leadership Europe.

His goal is to help people honor their true desires and to live happier and more productive lives. His approach fosters genuine commitment, essential for sustainable peak performance; his contribution enables people to build thriving teams and organizations and to make a constructive contribution to society.

Prior to his book *Coaching Across Cultures*, Rosinski's articles "Leading for Joy" and "Constructive Politics" had already shown how alternative and multiple perspectives complement traditional coaching and leadership development approaches for maximum impact.

Rosinski has presented sessions on coaching across cultures and coaching executive teams at international conferences. He has pioneered the integration of the cultural dimension into coaching, showing how coaching can deploy more human potential, leverage cultural differences, and more effectively address complex challenges in our global environment.

Prior to his career in coaching and leadership development, Rosinski spent six years in the engineering field as a software engineer in Silicon Valley, California, and as a project manager in Brussels.

Philippe Rosinski received an electrical and mechanical engineering degree from the Ecole Polytechnique in Brussels, a master of science degree

in electrical engineering from Stanford University, and the Cepac postgradu-
ate business degree from the Solvay Business School in Brussels. Rosinski is
also certified to use a broad variety of psychometric instruments.

Philippe Rosinski lives near Brussels with his wife Anne and their daughter
Arielle. He enjoys playing tennis, traveling, and reading.

Please visit www.CoachingAcrossCultures.com and www.philrusinski.com
for more information about the author, his book, and the services of
Rosinski & Company .